Sylvanus Dryden Phelps

## Songs for All Seasons

A Scriptural and Poetical Calendar for Holidays, Birthdays, and All Days

Sylvanus Dryden Phelps

**Songs for All Seasons**
*A Scriptural and Poetical Calendar for Holidays, Birthdays, and All Days*

ISBN/EAN: 9783337290245

Printed in Europe, USA, Canada, Australia, Japan

Cover: Foto ©Thomas Meinert / pixelio.de

More available books at **www.hansebooks.com**

# SONGS FOR ALL SEASONS [1]

## *A Scriptural and Poetical Calendar*

FOR

## HOLIDAYS, BIRTHDAYS, AND ALL DAYS

BY

## REV. S. DRYDEN PHELPS, D.D.

Every day will I bless Thee. — PSALM cxlv : 2.
Speaking one to another in psalms and hymns and spiritual songs. —
EPHESIANS v : 19.

## SILVER, BURDETT & COMPANY

NEW YORK    BOSTON    CHICAGO

1891

PRESSWORK BY BERWICK & SMITH, BOSTON.

# PREFACE.

THIS volume is a collection of the author's hymns and short poems, arranged as a poetical calendar for daily reading and reference, and for holidays, birthdays, memorial and other occasions. There is a poem for every day in the year, with consecutive dates, and preceding each and adapted to it are two passages of Scripture, one from the Old Testament and another from the New, making more than seven hundred choice selections from the Inspired Book—furnishing blessed supplies for devout meditation and texts for rich discourse. Some of these songs have a special significance and relation to the dates indicated—the day, the month, the year—the last shown by the appended figures that note also the time of their composition. The range is more than half a century. The earlier ones, culled from the author's three volumes of verse published at intervals, have been more or less revised. A portion of the later songs were printed in the *Christian Secretary*, while he was conducting it, the themes being those of the Sunday-school lessons. These the reader will readily recognise by the order in which they appear. Hymns and odes for particular occasions have been inserted at the dates when they were used. Others commemorate events which occurred at the dates given. It will be observed that a considerable number of the songs have been quite recently written, most of which appear now in print for the first time.

Hymns of the author's for many years past have found places in various church hymnals, Sabbath-school manuals, and collections for evangelistic and social services. Several of these have obtained a wide popularity, and it is gratifying to know that they have been to many persons spiritually uplifting, and comforting. Numerous testimonials in this regard are among the writer's sweetest and most precious treasures. In a note on the hymn, "Something for Thee," found at the end of this book, a few incidents are given and more might be added respecting the usefulness of this hymn and of several others also. Readers will observe that a few poems because of their length have been divided into two or more parts and inserted under fitting titles. A few of still greater length, which it seemed desirable to give a place in the volume, are included in an Appendix. None can be more sensible than the writer of the many imperfections of his work, but if God's blessing shall make these Daily Songs, with the accompanying Morsels of Manna, helpful and stimulating and cheering to any fellow-pilgrims along life's journey, he will rejoice in his labor of love.    s. d. p.

New Haven, Conn.

# INDEX OF TITLES.

v

### APPENDIX.

# Songs for all Seasons.

---

[JAN. 1.] Set thee up waymarks. JER. xxxi. 21.
For now is salvation nearer to us than when we first believed. ROM. xiii. 11.

## THE NEW YEAR.

AWAKE and watch, O heart of mine!
While passing o'er this mystic line:
Another wave, like those before,
Breaks on a new and unknown shore.

Upon its dark and troubled breast
Treasures of all the centuries rest;
The refluent tide a moment rolls,
Laden with memories, deeds, and souls!

How changeless all! I turn from these
To kindlier zones and calmer seas;
The land I touch, of variant form,
Is faintly viewed through mist and storm.

Nearer, 'tis vast and wide outspread,
It lures with hope, and chills with dread;
But oft to faith and courage bold
Vistas of beauty will unfold.

Brighter than all in years gone by,
Life's grand ideals waiting nigh,
Sweet friends and fields and skies benign
Greet him who walks in Light divine.

1

To live is Christ—O waves, roll on!
Ye bring me where my Lord has gone,
Where dawns the Year forever new—
The Crown of Life and Heaven in view!    1886

---

[JAN. 2.] Thou crownest the year with thy goodness. Ps. lxv. 11.
Every good gift and every perfect boon is from above. JAS. i. 17.

## ON THE BORDER.

KINDLY led and safely kept,
Lord, my grateful song accept:
Thought and heart to thee I raise,
Winged with sweet and joyful praise.

Constant as the Cloud and Flame,
Day by day thy blessing came—
Morning mercies, fresh and sure,
Evening comforts, precious, pure.

Folded in thy tender care,
Fullness of thy love to share,
Thou hast watched my pathway round,
Made thy grace and gifts abound.

While such goodness I review,
Think of what has been thy due,
What my poor returns for all,
Humbled at thy feet I fall.

Lord, if added years be mine,
Grant my life accord with thine,
Faithful in thy work and way,
Thou its daily strength and stay.    1888

[JAN. 3.]  Bless the Lord, O my soul, and forget not all his benefits. Ps. ciii. 2.

Singing and making melody with your heart to the Lord: giving thanks always for all things in the name of our Lord Jesus Christ to God. EPH. v. 19, 20.

## A SONG OF PRAISE.

THY name, O Lord, my soul shall bless
For mercies great and numberless;
The benefits thy bounty gives,
My heart shall prize while memory lives:
Let all within me join to raise
A grateful song of holy praise.

When sin and guilt my spirit bound,
Forgiveness full in thee was found,
When prostrate with disease and pain,
Thy healing power gave strength again:
Thou hast redeemed my life from ill,
And lovingkindness crowns me still.

Thy gracious hand has good supplied
Till want and taste are satisfied:
In sorrow's hour and joy's decline,
How like a father's pity thine:
How tender toward our frame of dust,
What loving care for those who trust.

With everlasting mercy, Lord,
Thou wilt thy faithful ones reward.
Oh, bless the Lord, ye angels strong,
Ye hosts of heaven, the notes prolong;
All works divine, the anthem roll;
Bless, bless the Lord, O thou, my soul!   1884

[JAN. 4.] I shall not die, but live, and declare the works of the Lord. Ps. cxviii. 17.

The things which are seen are temporal; but the things which are not seen are eternal. 2 COR. iv. 18.

## FORESHADOWINGS.

THE restless mind, in all its searchless powers,
The earnest longing of its thoughtful hours,
Harps in the soul, sweet melodies around,
Tell of a spirit realm where we are bound.

We seem at times to hear its music chime,
And oft the beating of its waves sublime,
As in the shadowy vale our friends depart,
As God's great truths come surging to the heart.

These voices heed, and let their cadence roll
Unceasing through the chambers of the soul:
Heed them, O youth! and let thy hope arise;
Heed them, O man! so near the mystic skies!

Cling to the Cross, with love divinely bright,
To Christ, who brings immortal life to light;
And let each new-born day, as it recedes,
Be rounded well with true and generous deeds.

Then, as the conflicts of this world are o'er,
And thou dost linger on its farther shore,
Thy view serene, like that of martyred Stephen,
Shall be entrancing as the Gate of Heaven.

As there thou lay'st thine armor down, thy rest
Shall be, like Jacob's sleep at Bethel, blest,
From whose lone pillow there did glorious rise
The angel stairway up to Paradise!

1856

[JAN. 5.] Awake, awake, put on thy strength, O Zion. Isa. lii. 1.

Now it is high time for you to awake out of sleep... The night is far spent, the day is at hand. ROM. xiii. 11, 12.

## A CALL TO VIGILANCE.

SWIFT the stream of time descending,
　　Priceless souls of glorious birth!
Here's the conflict and its ending—
　　Heaven is won or lost on earth!
Slumber not! life's days are waning,
　　Soon will come its latest night;
Up! improve the time remaining,
　　Ere your souls shall take their flight.

Wrapt in slumber? Heirs of glory,
　　Saved from sin and endless woe,
Bought with blood!—recall the story;
　　See from whence that blood did flow!
On the brow of Calvary gazing,
　　On the pit from which you came,
Wake! redeeming love be praising;
　　Let your spirits catch the flame!

Shadowy night is fast departing;
　　Dawn of day is near at hand;
Christian, up! from slumber starting,
　　Looms in view the brighter land!
Dashes round thy bark the billow,
　　Dangers threaten—seize the helm!
Sleeper, wake! and leave thy pillow;
　　Look! the day! the glorious realm!　　1845

[JAN. 6.] Wilt thou not quicken us again ? Ps. lxxxv. 6.

Repent ye therefore, and turn again, that your sins may be blotted out, that so there may come seasons of refreshing from the presence of the Lord. ACTS iii. 19.

## REVIVAL HYMN.

SEARCHING Spirit! make this hour
Witness thy reviving power;
Touch our hearts with sacred fire,
Faith and prayer and zeal inspire.

Some have left their early love,
Some have grieved thee, Holy Dove,
Proved unfaithful, worldly, cold,
Straying from the Shepherd's fold.

Call them back, for thou canst reach
Farthest ones with thy sweet speech;
Broken-hearted they shall come,
Find a joyful welcome home.

Others near us long have been
In the deadly sleep of sin,
Till their hearts refuse to move
At the plea of Jesus' love.

Show their guilt-imperiled state,
Hopes delusive dissipate,
Flash the truth upon their sight,
Bid them wake to life and light.

Oh, we long thy work to see,
Precious souls renewed by thee:
Let salvation now appear
Out of Zion, glorious here.

1875

[JAN. 7.] He believed in the Lord; and he counted it to him for right.
eousness. GEN. XV. 6.
Fear not, only believe. MARK v. 36.

## ONLY BELIEVE.

COME, trembling soul, be not afraid,
On Jesus all thy sins were laid,
And he thy hopeless debt has paid.
Only believe.

The Sufferer in the garden see.
The Lamb of God on Calvary,
And all that pain and death for thee.
Only believe.

The crimson stream, thy Saviour's blood,
Has power to bring thee nigh to God,
Cleansed in its precious, healing flood.
Only believe.

In wondrous love he calls to-day,
Cast now thy guilty doubts away,
Free pardon take without delay.
Only believe.

He bids the inward conflict cease,
He gives thy burdened conscience peace,
From all thy fears a sweet release.
Only believe.

For thee, O Christ! all things I leave;
To thee, my Saviour, now I cleave,
And I, as thou dost me receive.
Only believe. 1874

[JAN. 8.] He hath put a new song in my mouth, even praise unto our God. Ps. xl. 3.

That ye may shew forth the excellencies of him who called you out of darkness into his marvelous light. 1 PET. ii. 9.

## GRACIOUS DELIVERANCE.

My gracious Lord divine,
　　Thy works of might we trace,
But most thy glories shine
　　In soul-redeeming grace.
My grateful.heart shall never cease
To celebrate thy love and peace.

Thy mercy sought the pit,
　　The deep and miry clay,
Its horrid darkness lit,
　　And brought me into day.
How glad was I the light to see,
And bless the Hand that rescued me!

Upon the Rock so strong
　　My feet were firmly set,
My mouth received a song
　　My heart shall ne'er forget—
A song so new and wondrous sweet
That I shall evermore repeat.

The world around shall learn
　　What grace has done for me,
Saints shall thy power discern,
　　And sinners trust in thee.
O Lord, my Life! how blest the state
Of those who trust and serve and wait! 1884

[JAN. 9.] Arise and thresh, O daughter of Zion...and thou shalt beat in pieces many peoples : and..devote their gain unto the Lord. MIC. iv.13.

Let us go elsewhere into the next towns, that I may preach there also. MARK i. 38.

## MISSIONS IN OUR COUNTRY.

Sons of day! arise from slumbers,
    For the sluggish night is gone;
Swell the Saviour's marshaled numbers,
    Marching where he leadeth on.

Soldiers of the cross, appointed,
    Girded for the glorious war,
In the name of God's Anointed,
    Spread your victories afar.

Bid the trumpet of redemption
    Greet our country's farthest shore;
Boldly claim our Lord's preëmption,
    For the agonies he bore.

On the prairie and the mountain,
    In the valley rich and fair,
By the river and the fountain,
    Plant the sacred standard there.

Where the infant city 's founded,
    Where the hamlet dots the plain,
Let the Gospel-call be sounded,
    Let the Church a foothold gain.

So shall error be supplanted,
    So shall Truth her vanguard keep,
So shall temple-homes be granted
    To the Shepherd's wandering sheep.   1857

[JAN. 10. ] How beautiful upon the mountains are the feet of him that bringeth good tidings,.. that publisheth salvation. ISA. lii. 7.

And lo, I am with you alway, even unto the end of the world. MAT. xxviii. 20.

## A MISSIONARY HYMN.

HERALDS of the Cross! Selected
  For the highest service known,
Spirit-called and Heaven-protected,
  Jesus shall your labors own,—
    With you always,
  Every deed of love to crown.

On Jehovah's might depending,
  Ever hopeful, strong in prayer,
Armed by faith, in love contending,
  Gracious victories you share:
    Desert regions
  Bud and bloom as gardens fair.

Ripened under showers of blessing,
  Sheaves rejoicing reapers bring—
Souls redeemed, their Lord confessing,
  Harvest home the toilers sing,
    While the angels
  Chant the joy before their King.

Sweet your rest and labor leaving,
  When is closed this work of love,
Gratefully from Christ receiving
  Glorious crowns of life above!
    Oh, what kingdoms
  Wait for those who faithful prove! 1876

[JAN. 11.] Strength and beauty are in his sanctuary. Ps. xcvi. 6.

A holy temple in the Lord; in whom ye also are builded together for a habitation of God in the Spirit. EPH. ii. 22.

## THE DIVINE HABITATION.

How GLORIOUS is thy dwelling,
    O Lord of hosts on high,
Where angel anthems, swelling,
    Fill all the boundless sky.
In more than Eden splendor,
    The heavenly mansions shine,
Where praise the ransomed render,
    In worship all divine.

On earth, among the lowly,
    Thou hast a gracious reign—
The kingdom of the holy,
    The Church, the born-again;
And temples, reared by mortals,
    The homes of truth and love,
Are hallowed as the portals
    Of Paradise above.

Make this thy habitation,
    And here thy name record;
With blessing and salvation
    Our prayers and toils reward;
Let dews of grace descending,
    On every heart distill,
And humble throngs come bending
    To know and do thy will.

The Spirit's living beauty
　　To all thy servants give,
And strength for every duty,
　　That each to thee may live;
Till, in his chariot gleaming,
　　The Saviour comes to bear
The souls of his redeeming
　　To heavenly mansions fair.　　1850

---

[JAN. 12.]　I will set up shepherds over them who shall feed them.
JER. xxiii. 4.

Remember them that had the rule over you, who spake unto you
the word of God.　HEB. xiii. 7.

## A PASTOR'S RECEPTION.

PASTOR! joyfully we meet thee—
　　Flock around their shepherd dear—
And with choicest wishes greet thee,
　　At the opening of the year.

Words of sacred truth, with gladness,
　　Oft we 've heard dispensed by thee;
They have banished clouds of sadness,
　　Hanging o'er life's troubled sea.

Though the season's gifts we proffer
　　Be not large in earthly shares,
To the Lord, for thee, we 'll offer
　　Faithful hearts and fervent prayers.

Long may Heaven, thy life protecting,
　　Make thy labors richly blest,
Faith confirming—souls directing
　　To the Lord our hope and rest.　　1843

[JAN. 13.] All that thou hast commanded us we will do. JOSH. i. 16.
Be thou faithful unto death, and I will give thee the crown of life.—
REV. ii. 10.

## CROSS BEFORE CROWN.

COME, friends, and let our hearts awake,
　　To Jesus' call attending;
The cross we 'll take for his dear sake,
　　Our toils and praises blending.

Gird on the heavenly armor bright,
　　And standing up for Jesus,
Watch, pray and fight as sons of light,
　　Till from the war he frees us.

'Tis sweet to trust his glorious word,
　　His name and grace confessing;
Who serve the Lord have great reward,
　　And share his richest blessing.

Let Jesus' love fill every mind,
　　Our faith and hope inspiring;
What worldlings find, we leave behind,
　　Immortal crowns desiring.

The painful cross for us he bore,
　　And bowed in death's cold river—
Oh! for the power to love him more
　　Who did our souls deliver.

When he shall come and bring us home,
　　Where rest and joy end never,
The cross laid down, we 'll wear the crown,
　　And shout his praise forever.

1858

[JAN. 14.]   I will dwell in the house of the Lord for ever.   Ps. xxiii. 6.
  If the earthly house of our tabernacle be dissolved, we have a build-
ing of God, a house not made with hands, eternal, in the heavens.—
2 Cor. v. 1.

### THE CHRISTIAN'S HOME.

Beyond the utmost verge of time,
There is a broad resplendent clime,
Where glories rapturous and sublime
    In untold grandeur rise ;
And mid those fair celestial lands,
In undecaying beauty stands
A building never made with hands,
    Eternal in the skies.

The glorious Sun of righteousness
Sheds there his radiant beams to bless,
While all the heavenly hosts confess
    The honors of their King ;
The ransomed throng his grace admire,
They join the vast angelic choir,
With sweetest voice and tuneful lyre,
    His lofty praise to sing.

Bright land of bliss ! where all is peace,
Where cares and fears and sorrows cease,
Pleasure divine and love increase,
    To thrill the raptured soul.
Thrice happy home ! for ever blest !
How sweet the weary pilgrim's rest,
What holy calm fills every breast,
    As endless ages roll !

Look thence! and like the tireless sun
The Christian race with patience run,
Nor deem thy work on earth is done
    Till life's last breath be given:
Then thou shalt soar to that blest home,
Far from the reach of sin and gloom,
Beyond the portals of the tomb—
    Eternal, and in Heaven.        1839

## CLOSE OF SOCIAL SERVICE.

[JAN. 15.]  Then they that feared the Lord spake one with another.—
MAL. iii. 16.
Rabbi, it is good for us to be here. MARK ix. 5.

WE meet, we part—how blest the scene,
    Where Christians sing and pray:
Soft on our souls falls light serene
    From the eternal day.

The heavenly frame, the humble plea,
    The earnest witness-word,
The thrill of praise—such bliss have we
    In waiting on the Lord.

When earthly toils and cares are past,
    And here no more we come,
How sweet the Saviour's voice at last,
    That bids us welcome home.

But now, in union, faith and love,
    We 'll live, a pilgrim band;
Then strike our tents, and soar above,
    To our Immanuel's land.        1857

[Jan. 16.]   Be thou strong therefore, and show thyself a man.—
1 Kings ii. 2.

And he said, Young man, I say unto thee, Arise.  Luke vii. 14.

## DAWN OF MANHOOD.

Well garnered in the past,
  Are happy childhood scenes,
That sure will always last,
  Whatever intervenes :
Heart-treasures they, linked to the skies,
By heavenly ties, that ne'er decay.

Lo, a new day! the time
  When boyhood's bird-like songs,
With manly music chime,
  And life itself belongs,
From this birth-hour, to eras new
That rise to view—the dawn of power!

The fount becomes a stream,
  The fruits succeed the flowers,
Life's fancy-gilded dream
  Turns into sober hours.
The world of fact, full of its needs
For earnest deeds, calls now to act.

So shall the future, blest,
  Be filled with welcomes bright ;
When comes the day of rest,
  Its evening time be light !
Glad the survey, as o'er long years,
This date appears—Life's true birthday.   1855

[JAN. 17.] As one whom his mother comforteth, so will I comfort you.  ISA. lxvi. 13.

The Father of mercies and God of all comfort; who comforteth us. 2 COR. i. 3.

## DIVINE MOTHERLY COMFORT.

LORD, how thy royal tenderness
    Stoops to our human needs!
Borne on thy love, its dear caress
    Our fondest thought exceeds.

Words wonderful it uttereth—
    Thy voice in kindness true:
"As one his mother comforteth,
    So will I comfort you."

Oh, promise doubly sweet and clear,
    Ill's quick and blest relief,
As it recalls the mother dear,
    Who soothed our childish grief.

Close to her heart, in fear's alarms,
    She drew us sobbing sore,
And, held in love's enfolding arms,
    Our sorrows soon were o'er.

So, Lord, thy child, to thee I come,
    When cares or woes abound,
And seem as in my early home,
    With mother's comfort crowned.

Peace fills my spirit, calm, composed,
    And pillowed on thy breast,
With "everlasting arms" enclosed,
    I find a heavenly rest.

1888

[JAN. 18.]  They shall enter into the king's palace.  Ps. xlv. 15.

This woman was full of good works and almsdeeds which she did.—
ACTS ix. 36.

## THE KING'S DAUGHTERS.

THERE are beautiful labors unseen by the proud,
  But welcomed by gratefulest hearts,
As the silvery light, from their gloomiest cloud,
  At whose shining, the tempest departs.

Your love-gifts in kindness the world may not know,
  Ye friends of the poor and the sad;
Yet from many a heart they shall banish its woe,
  And bid it look up and be glad.

If not in full splendor on fame's blazing scroll,
  Your charity-deeds may be found,
They sure are recorded—engraved on the soul—
  To last through eternity's round.

Then onward! rejoicing earth's lorn ones to bless,
  The orphan to teach and to aid,
To comfort the widow in want and distress—
  And ye shall be richly repaid.

When bright in the gathering clouds of the heaven,
  Your Master descending ye see,
Whate'er to his needy ye kindly have given,
  He'll say, "Ye have done it to me."

"And ye shall be mine, my own jewels so pure,
  For mansions celestial arrayed;
Come up to my kingdom all glorious and sure—
  To honors that never shall fade."            1841

JAN. 19.] The Lord opened the eyes of the young man; and he saw. 2 KINGS vi. 17.

Then shall he send forth the angels, and shall gather together his elect. MARK. xiii. 27.

## A CELESTIAL ARMY.

SOFT on the prophet's servant fell
A ray divine, a sacred spell,
That touched with holy fire his soul,
And held him in a blest control.

The earthly veil before his face
Was drawn aside, and in its place
There came a medium, crystal clear,
In which celestial things appear.

What splendors rush upon his sight!
What heavenly forms and visions bright!
A glory, crowning Dothan's hills,
His raptured spirit strangely thrills!

On every hand afar he sees,
Amid the rocks and through the trees,
A white-robed host in armor bright—
Chariots of fire and steeds of light!

Ten thousand thousand there they stood,
The angel helpers of the good:
Before that throng the Syrian band
Seemed like a single grain of sand.

A great deliverance, timely given—
The mountain camp of hosts of heaven,
Disclosed to mortal vision fair,
The answering aid of holy prayer.　　1854

[JAN. 20.]   There shall come forth a star out of Jacob. NUM. xxiv. 17.
  A light for revelation to the Gentiles, and the glory of thy people Israel. LUKE ii. 32.

## THE JACOB STAR.

SEERS, looking from afar,
Hailed thee, O Jacob Star!
   Of princely name:
Thy praise tuned many a tongue
The Gentile race among—
Thy love the martyrs sung
   Amidst the flame.

Now to unnumbered ones
Of God's enfranchised sons
   Thou art the Guide,
Imparting light and peace,
Bidding their joys increase,
And fearful tempests cease,
   On life's dark tide.

And countless more shall find
That thou canst calm the mind,
   And set it free,
When filled with boding fears,
When fall the bitter tears,
When aid nowhere appears,
   Except from thee.

Ambition's star may set,
Friends even may forget,
   Earth's hopes decay—
The star of wealth shall wane,

Pleasure soon yield to pain,
But thou shalt still remain,
  Beaming for aye.    1842

---

[JAN. 21.] I have loved thee with an everlasting love. JER. xxxi. 3.
The Son of God who loved me, and gave himself for me. GAL. ii. 20.

## JESUS LOVES ME.

JESUS loves me, came to save me,
 When my soul in sin was lost,
For my life his own he gave me—
 Oh, how much my ransom cost!

Jesus loves me, ne'er forsakes me,
 Gives me peace and joy and grace;
By his loving presence makes me
 Dwell as in a heavenly place.

Jesus loves me, mercy sends me,
 Cheers me on my pilgrim way;
From my foes and fears defends me,
 Strength imparts for every day.

Jesus loves me, always loves me,
 In my darkness as in light;
By my pains and trials proves me,
 To reveal his face more bright.

Jesus loves me, feasts and guides me,
 Asks if I my Saviour love;
Dearest Lord, I've none besides thee,
 Here on earth, in heaven above.   1858

[JAN. 22.] The people that walked in darkness have seen a great light. ISA. ix. 2.

When they saw the star, they rejoiced with exceeding great joy.—
MATT. ii. 10.

## THE BETHLEHEM STAR.

DARK was the night of time
When first thy rays sublime,
 Celestial Gem,
Descending from on high,
Illumed the somber sky,
And met the shepherds' eye,
 In Bethlehem.

Ere toward the Light of God,
With hasty steps they trod,
 An angel's voice,
In new and rapturous song,
Joined by a heavenly throng,
The anthem to prolong,
 Bade them rejoice.

Star of celestial ray,
Beam thou upon my way,
 With guiding light;
In trial's gloomiest hour,
When pain may overpower,
When life's last clouds shall lower,
 Dispel their night.

Then thee shall I behold,
On shining streets of gold—
 From earth afar—

Where shadows never fall,
Where death shall ne'er appall,
Where thou art All in all,
Sweet Bethlehem Star! 1842

[JAN. 23.] My presence shall go with thee, and I will give thee rest.
Ex. xxxiii. 14.
Now they desire a better country, that is, a heavenly. HEB. xi. 16.

## HEAVENWARD BOUND.

My Saviour from his throne,
Regards his servant here,
And in the blessèd Comforter,
I feel that he is near.

Oft with dear saints I meet,
And glory seems to dawn:
Gladness and strength my soul refresh,
And so I journey on.

If Marah I must taste,
Sweet hope my spirit calms,
And soon I drink at Elim's wells,
And rest beneath its palms.

So through my pilgrim course,
E'en to the darkling tide,
I will not fear, but love to think
Of scenes the other side.

Oh, the transporting bliss,
When I am safely o'er,
To find my Lord, my home, my heaven,
And leave them nevermore! 1875

[JAN. 24.] The Lord shall be unto thee an everlasting light. Isa.lx.19.
I am the root and the offspring of David, the bright, the morning
star. REV. xxii. 16.

## THE MORNING STAR.

THOUGH lowly was thy birth,
Among the sons of earth,
    Bright, Morning Star!
Yet, with the victor's prize,
Triumphant thou didst rise,
And highest in the skies
    Thy glories are.

When perisheth the sun,
And planets cease to run,
    Leaving the sky;
When God's consuming ire
Shall wrap the world in fire,
And time itself expire,
    Thou shalt not die.

In loftier heavens above,
Where all is peace and love,
    Thy radiance fair,
Beaming from pole to pole,
Shall feast the ransomed soul,
While circling ages roll
    Eternal there.

Let now thy rays divine,
On every nation shine,
    Through earth abroad,
Till all thy light shall see,

Till all by truth be free,
Till all shall bow the knee,
And worship God. 1842

---

[JAN. 25.] Out of Zion, the perfection of beauty, God hath shined forth. Ps. l. 2.

The church of the living God, the pillar and ground of the truth.—1 TIM. iii. 15.

## THE CHURCH OF GOD.

NAUGHT so conserves the truth and right,
As God's pure Church, the world's best light;
Her source on high, divine her birth,
Heaven's life made manifest on earth.

Hers to embody Christ the Lord,
Unfold the purpose of his word,
The one grand means that God bestows
To save our race, and cure its woes.

For this, the blest Incarnate One
A wanderer was beneath the sun,
The Garden sorrow's whelming flood,
The Cross—its death and sacred blood.

For this he rose, to plead above,
Give conquests of almighty Love,
Augment the Church's matchless worth,
And make her regnant o'er the earth.

O Church! in purity and power,
Assert and prove thy priceless dower!
To thee thy Head, as he doth live,
The kingdoms of the world shall give. 1869

[JAN. 26.] Behold, he spreadeth his light around him. JOB xxxvi.30.
The city hath no need of the sun, neither of the moon, to shine upon it: for the glory of God did lighten it. REV. xxi.23.

## AURORAL LIGHTS.

ALONG the clear and lofty arch,
    With shimmering banners lifted high,
In brilliant robes they form and march,
    Auroral armies of the sky.

Some, pale and spectral as they shine,
    Like spirits wandering near us seem,
While vaster columns throng the line,
    And crimson splendors o'er them stream.

The white and red o'erlap the blue,
    Where flash the gems of starry light;
A heavenly host breaks forth to view,
    And scales the sapphire dome of night.

Ah! whence this mingled grand array,
    That half the concave fills and sweeps,
Glintings of some pure sphere are they,
    In the far space of upper deeps?

Are these reflections from the sea
    That wraps and warms the distant pole,
Whose gleaming waves, from winter free,
    Wait the adventurer's daring stroll?

Come these celestial bannered hosts,
    Within our dim horizon's bound,
To lure us to sublimer coasts,
    Where hope's ideal realm is found?

Are they but shadows of that world
  Where sainted spirits dwell and sing?
The twilight of those skies unfurled
  Above the City of the King?

Oh, what must be the splendors rare,
  The hues that zone that high abode,
The radiant glories streaming there,
  Lit by the throne and smile of God!   1869

---

[JAN. 27.]   Our redeemer, the Lord of hosts is his name. ISA. xlvii. 4
In whom we have our redemption through his blood. EPH. i. 7.

## SONG OF REDEMPTION.

O PRINCE of Peace! extend thy reign,
Make earth a Paradise again:
Banish the woe and wail of sin,
Bring songs of joy and gladness in—

The songs whose chorus, angel-given,
Augments the growing bliss of Heaven,
Lifts up our souls on faith's strong wing,
Till charmed by psalms immortals sing.

The "new song" there, that never tires—
Redemption—sung by ransomed choirs,
Hath echoes lingering here in strains
Akin to those o'er Bethlehem's plains,

Breathed in the life and matchless love
Of Him who sought us from above,
Dropt from his deeds and sympathies,
Prolonged in lives that image his.   1857

[JAN. 28.] Woe unto him that giveth his neighbor drink, that addest thy venom thereto, and makest him drunken also. HAB. ii. 15.

Nor covetous, nor drunkards . . . shall inherit the kingdom of God.— 1 COR. vi. 10.

## HOW LONG, O LORD?

How LONG, O Lord! must suffering mortals wait,
As held in iron shroud or prison gate,
Despairing, sink beneath their crushing fate?

How long these streams of bitter anguish flow,
These tides of grief and desolating woe,
These fiery, soul-engulfing torrents go?

Shall brilliant stars still fade or fall from heaven?
Shall to this Moloch dread the best be given?
Shall brightest hopes in darkest night be riven?

My soul shrinks back, with horror all aghast,
To think of miseries so deep and vast,
Of what such souls defiled must be at last!

And still we let the awful work proceed;
What thousands aid it in their love of greed,
Though God forbids, and helpless sufferers plead!

O sluggish hearts, and slumbering hosts, awake!
Lethargic bands, inaction's fetters break!
Go forth! the foe's defiant ramparts take!

It can be done—united souls are strong;
Move thus in force, the fight need not be long,
But surely bring the glad victorious song!

I hear that song amidst the noise and din
Of mighty struggles with the giant sin—
The shout of armies that we know must win! 1886

[JAN. 29.]   Look unto me, and be ye saved, all the ends of the earth:
for I am God, and there is none else. ISA. xlv. 22.
He went on his way rejoicing. ACTS viii. 39.

## BELIEVING AND OBEYING.

OH, loving Saviour, dying Lamb!
The bearer of my sin and shame,
Wilt thou receive me as I am,
    A wretched, helpless soul?
Vain is the world, and all my deeds,
As broken cisterns, useless weeds,
They ne'er can meet my deepest needs;
    O Jesus, make me whole!

I do believe, give all to thee,
Nothing to what thou givest me—
Thy life, thy blood, thy grace so free,
    On which alone I rest.
Lord, I am thine, no more to stray
From thee and thy dear cross away,
But there to love, adore, and pray,
    And be supremely blest.

How long I sought thy grace to know,
Groping in darkness, doubt, and woe;
But thou didst find and love me so,
    I must thy word obey.
To tread where I thy footprints see,
To take my cross, to follow thee,
To do thy will, is sweet to me,
    And brightens all my way.

1867

[JAN. 30.]   There is a friend that sticketh closer than a brother.—
PROV. xviii. 24.

Greater love hath no man than this, that a man lay down his life for
his friends.   JOHN xv. 13.

## THE HEAVENLY FRIEND.

CHRIST is a faithful friend,
In whom the trembling soul, in hope confiding,
May safely trust; his love is strong, abiding
    Even to the end.

His sympathy, how sweet!
Like softest music o'er the spirit stealing,
It soothes the troubled heart with balmy healing,
    And joy complete.

His words of glorious truth,
Like cadences of love from heaven descending,
Allure and guide to scenes of bliss unending,
    And fadeless youth.

He, with almighty power,
Can give support when earthly hopes are dying;
Safe is each soul to this dear refuge flying
    In trial's hour.

Celestial, peerless Friend!
Around me close thy soft and sheltering pinions;
And take my spirit to thy blest dominions,
    When life shall end.

Oh, give this gracious Guest
A throne in every heart, earth's sons and daughters!
His friendship is a fount of living waters,
    And heavenly rest.

1847

[JAN. 31.] Ask of me, and I will give thee the nations for thine inheritance. Ps. ii. 8.

Come over into Macedonia and help us. ACTS xvi. 9.

## THE MACEDONIAN CRY.

HARK! from o'er the distant waters
  Myriad voices sweep along;
Heathen sons and heathen daughters
  Vainly round their idols throng.

Piteous wails, to heaven ascending,
  Roll along the leaden sky:
Christian, wake! thine ear be lending,
  List the Macedonian cry!

Quickly send the bread of heaven,
  Ere they die in pagan gloom,
Ere their priceless souls are given,
  Blindly, to despairing doom.

Must they downward rush forever,
  Plunging still in misery's tide?
Shall the message reach them never,
  "Ho! for you the Saviour died!"

Jesus! shall thy ransomed number
  Cease thy burning words to keep?
O'er the dying nations slumber,
  While they grope in darkness deep?

Oh! in view of death's dread portal,
  And of Life's all-glorious gift—
Real things, unseen, immortal—
  From our hearts inaction lift!

1845

[FEB. 1.]　He shall be as the light of the morning, when the sun riseth,
a morning without clouds. 2 SAM. xxiii. 4.

The true light already shineth. 1 JOHN ii. 8.

## THE BEACON LIGHT.

WHILE on life's stormy sea
　　My bark is driven,
From a fair coast to me
　　Sweet light is given,
Gleaming around my way,
Changing dark night to day,
Blending its golden ray
　　With hues of heaven.

That beacon light I have,
　　And lose all fear;
The Saviour walks the wave—
　　His voice I hear—
My precious, perfect Guide,
Bidding the storm subside,
Showing, beyond the tide,
　　Skies heavenly clear.

I feel thy magnet powers,
　　Bright world to come!
Faith sees thy glorious bowers
　　Where angels roam;
Where loved ones, gone before,
Now beckon from the shore,
And make me long the more
　　For them and home.

1862

[FEB. 2.] In six days the Lord made heaven and earth, the sea and all that in them is. EX. xx. 11.
He himself giveth to all life, and breath, and all things. ACTS xvii. 25.

## CREATIVE DAYS—FIRST THREE.

WAS it once a globe of darkness
    In its early birth?
A revolving mass of vapor,
    All this wondrous earth?
Through it swept the Voice eternal,
    Thrillingly it rung,
Piercing all its gloomy chambers
    Like a fiery tongue;
"Let there light be!" Flashing, dancing,
    O'er it light upsprung.

Was it once a ball of fire—
    This old wondrous world—
Blazoned with electric lightnings,
    As it onward whirled?
Chaos trembled into order,
    At the fiat given,
And the firmaments commingled
    Were asunder riven,
And from out the parting waters
    Rose the air of heaven.

Was it once all o'er enshrouded
    With a shoreless sea,
But a swinging sphere of billows,
    Bounding in their glee?
Back Jehovah rolled the waters
    From their rocky floor;

Mountains climbed from out the oceans,
    Hills, plains, flecked them o'er;
All along the mazy distance
    Lay the sea and shore.

[FEB. 3.]   There was evening and there was morning, a fourth day.—
GEN. I. 19.

Worship him that made the heaven and the earth and sea. REV. xiv.7.

## CREATIVE DAYS—LAST THREE.

WAS the world all sunless, starless?
    Day and night the same?
God furled up the vapory curtains—
    Light from heaven came!
There the sun broke out in glory,
    Crowned the king of day;
There the moon, revealed in splendor,
    Chased night's gloom away;
There each star, with smiling glances,
    Earthward threw its ray.

Growing into form and beauty,
    Lifeless was the earth?
Then the good and great Designer
    Gave its tribes their birth.
First the seas held creatures moving—
    Life their waters stirred;
But, amid earth's awful silence,
    Not a voice was heard,
Till, a brighter era dawning,
    Sang the earliest bird.

O'er the plains, along the mountains,
    Roamed no flock or herd?

Then they came—the wild, the docile,
  At the mighty Word!
But no form, erect and human,
  No observant eye,
No pure mind to heaven aspiring,
  Till, with purpose high,
Man was made in God's own image;
  Made to live—not die!          1856

---

[FEB. 4.]   In Eden .. he put the man whom he had formed. GEN. ii. 8.
  To him that overcometh, to him will I give to eat of the tree of life,
which is in the Paradise of God. REV. ii. 7.

### PARADISE.

In Eden's blessèd bowers
  The primal man was placed;
With bright and fragrant flowers
  His happy home was graced.

The skies smiled sweetly o'er him,
  And bird-songs echoed near,
While every view before him
  Was beautiful and dear.

For him, through all its stages,
  Each period-day had wrought;
To him the lingering ages
  This lovely scene had brought.

For man, is still progressing,
  Through time's long weary swing,
A grander work and blessing—
  The Eden Christ shall bring.          1889

[FEB. 5.]   God blessed the seventh day and hallowed it: because that in it he rested from all his work. GEN. ii. 3.

I was in the Spirit on the Lord's day. REV. 1. 10.

## THE SABBATH.

CREATIVE days were ended,
　　Earth's beauty spread afar,
The gemmed expanse extended
　　To heaven's remotest star—
His perfect work Jehovah blest,
And o'er it came his hallowed rest.

With joy this wondrous splendor
　　Man, latest formed, could view,
And he alone could render
　　The thoughtful homage due
To him who made the sabbath blest
For sacred worship, praise, and rest.

Bright, on these earliest pages,
　　The sabbath light is shed;
It gleams along the ages,
　　By Law and Gospel led;
And still the world is richly blest
By God's thrice-hallowed day of rest.

The grandest work was ended
　　The world has ever known,
When Christ arose—ascended—
　　From sepulcher to throne:
Oh, resurrection day of rest,
Our Lord's memorial, ever blest!

We hail its sweet returning,
  Its Lord we love to see;
Our hearts, with worship burning,
  Would in the Spirit be:
Thus shall the day, so honored, blest,
Foreshadow our eternal rest.          1880

---

[FEB. 6.]  Worship before the Lord thy God : and thou shalt rejoice in all the good which the Lord thy God hath given unto thee. DEUT. xxvi. 10, 11.

They were all together in one place. ACTS ii. 2.

### INVOCATION.

GOD of glory! great, eternal,
  Robed in majesty and light,
Worshiped, on thy throne supernal,
  By adoring spirits bright,
      Gladly crowning
  Thee with honor, praise, and might :

Humbly at thy footstool bending,
  Here we come to pay our vow;
Let thy grace, like dew descending,
  Sweetly rest upon us now,
      While before thee,
  Lord, with grateful hearts we bow.

Grant to us thy richest blessing—
  Presence of the Holy Dove,
Peace and joy our souls possessing,
  Through the Saviour's dying love;
      Make our worship
  Like the praise in heaven above.          1841

[FEB. 7.] Her seed : it shall bruise thy head, and thou shalt bruise his heel. GEN. iii. 15.

Through one man sin entered into the world, and death through sin. ROM. v. 12.

## THE FALL AND THE PROMISE.

OH, why should the beauty of Eden be marred,
   Its radiant loveliness fade?
And why from its splendors immortals be barred,
Their innocent souls sin-smitten and scarred,
   In shame and in sorrow arrayed?

Why over the glory of nature a blight,
   And briars with roses be found?
Sad curses commingled with scenes of delight,
All pleasures to poison, all prospects to smite,
   And leave a death-wail o'er the ground?

The Word of the Lord was unheeded, unkept;
   The tempter, persuading apace,
Deep into the soul how unwarily crept,
Its powers to bewilder while consciences slept ;
   So ruin was wrought for the race.

The shock of man's sin, how it jarred all the world,
   And dashed on eternity's shore!
The lovely and fair to guilt's doom it has hurled ;
And over earth's realms a black banner unfurled
   Waves dismally sad evermore!

No! not evermore bides the curse that we dread;
   A promise rings out o'er the tomb!
The Seed of the woman shall bruise the foe's head:
Life, life, shall return unto souls that are dead,
   And earth a new Paradise bloom!              1880

[FEB. 8.] He shall come again with joy, bringing his sheaves with him. Ps. cxxvi. 6.

The harvest is the end of the world; and the reapers are angels.— MATT. xiii. 39.

## THE GRACIOUS HARVEST.

THE kingdom of the holy
　　Springs from the seed divine;
The gracious world-wide sowing,
　　O blesséd Christ! was thine—
Through toilsome, weary journeys,
　　In words and works of might,
Lone sorrows of the Garden,
　　Death-woes in Calvary's night!

Alas! that seeds of evil,
　　Through Satan's wily snares,
Should on the field be scattered—
　　The worthless, blighting tares:
But in the march of ages,
　　As his supreme reward,
Shall spread o'er earth in splendor
　　The kingdom of the Lord.

When come the angel reapers
　　To sever souls depraved
From Christ's obedient followers,
　　The myriads of the saved—
These like the sun in glory,
　　Shall near their Father shine,
And sing through endless cycles
　　Redeeming love divine.

1887

[FEB. 9.]   The Lord had respect unto Abel and to his offering.   GEN.
iv. 4.
And through it he being dead yet speaketh.   HEB. xi. 4.

## ABEL, THE FIRST SAVED.

RIGHTEOUS Abel! first to tread
The dark valley to the dead;
First to pass the mystic gate,
By a brother's vengeful hate;
 First of martyrs, first of souls
 Crossing o'er the untried shoals
 Where life's sea eternal rolls.

First of all the sons of earth
Welcomed to a heavenly birth;
First of mortals to behold
Jasper walls and streets of gold;
 First of all the mighty throng
 That to Christ the Lord belong,
 First to sing redemption's song.

Through the gateway as he trod,
Safe within the realm of God,
O'er him Heaven's all-glorious skies,
Round him angels' eager eyes,
 Wondering whence this stranger fair,
 Whence the robe they see him wear,
 Brighter both than any there.

Wondering still they list the strain
Abel sings and sings again,
Sings so sweet, so strange, so new,
Hosts from farthest bounds it drew;

Ne'er on all the heavenly shore
Strain like that heard they before,
Thrilled to hear it o'er and o'er.

Ah! redemption's song on high
Wakes the wonder of the sky,
Still increasing since the hour
Abel first disclosed its power.
　Vast the throngs its music share,
　Vaster yet as ages wear,
　Countless when all gathered there.　1879

---

[FEB. 10.]　The Lord is my shepherd ; I shall not want. Ps. xxiii. 1.
　My sheep hear my voice, and I know them, and they follow me : and
I give unto them eternal life ; and they shall never perish. JOHN
x. 27, 28.

## DEVOTION TO CHRIST.

Jesus, my shepherd and my guide,
　Oh, keep and shelter me!
With thy dear flock I would abide,
　Thy true disciple be.

Dear Jesus, thou hast loved me so,
　And sought me from above—
Oh, never let me cease to know
　The sweetness of thy love.

Blest Jesus, take and rule my heart,
　Each thought, all life be thine;
Then may I see thee as thou art,
　And in thy glory shine.　1858

[FEB. 11.]   I do set my bow in the cloud, and it shall be for a token of a covenant between me and the earth.   GEN. ix. 13.

There was a rainbow round about the throne, like an emerald to look upon.   REV. iv. 3.

## THE RAINBOW.

As PENDENT from the bending sky,
   Behold the storm-cloud grandly march!
And as we gaze the wondering eye
   Discerns the rainbow's lovely arch.

What soft clear hues, divinely bright,
   Along the curving glory shine,
Blending in matchless lines of light,
   Our Father's work and covenant-sign.

It seems, on that back-ground of wrath,
   Sweet Mercy's form with smiling grace,
To show a blest and radiant path
   That leads us to the holy place.

For evermore it speaks to man,
   As time shall pass and earth endure:
See, as the bow the cloud shall span,
   Jehovah's promise bright and sure!

Not e'er again wild deluge-wave
   Our sin-scarred world with ruin sweeps;
From wrath deserved the Lord shall save
   The race his long forbearance keeps.

So man may live and turn to him,
   The beast beneath his care repose,
And naught his wondrous love shall dim
   Till time and calls of mercy close.

Oft shall repeat the cloud and shower,
  To eyes and hearts that see and know,
God's lovingkindness, grace, and power,
  Blent in the circling radiant bow.

Fair bow of promise!—mercy's sign—
  Thy lessons sweet I gladly own,
And may I in the land divine
  Behold the rainbow round the throne.   1880

---

[FEB. 12]  He shall dwell on high.  ISA. xxxiii. 16.

  Willing rather to be absent from the body, and to be at home with
the Lord.  2 COR. v. 8.

### THE HOME ABOVE.

THERE is a home of love and joy,
  That knows no shade of gloom,
Where charming flowers, that never fade,
  In radiant gardens bloom.

Soft angel fingers gather them,
  As o'er those fields they tread,
To weave a glorious coronal
  For every saintly head.

In that fair land of purest bliss
  No sorrow e'er appears,
For God will bring his children there,
  And wipe away their tears.

Oh, bless'd home! sweet place of rest!
  Where friend ne'er parts with friend,
And all shall sing their Saviour's praise
  In songs that never end.   1840

[Feb. 13.]  For a small moment have I forsaken thee; but with great mercies will I gather thee. Isa. liv. 7.

Death shall be no more; neither shall there be mourning, nor crying, nor pain, any more. Rev. xxi. 4.

## SORROW AND FAITH.

Bereft again!  Who shall the grief reveal,
  When thus are sundered life's endearing ties;
What untold anguish may the heart conceal,
  When its own self in its belovéd dies!

Ah! none can tell the sorrow of the hour,
  Save he whose spirit knew its keenest pang,
When voices of the past, with throngful power,
  Through memory's halls in saddest cadence rang.

But, breaking thro' the thick enswathing gloom,
  Come the sure promises of truth divine;
They bear the soul aloft, while o'er the tomb
  Their clustering beams in glorious beauty shine.

Faith cleaves the sky, as in an upward flight
  She wings her way to opening realms of bliss,
And views those spirits in the world of light
  So fondly loved while they sojourned in this.

She whispers: Thou, erelong, shalt meet them there,
  No more to part while endless ages roll;
For Heaven's eternal life excludes all care,
  And Heaven's eternal love fills all the soul.

Now, lost in light the darkest scenes of time,
  Faith bids the toil-worn pilgrim's heart rejoice,
Speaks of the raptures of that holier clime,
  And restful trust is in her cheering voice.      1846

[FEB. 14.] The flowers appear on the earth; the time of the singing
of birds is come. CANT. ii. 12.
Solomon in all his glory was not arrayed like one of these. MAT. vi. 29.

## FRIEND AND FLOWERS.

How LIKE to thee
The flowers, so sweetly beaming,
While beauty o'er them gleaming,
And light around them streaming,
They smile in glee.

Like thee the birds,
So gaily singing o'er thee,
All nature bright before thee;
Let not thy heart deplore thee,
In saddening words.

But know that soon
Flowers fade as dreams of pleasure,
Earth's joys expend their measure,
Fickle as fancy's treasure,
Or clouds at noon.

Be thine, dear one,
A friend of true affection;
Be Christ your first selection,
And yours his kind protection,
Till life is done.

Then shall you rise,
All earthly hopes releasing,
To scenes of bliss unceasing,
Where joys are still increasing,
In Paradise.

1844

[FEB. 15.] Get thee out of thy country, and from thy kindred, and from thy father's house, unto the land that I will shew thee. GEN. xii. 1. And he went out, not knowing whither he went. HEB. xi. 8.

## THE CALL OF ABRAHAM.

WITH strength of faith sublime,
O'er all of olden time,
　　The patriarch weighed
The call that stirred his heart,
That bade him rise and start,
From home and kindred part,
　　And quick obeyed.

Forth on the untried path,
Taking what each day hath,
　　He journeyed strong:
God would his footsteps guide,
All needful things provide,
And let no ill betide,
　　His way along.

O'er plain and stream he went,
And nightly pitched his tent,
　　And slept and dreamed,
Till Canaan's land of rest,
The end of march and quest,
The promised country blest,
　　Before him beamed.

Oh, thus to walk by faith,
In what the dear Lord saith,
　　Led by his hand;
To know each day is right,

Though oft come clouds and night,
The end to be all bright,
And Canaan's land!                     1880

---

[FEB. 16.] The Lord..will send his angel with thee, and prosper
thy way. GEN. xxiv. 40.

The Lord hath sent forth his angel and delivered me out of the hand
of Herod. ACTS xii. 11.

## GUARDIAN ANGELS.

Its beautiful angels kind Heaven oft sends
To saints here sojourning, as guardian friends;
They linger about us, give hints of alarm,
A vigil most helpful to shield us from harm.

In visible forms once they wandered earth o'er,
By patriarchs seen at their humble tents' door;
The prophets beheld them in peril's dark hour,
Eluded dread foes by the aid of their power.

When once our Redeemer abode among men,
How Heaven's sweet angels attended him then!
They came to apostles on land and on sea,
Their safety assured, or from prison set free.

Not now to our sight do these guardians appear,
Still oft they come earthward and tenderly near;
Their soft wings are o'er us as banners of love,
Their watch ceases not till they bear us above.

God's grace in salvation they long to survey,
Its mysteries scan, and its glories portray:
Its victory sure, in each soul that's forgiven,
Enhances their joy and they chant it in heaven.   1889

[FEB. 17.]   Lot dwelled in the cities of the Plain and moved his tent as far as Sodom.   GEN. xiii. 12.
Remember Lot's wife.   LUKE xvii. 32.

## THE CHOICE OF LOT.

FROM the hill above Bethel rose full on Lot's vision
    A landscape enchantingly fair;
The deep Jordan valley—an Eden elysian—
    Reposed in its loveliness there.

The beautiful river oft winding descended
    Through richest of verdure-clad fields,
While fringing its banks to the sea where it ended
    Were the palms and the balsams it yields.

Not the right nor the left of the patriarch's offers
    Would the venturing nephew accept;
The passion for wealth, for enlarging his coffers,
    To the depths of his spirit had crept.

So down toward the city of Sodom polluted,
    He pitched his white tents on the Plain;
And they laughed as he often their errors refuted,
    While into his home came the stain.

The riches he gained, while forgetting the altar,
    Were lost in a moment at last;
And the wife of his bosom in fleeing would falter,
    O'erwhelmed in the dread judgment-blast.

Oh, pitch not thy tent with the wicked, forsaking
    God's people and service of love!
For what are the riches the Godless are making,
    Compared with the treasures above?    1880

[FEB. 18.] He was priest of God Most High. And he blessed him, and said, Blessed be Abram. GEN. xiv. 18, 19.

The author of eternal salvation; named of God a high priest after the order of Melchizedek. HEB. v. 9, 10.

## MELCHIZEDEK.

THE Most High God, to do his beck,
Chose Salem's king, Melchizedek;
A king and priest, though not in line,
An earthly prince with ken divine:
He goes to Shaveh's lovely vale
The gallant Abraham there to hail,
Returning now, a victor bright
O'er federate foes of plundering might.

Who is this wondrous king of peace,
This earliest priest of righteousness,
Who blessings poured on Abraham's head,
And offerings gave of wine and bread?
Type of a greater King he stands,
Sovereign at length of all the lands,
The Priest whose offering was to die,
Who lives and pleads for us on high.

Oh, precious truth, so early given,
To lead the way to hope and heaven;
The light that cheered the saints of old,
The story of redemption told:
Oh, blesséd truth, the Christ divine,
Who gives our souls the bread and wine;
Our All in all while here we stay,
Our King and crown in endless day.  1880

[FEB. 19.]  I am thy shield and thy exceeding great reward. GEN.
xv. 1.

To Abraham his faith was reckoned for righteousness. ROM. iv. 9.

## GOD'S PROMISES TO ABRAHAM.

FEAR not, Abraham, saith the Lord,
　I'm thy shield and great reward;
I will bless thee now and ever,
Naught from thee my love shall sever.

　Promises that I have made,
　All the words my mouth hath said,
I'll fulfill them to the letter—
Than thy fears thy God is better.

　I from Ur, with guiding hand,
　Brought thee to this chosen land;
I have seen thy faith's true merit,
Thou this country shalt inherit.

　Would'st thou have a certain sign
　That the blessing shall be thine?—
Canst thou count the stars of heaven?
So shall seed to thee be given.

　From a land of trials sore,
　After bondage years are o'er,
They shall here repeat the story
Of their triumph and my glory.

　Abraham then his Lord believed,
　And the great reward received:
So may all the souls that love him
By their faith unwavering prove him.　1880

[FEB. 20.] Lovely and pleasant. 2 SAM. i. 23. But sleepeth. M'K v. 39.

## THE ONLY CHILD.

PLAYFUL darling, blooming maiden,
  Precious gift and only child,
Dearly loved and beauty-laden—
  Heaven upon our home had smiled.
    Loving eyes were often glancing
    On her winning ways entrancing,
    Toward maturing years advancing.

Angel daughter, fondly cherished,
  How our hearts around thee twined!
Brightest hopes in thee have perished,
  All the world seems dumb and blind!
    Night upon our souls is falling,
    Deep to solemn deep is calling,
    Ah! the shadows are appalling!

Lingering gently at the border,
  While no fear her spirit vexed,
Sweet she spoke her love's true order:
  "Jesus first and parents next."
    Farewells given, forth she ventured,
    All her hopes in Jesus centered,
    As within the veil she entered.

There, amid celestial splendors,
  Angel hosts and ransomed throngs,
Praises to the Lamb she renders,
  Joining in their glorious songs:
    There she waits for us to meet her,
    Then with rapture we shall greet her;
    Oh, what thought or hope is sweeter?  1884

[FEB. 21.]  In great affliction. NEH. i. 3.  Reserved in heaven. 1 PE. i. 4.

## BEREAVEMENT.

WHO parental love can measure,
  Tell its strength, its depths unfold?
Who can estimate the treasure
  Which the heart's affections hold?
    When the tie by death is broken,
    When fades out love's sweetest token,
    Can the sorrow e'er be spoken?

Saviour, lift the cloud of sadness,
  Show us thy dear face divine;
Bring our hearts a ray of gladness,
  O'er them let thy pity shine:
    Sure the soul that deeply grieveth,
    Comfort sweet and calm receiveth,
    As thy promise it believeth.

Passing through the heavenly portal,
  Fading from our earthly sight,
She has found a home immortal,
  In the world of life and light:
    Left forever tears and sighing;
    Blesséd change, from pain and dying,
    Endless bliss the soul supplying.

Lord, we trust thee; thou art gracious;
  Thou didst give the jewel fair;
Oh, to us how bright and precious!
  And to thee what treasure rare!
    Ours and thine, Lord, thou hast taken;
    We're bereaved, but not forsaken;
    Her from sleep thy voice shall waken.   1884

[FEB. 22.] Men of renown. GEN. vi. 4. Hazarded their lives. AC. xv. 26.

## OUR TRIUMVIRATE.

GOD gave us Washington,
When freedom must be won,
    As here proclaimed.
He, strong through battles dread,
Our arms to victory led,
Became his country's head,
    Its father named.

As discord shook the state,
In fierce rebellion's hate,
    And sought its grave,
Our greatheart Lincoln then,
Heaven's chosen of our men,
With faith's courageous pen,
    Freed every slave.

A matchless hero leads
Our hosts to valorous deeds,
    Excelled by none—
The silent soldier Grant,
Whom naught could swerve or daunt,
Who met the Nation's want,
    And kept it one.

Heart-shrined, their names shall live,
And inspiration give,
    While ages roll:—
Illustrious dead, and great,
Peerless in field and state,
Sublime triumvirate,
    In act and soul.

1885

[FEB. 23.] **Thy people shall be my people, and thy God my God.—**
RUTH i. 16.

Chosen the good part, which shall not be taken away from her.—
LUKE x. 42.

## RUTH'S CHOICE AND HONOR.

MOAB daughter! leave thy mountains,
　　Leave the plains along the sea;
Leave the flowers, the sunny fountains,
　　And the graves so dear to thee!

Leave the gods where, often kneeling,
　　Thou hast poured the tears of woe:
Broken hearts they give no healing,
　　Let those senseless idols go!

Heavenly voices, sweetly tender,
　　Through thy spirit-chambers ring;
To their call obedience render,
　　To the hand that beckons cling.

Thoughtful, tearful, mid derision,
　　Thou hast made the highest choice;
Heaven records the grand decision,
　　God has heard thy earnest voice.

Humble gleaner, loved, protected,
　　Trusting under wings divine,
Thou, for high renown selected,
　　Risest to the royal line!

God shall bless thee, and thy story
　　To the farthest age shall live;
He shall crown thy choice with glory,
　　Thee immortal honors give.

1868

[FEB. 24.] Orpah kissed her mother in law; but Ruth clave unto her. RUTH i. 14.
I will follow thee whithersoever thou goest. MATT. viii. 19.

## RUTH AND NAOMI.

I WILL go where faith shall lead me,
 Fearing not the way untried;
Hands unseen shall guide and feed me,
 Though I pass the Jordan tide.

Where thou goest, dear Naomi,
 I will surely go with thee;
Moab's land no more shall know me,
 From its gods I'm ever free.

Where thou sleepest I will slumber,
 Sharing all the lot of thine;
I will join thy people's number,
 And thy God shall hence be mine.

In life's evening where thou diest,
 Is the place where I will die;
In the tomb wherein thou liest,
 Buried there, my dust shall lie.

Heaven records my declaration;
 Naught but death can us divide;
Henceforth be my joyful station,
 Loved Naomi, at thy side.

Gentle spirit, angels cheer thee,
 In a path untried before,
Watching, guarding, camping, near thee,
 Till thy pilgrimage is o'er.

1868

[FEB. 25.] Bethlehem .. out of thee shall one come forth unto me that is to be ruler in Israel. MIC. v. 2.
And he called his name JESUS. MATT. i. 25.

## THE CHRIST CHILD.

How BEAUTIFUL the morn,
   That breaks in heavenly song,
As Christ the Lord is born,
   The Saviour promised long.
Earth too may sing, as angels bright
On wings of light the tidings bring.

In Bethlehem's manger low
   The Christ-child sweetly lies;
There favored shepherds go,
   And feast their wondering eyes.
The story they to all repeat,
As haste their feet along the way.

The wise men leave their home,
   And westward journeying far,
To the Child Jesus come,
   Led by the guiding star.
They bow before the new-born King,
And rich gifts bring from out their store.

Oh, sweet and blesséd truth—
   Our Lord was once a child!
He knows the hearts of youth,
   He's near the meek and mild.
He took our place he loved us so,
That we might know his saving grace.

Children, how great his charms!
   Jesus, of lowly birth;

He calls you to his arms,
As once he did on earth.
Hear and obey, your young hearts give,
And for him live from this glad day. 1884

---

[FEB. 26.] He made it glorious, by the way of the sea, beyond Jordan,
Galilee of the nations. Isa. ix. 1.
Come ye after me, and I will make you fishers of men. Mat. iv. 19.

## JESUS AT THE SEA OF GALILEE.

From honored Bethlehem's lowly cave,
From Nazareth's vale in Galilee,
From wondrous scenes at Jordan's wave,
Jesus now stands beside the Sea.

How sweet in such a favored hour,
From lips divine the gospel sounds;
The heavenly kingdom comes in power—
Repent, believe, while grace abounds.

Toilers along that pebbly shore
Hear calls that memory ne'er forgets;
The tones their inmost souls explore,
And draw the fishers from their nets.

In new-born love to Christ they cling,
Feast on his words of life and peace;
To earth's far bounds those words they ring,
Fishers of men till time shall cease.

Oh, wondrous Voice, divinely sweet,
The call of Jesus, Follow me:
What countless tongues the call repeat—
To-day it comes, dear soul, to thee. 1882

[FEB. 27.]   Surely he hath borne our griefs, and carried our sorrows. ISA. liii. 4.
He laid his hands on every one of them and healed them. LU. iv. 40.

## HEALING THE SICK AT SUNSET.

O'ER Carmel's ridge declining,
    The sun is sinking low;
On Gilead's brow his shining
    Is but a lingering glow,
While waiting shadows rally,
    As day-beams gently flee,
To fill the Jordan valley,
    And veil Gennesaret's sea.

But such a day of blessing
    Was never known before—
Capernaum Christ possessing,
    While thousands throng the shore
To hear the loving Preacher,
    And see in mercy's hour
The wonder-working Teacher
    Subdue the demons' power.

From homes of grief and sighing,
    That sabbath evening came
The sick, the crazed, the dying,
    Drawn by the mighty Name.
Their woes and sorrows feeling,
    He rent their heavy chains;
His gracious power of healing
    Brought joys for all their pains.

When shadows o'er us falling,
    And hearts are troubled sore,

He hears the burdened calling,
    His words the soul restore.
O Healer, great and tender!
    O Saviour, throned above!
Strong Leader and defender,
    We trust thy matchless love.    1882

[FEB. 28.] While they are yet speaking I will hear. ISA. lxv. 24.
Ask and ye shall receive, that your joy may be fulfilled. JOHN xvi. 24.

### SOCIAL PRAYER.

DEAR Saviour! teach us how to pray,
    To bring thy blessing from above;
Our faith upon thy promise stay,
    And fill our souls with peace and love.

Oh, grant to us the Spirit's power,
    Uplift our hearts with thine to blend,
That we may share, this sacred hour,
    A heavenly joy that ne'er shall end.    1838

[FEB. 29.] By my spirit, saith the Lord of hosts. ZECH. iv. 6.
Put on the whole armor of God. EPH. vi. 11.

### EQUIPMENT.

BREATHE upon us, Holy Spirit,
    Permeate our souls with light;
Let us life from thee inherit,
    Clothed with resurrection might.

In thy pure and ample showers
    Bathe the hosts that hesitate;
Energize their dormant powers
    Till for God they work and wait.    1889

[MAR. 1.]   Who forgiveth all thine iniquities; who healeth all thy dis-
eases.  Ps. ciii. 3.

Jesus seeing their faith saith unto the sick of the palsy, Son, thy sins
are forgiven.  MARK ii. 5.

## RESTORED AND FORGIVEN.

At home by the lake, encompassed by throngs,
  The wonderful Prophet was eagerly sought.
The healed had proclaimed him in jubilant songs,
  And still to his feet were the suffering brought.

How sweet were the words that he graciously spoke,
  Unfolding the heavenly kingdom of love:
How dark were the clouds that he lifted and broke,
  How cheering the rays that he flashed from above.

No room in the dwelling, vast crowds at the door,
  With eagerness pressing the message to hear:
A prone paralytic, borne thither by four,
  Would fain to the Miracle-worker draw near.

All helpless they take him, the house-top ascend,
  And over the head of the Master below,
The roof intervening they hasten to rend,
  And gently let down their sad burden of woe.

'T was marvelous faith!  He beheld it and said,
  Thy sins are forgiven, rise up and depart:
'T was full restoration! and grasping his bed
  He bounded away in what gladness of heart!

Dear pitying Healer, still mighty to save,
  And waiting for faith the poor helpless to bring:
Come, come, ye sin-smitten, recovery crave—
  Restored and forgiven—then evermore sing!  1882

[MAR. 2.]  Another shall subscribe with his hand unto the Lord.—
ISA. xliv. 5.
He stretched it forth: and his hand was restored.  MARK iii. 5.

## THE WITHERED HAND.

Son of man and Son of God,
While our sinful earth he trod,
Precious gifts diffused abroad.

Words of truth and life he spoke,
Bonds of sin and Satan broke,
Healed the sick, the dead awoke.

See him with a sweet command,
Bid the man with shriveled hand,
Forth before the crowd to stand.

Once a limb of strength and pride,
Now of vital force denied,
Hangs how helpless at his side.

Past all earthly aid or cure,
Pain and weakness to endure,
Seems till death his burden sure.

Ah, that voice of sweet command,
Like a note from heaven's own land,
Thrills his soul: *Stretch forth thy hand!*

Instantly, as he obeyed,
Christ the needed strength conveyed,
Whole the withered arm was made.

Heed the lesson, souls in sin,
Would you life eternal win?
See the gate, and enter in.                1882

[MAR. 3.]  I took twelve men of you, one man for every tribe. DEUT. i. 23.

He continued all night in prayer to God. And when it was day, he called his disciples: and he chose from them twelve. LUKE vi. 2, 13.

## JESUS AND HIS CHOSEN.

FROM all the regions round,
Crowds came to Christ and found
　　His mighty will
Subdued their mortal foes,
Availed for all their woes,
And gave them glad repose
　　From torturing ill.

Ah, thus how much he bore,
What burdens great and sore,
　　What weary grief!
For rest, so long denied,
He left the water side,
And o'er the upland wide
　　Sought sweet relief.

Lone, on the mountain's brow,
The still hours saw him now
　　All through the night:
A new work on him weighed,
Whose vastness was surveyed,
As peacefully he prayed
　　Till morning light.

Joy fills his sacred soul,
As here he calls the roll
　　Of chosen friends,
Who to their Lord shall cling,

Go forth and trophies bring,
Till earth before her King
　　In reverence bends.

We have our burdens too,
Our work assigned to do,
　　Our night of prayer:
Oh, chosen of the Lord,
For service and reward,
Can any task be hard
　　Under his care?　　　　1882

---

[Mar. 4.] The Lord bless thee, and keep thee:
　The Lord make his face to shine upon thee, and be gracious unto thee:
　The Lord lift up his countenance upon thee, and give thee peace.—
Num. vi. 24–26.
　Peace I leave with you: my peace I give unto you. John xiv. 27.

### A BENEDICTION.

The Lord his blessing give to thee,
For none can richly bless as he;
And always thee in safety keep,
At home, abroad, awake, asleep.

The Lord's dear face upon thee shine,
Illume thy way with smiles benign;
And through all scenes of joy or ill,
Be kindly gracious to thee still.

The Lord lift up his countenance
On thee, in sweet approving glance;
And give to thee till life shall cease
Abundance of his blessèd peace.　　　1889

[MAR. 5.]   I will put a new spirit within you. EZEK. xi. 19.
The kingdom of God is within you. LUKE xvii. 21.

## THE KINGDOM WITHIN.

WONDROUS is the new creation,
  Here in mortal lives begun;
Dawn of light, an emanation
  From the glorious central Sun.
See it rise, the darkness fleeing,
  As it holds its upward way,
Till the Heaven-illumined being
  Shines serene in perfect day.

Like the grain the human sower
  Casts with faith in mellow earth,
Jesus, truth's divine bestower,
  Gives to souls immortal birth.
Now the tender blade appearing,
  Then the ear, the ripened corn,
Ay, the harvest, full and cheering,
  In the coming cloudless morn.

Oft how small this life's beginning,
  Like the seed we scarcely see;
Up it springs, a grandeur winning,
  As a fair and stately tree.
Rarest birds, the branches filling,
  Sing all day, nor cease at night;
Blesséd music, spirit-thrilling,
  Foretaste of the songs of light.

With this life forever bless me,
  Let it all my nature claim,
In thy fullness, Lord, possess me,

On my soul inscribe thy name;
Let the light, the word, the gladness,
Grow within me, ne'er depart;
Shine away all sin and sadness,
Build thy kingdom in my heart. 1882

[MAR. 6.] My beloved is mine, and I am his. CANT. ii. 16.
Whosoever shall do the will of God, the same is my brother, and sister, and mother. MARK iii. 35.

## KINSHIP WITH CHRIST.

How RICH the tenderness and grace,
Shown in the Saviour's loving care;
Deep in his heart he gives us place,
And owns the tie that binds us there.

What high relationship is mine,
If to the Father's will I bow;
How wonderful the truth divine,
That names me Jesus' brother now!

Christ's love and sympathy so kind
Brings gentle, trusting spirits near:
Sweet soul, if in that love enshrined,
Thou art his precious sister dear.

And ye that serve through many cares,
Oft suffering much with scant reward,
Think who your every burden shares,
And calls you mothers of the Lord!

Oh, what the pride of earthly fame,
The rank from royal blood that springs?
We bear a far more glorious name,
A kinship with the King of kings! 1882

[MAR. 7.]   He hath sent me to bind up the brokenhearted, to proclaim
liberty to the captives. ISA. lxi. 1.

Tell them how great things the Lord hath done for thee, and how
he had mercy on thee. MARK v. 19.

## THE SAVED DEMONIAC.

WHERE, mid rock bluffs and gaping tombs,
 The wild demoniac made his lair,
 In raging madness and despair,
The Prince of peace with blessing comes:
 'T is he who bid the sea be calm,
 Brings to this soul a healing balm.

At his command the Legion foe
 Released his prey, tormented long;
 The Stronger now had bound the strong,
And made the captive freedom know.
 To him, so wondrously redeemed,
 At Jesus' feet a heaven seemed.

What selfish souls that bade the Lord,
 Who in great mercy wrought the change,
 And waited still for wider range,
Depart and leave no other word.
 Oh, fearful, when the boon's so nigh,
 To thrust it hence, and hopeless die!

The ransomed would to Jesus cling,
 Go with him o'er Gennesaret's tide,
 Linger most grateful at his side,
And never cease his praise to sing.
 How can he see his soul's delight
 Float from the shore and fade from sight!

With loving look and tender tone:
  "Go to thy home, let kindred see
    The work thy Lord hath done for thee,
And they this marvel great shall own;
    And so thy Master still will stay
    With thee and them, though sent away."

Oh, bléssed task, this grace to tell,
    To publish far in mercy's hour
    The matchless love, the mighty power,
That saves from Satan and from hell.
    Go forth, ye rescued, and proclaim
    Salvation free in Jesus' name.      1882

---

[MAR. 8.]  I will be as the dew unto Israel. Hos. xiv. 5.
  Ye have heard of the patience of Job, and have seen the end of the Lord, how that the Lord is full of pity, and merciful. JAS. v. 11.

### DIVINE GOODNESS.

FATHER! the nations saw and knew
Thou wast to Israel as the dew;
Thy tender love and kindly care
Were benedictions everywhere.
Through all the years thou art the same,
Thy people know and trust thy name.

Longsuffering still, wrath laid aside,
Dear Lord, thou dost not always chide;
As heaven o'er earth is high above,
So great thy mercy, rich thy love;
Far as the east is from the west,
Are our transgressions from us cast.     1889

[Mar. 9.] He shall save the children of the needy. Ps. lxxii. 4.

He, taking her by the hand, call'd, saying, Maiden, arise. And her spirit returned, and she rose up immediately. Luke viii. 54, 55.

## JAIRUS'S DAUGHTER.

How SAD the sound to anxious ears,
 The child is dead!
But Jesus quells the dreadful fears:
 By faith be led.

They near the home—the wail is wild
 The mourners make.
Why all this tumult, when the child
 But sleeps to wake?

They laugh to scorn, as forth he sends
 The heartless throng.
The mourners true, the chosen friends,
 He leads along.

The silent chamber holds them now:
 How still is death!
The pallid seal is on that brow—
 Hushed the last breath.

For breaking hearts is there surprise?
 Her hand he takes:
*Talitha cumi*—Dear one, rise!—
 She moves, she wakes!

At once she rose in health's full glow,
 And walked apace:
Parental hearts in love's o'erflow
 Their child embrace.

O Son of God! this work of thine
   My faith shall keep:
Death is not death—thy voice divine
   Shall break its sleep!     1882

---

[MAR. 10.]  A bruised reed shall he not break, and the smoking flax shall he not quench.  ISA. xlii. 3.

Is not this the carpenter's son? is not his mother called Mary?—MATT. xiii. 55.

## MEEK AND LOWLY.

JESUS! God's dear and only Son
Ere earth was formed or time begun:
For us he left his home on high,
And laid his throne and glory by.

Among the lowly see him move,
His heart all tenderness and love;
The child, the youth, the man of care,
He comes their lot and toil to share.

Dear Son of Mary, King of kings!
Treasures of peace and joy he brings;
Salvation's gift for every soul,
With power to make the dying whole.

His gracious words of truth and light
Would banish woe and heavy night;
His kindly help, his mighty deeds,
Relieve at once the deepest needs.

Each choice he notes and, filled with grief,
He marvels at their unbelief
Who spurn the grace and gift of God,
While ways of sin and death are trod.   1882

[MAR. 11.] His violence shall come down upon his own pate. Ps. vii. 16.
Herod, when he heard thereof, said, John, whom I beheaded, he is
risen.  M'RK vi. 16.

## HEROD'S CONSCIENCE.

BY sea side and mountain, wherever he trod,
The works of the Saviour revealed him as God,
And published his fame to the people abroad.

To the palace of Herod these wonders have sped;
They recall what a horror that never has fled,
Since he gave to Salome the Forerunner's head!

The birth-feast with nobles revisits his glance,
The oath to the damsel, bewitched by her dance,
The mother's revenge as she seizes her chance.

His conscience awakes—it can never expire;
Of guilt it accuses, and flashes fierce ire,
While whelming his soul like a torrent of fire!

It wrings the confession: "These marvels of might
Are works of the prophet I murdered that night;
He's risen again and walks forth in the light.

I knew he was right as my vices he named;
I knew I was wrong as excuses I framed;
I felt all the truth he so boldly proclaimed.

This John I beheaded—most royal of men;
His pale, bleeding face—I behold it as then;
He comes from the dead to confront me again!"

Ah, mortal, beware! for the truth you despise,
The good you discarded for folly or lies,
Will flash on your soul as in future they rise!     1882

[MAR. 12.]  They that sow in tears shall reap in joy.  Ps. cxxvi. 5.

Those are they that were sown upon the good ground; such as hear the word and accept it.  M'RK iv. 20.

## SOWER AND HARVEST.

O LORD, thy blesséd word
    To countless souls is taught,
And where its truth is heard,
    Salvation free is brought.
As rain and snow descend from heaven,
This gospel grace to men is given.

While sowers cast the seed
    Upon the favored ground,
If sinners felt their need,
    What harvests would be found!
In hearts long dead new life would spring,
And peace and joy with pardon bring.

The quickening Spirit warns
    Against each hindering foe—
The birds, the rocks, the thorns—
    Lest fruits should fail to grow,
And toil and blood of priceless cost
On souls of sordid care be lost.

O Sower, blest, divine!
    My heart the good ground be,
Where every word of thine
    Shall something yield for thee—
A hundredfold in works of love,
A hundredfold in wealth above.

1882

[MAR. 13.]   He shall feed his flock like a shepherd.  ISA. xl. 11.
They that did eat were about five thousand men, beside women and children.   MATT. XIV. 21.

## FEEDING THE MULTITUDE.

TEN thousand souls were feeding
　　On truth and love divine,
Till bread the crowds were needing,
　　As day was toward decline.
To meet their urgent wishes,
　　The present scanty fare—
Five barley loaves, two fishes—
　　Would count as little there.

Christ, pitiful and tender,
　　Said, Give ye them to eat,
Let faith true service render,
　　And see its aim complete.
Mysterious is the blending
　　Of human and divine—
We act, but in the ending,
　　The work, O Lord, is thine.

Along Bethsaida's border,
　　On verdant lawn arrayed,
To all the ranks in order,
　　The food is soon conveyed.
As Jesus gives his blessing,
　　The loaves are multiplied,
His wonder-work confessing,
　　Till all are satisfied.

O Shepherd! for us dying,
　　Compassionate as then,

What starving souls are sighing
    To know thy gifts for men!
Intrusted with these treasures,
    While almoners we live,
Bless and increase the measures
    As we thy bounty give.     1882

---

[MAR. 14.] This people .. with their lips do honor me, but have re-
moved their heart far from me. Isa. xxix. 13.
    But Christ is all, and in all. Col. iii. 11.

## CHRIST—NOT TRADITION.

Forms are a broken reed,
    Fails every human rite;
No wayside fount can meet my need,
    Or wash my spirit white.

O Lord of life divine,
    Thyself my being craves;
No sacrifice avails but thine—
    Thy blood redeeming saves.

This cleanses me from sin,
    Appeals to God above;
My soul is purified within,
    And filled with peace and love.

No more is self my stay,
    Thy truth has made me free;
How blesséd is salvation's way,
    O Jesus, taught by thee!

To worship thee, my Lord,
    E'er follow thy dear feet,
Rest wholly on thy precious Word—
    Ah, this is joy complete.     1882

[MAR. 15.]  A little child shall lead them.  Isa **xi. 6.**
He took a little child and set him in the midst of them.  MK. **ix. 36.**

### THE CHILD LESSON.

SWEET the scene in Galilee,
When, at home beside the Sea,
To his own the Master turns,
And their inmost thought discerns.

They disputed by the way
Of the kingdom's outward sway,
Who should high in honor stand,
Greatest mid the favored band.

Ah! not thus, proclaims the Lord,
Comes position or reward:
First is he among the blest,
Who shall humbly serve the rest.

Jesus then before them brings
A sweet child that to him clings,
Whom in loving arms he takes,
Emblem of his kingdom makes.

"Who for me, in spirit mild,
Welcomes such a little child,
Me receives and God above,
Crowned at last through toil and love."

Oh! to rest in Jesus' arms,
There to find immortal charms:
Who his humble service bear
Shall his throne of glory share.

1882

[MAR. 16.] Then shalt thou walk in thy way securely. PROV. iii. 23.

Greater joy have I none than this, to hear of my children walking in the truth. 3 JOHN 4.

## BEGINNING TO WALK.

COME, my darling, come to me,
Laughing, crowing in your glee;
See, your father's beckoning arms
Wait to shield from hurts and harms:
Ha! you've started, tripping, running,
Hands outstretched, and steps so cunning.

Oh, my precious baby boy,
Father's pride and mother's joy,
Many charms in thee are found,
Many hopes in thee are bound,
Kindest hands to thee are proffered,
Earnest prayers for thee are offered.

All alone, my blessèd child,
Now so winning, sweet, and mild,
Though with crowds, along the way
Of life's opening, closing day,
Thou must walk, thyself immortal,
Toward the future's solemn portal.

Take no evil path, my boy,
Make not bitter all our joy;
Oh, may every step of thine
Guided be by love divine:
Walk alone the path of duty—
Path of safety and of beauty.

Then thy faithful feet at last,
When this earthly scene is past,
Shall, within the heavenly gate,
Walk, with highest joy elate,
On the banks of Life's pure river,
Bright with glories fading never.          1855

---

[MAR. 17.] When thou passest through the waters I will be with
thee. ISA. xliii. 2.

He cometh unto them, walking on the sea. MARK vi. 48.

## CHRIST ON THE WAVES.

IF on some stormy flood we go,
　　As fades the sunset ray,
From yonder mount, 'tis sweet to know,
As threatening billows round us flow,
　　That Jesus sees our way.

If gloom appalls while surges rave,
　　And struggles vain appear,
Ah! then, as needed help we crave,
He treads sublime the darkling wave—
　　The mighty Saviour near.

Why tremble at the wondrous sight?
　　'Tis Jesus whom we know;
He comes to guide us through the night,
To scenes of peace and rapt delight,
　　Beyond all present woe.

In blinding grief and boding fear,
　　As doubts the soul invade,
How sweet that Voice, so calm and clear,

So fraught with hope and joyous cheer,
"'Tis I, be not afraid."

Welcome, dear Lord! O Saviour blest,
 Come to these weary hearts;
Thy words the raging winds arrest,
Thy presence soothes each troubled breast,
 And life and strength imparts.

How safe the voyage with Christ along!
 How bright the beckoning shore!—
The home of rest, the land of song,
The palms, the crowns, the ransomed throng,
 The Lord whom we adore!     1882

---

[MAR. 18.]   Anointed to preach good tidings unto the meek. ISA.
lxi. 1.
The common people heard him gladly.   MARK xii. 37.

## CHRIST'S PREACHING.

THE people heard the Saviour gladly,
 His Gospel was so sweet;
Their grievous burdens, borne so sadly,
 Fell off at his dear feet.

His gracious message of salvation,
 As morning to the night,
Disclosed a new and blest creation—
 A world of life and light.

O Jesus! mortal man hath never
 Spoken God's love like thee:
To humbly trusting souls thou'lt ever
 Speak peace and pardon free.     1889

[MAR. 19.]   The tongue of the dumb shall sing.  ISA. xxxv. 6.
He sighed and saith unto him, Ephphatha, that is, Be opened.   MK
vii. 34.

## EPHPHATHA.

THIS is the very word
    The mighty Master spoke;
The deaf the mandate heard,
    The dumb his silence broke;
The opened ears drank in the sound;
Praise moved the tongue at once unbound.

Ah! sad and lonely state—
    No voice of friend to hear,
While mute the soul must wait
    Mid scenes of social cheer;
The sun of life in dim eclipse,
No music's tone on ear or lips.

"Be opened!"  Oh, what bliss
    The wakened spirit thrills,
As rapture such as this
    The ransomed senses fills!
It never dreamed such joy to know,
Such sweet release from helpless woe.

But duller ears are found
    To sweeter music sealed;
The Gospel's blessèd sound
    In vain for them is pealed;
They will not list the voice from heaven,
That speaks of Christ and sins forgiven.

And palsied tongues there are,
    By sin enslaved, and weak,

That raise to God no prayer,
   Nor love of Jesus speak;
No soul-uplifting song is sung—
Ah, what a bondage chains the tongue!

"Be opened!" Lord, that word
   To deadened spirits ring!
What wonders will be heard,
   What music it shall bring!
And tongues unloosed will speak abroad
The grace and glory of our God.

Ye whom the Lord has freed,
   And made each sense rejoice,
Bid souls in dying need
   To hear his saving voice,
That they may know and gladly tell
How Jesus doeth all things well.            1882

---

[MAR. 20.]  There are many devices in a man's heart; but the coun-
sel of the Lord, that shall stand.  PROV. xix. 21.
The word of God, which liveth and abideth.  1 PET. i. 23.

### DIVINE TRUTH.

BEHOLD, along the track of years gone by,
The scattered wrecks of faithless theories lie;
Like Jonah's gourd they flourished for a day,
Felt the keen edge of truth and passed away.

The ages roll, and grander grows the truth,
Its birth divine, its life immortal youth;
Its reign is certain as its Lord sublime,
Desire of Nations to the end of Time!            1873

[MAR. 21.] The Lord openeth the eyes of the blind. **Ps. cxlvi. 8.**
They bring to him a blind man, and beseech him to touch him.—
MARK viii. 22.

## THE BLIND RESTORED.

DARK is the world to sightless eyes;
No sunlit day or star-gemmed skies,
　　No garden, field, or streamlet there,
No summer blooms or autumn dyes,
　　No lovely vale or mountain rare,
　　No form of friend or visage fair.

The Lord of life, so sweet and kind,
Leads gently forth the lonely blind—
　　Oh, to be led by such a Hand,
Its touch to feel, its power to find!—
　　He hears the soft yet strong command,
　　And men as trees before him stand.

Sight he receives, but naught is plain,
The Master touched his eyes again;
　　He looks abroad and sees how bright
The blooming land, the sparkling main:
　　Broken the long and weary night,
　　With joy he hails the day's full light!

O blesséd Saviour! thou dost find
Our souls by nature dark and blind,
　　And straying far from light and thee.
To visit us, how gracious, kind;
　　To touch our eyes and bid us see,
　　What wondrous love, how rich and free!

Our sight, dear Lord, is often dim,
Narrow our low horizon's rim;

We crave a higher, clearer scope,
A vision like the seraphim,
   A view of things for which we hope:
   Touch our dull eyes, and they shall ope!

How many souls in sin's dread night
Know not thou art the world's true Light;
   Help us to bring them, Lord, to thee,
That thou mayst touch and give them sight:
   Oh, glorious change! from blindness free,
   The loving Christ to know and see!   1882

---

[MAR. 22.] I wholly followed the Lord my God.  Jos. xiv. 8.
   If any man would come after me, let him deny himself, and take
up his cross, and follow me.  MATT. xvi. 24.

## FOLLOWING CHRIST.

SAVIOUR, I would ever hear thee,
Trace thy footsteps and be near thee,
   Bear whatever cross:
Make of self complete denial,
Firmly stand in every trial,
   Be it gain or loss.

Souls but devotees of pleasure
Sacrifice the noblest treasure,
   Bartering life away.
Who for Christ this vain world losing
Are celestial riches choosing,
   Life and endless day.

When the mortal vale descending,
Where all human scenes are ending,
   Be the world attained,

What would all its wealth avail me,
Just as life itself should fail me?
    What the profit gained?

When the soul, repenting never,
Finds redemption cease forever,
    Can exchange be given?
O'er the bound of man's probation,
Passed the limit of salvation,
    Lost both earth and heaven!

Not ashamed, but thee confessing,
Lord, I would thy grace possessing,
    Live to thee alone;
So, when thou shalt come in glory,
I may sing thy love's sweet story,
    Safe among thine own.                    1882

[MAR. 23.]  Mine eye poureth out tears unto God.  JOB xvi. 20.
Jesus wept.  JOHN xi. 35.

## DID JESUS WEEP FOR ME?

DID Jesus weep for me?
    And sigh o'er sinners here?—
My soul that weeping Saviour see,
    And shed thyself a tear.

Did Jesus pray for me?
    For such a wanderer care?—
My heart subdued and broken be,
    And drawn to him in prayer.

Did Jesus die for me?
    Oh, depth of love divine!—
I die to sin—I'll live to thee;
    O Saviour, make me thine!                1858

[MAR. 24.] I have trodden the winepress alone. ISA. lxiii. 3.
  Over the brook Kidron, where was a garden, into which he entered.
JOHN xviii. 1.

## IN GETHSEMANE.

ONE day, to memory dear, I knelt
    In lone Gethsemane,
On the same ground where Jesus felt
    What none could feel but he.

While praying there it truly seemed
    The Lord himself is here;
I scarce before had thought or dreamed
    That he could be so near.

Among those great old olive trees
    A low wind faintly moans;
'Twas Jesus' prayers upon the breeze,
    With agonizing groans.

I note the soft dew still appears
    On rose-leaves lingering yet;
The pearly drops were Jesus' tears
    That this sad garden wet.

The crimson flower and scarlet bud
    Are blooming sweetly round;
Ah! they are those great drops of blood
    Once falling to the ground.

I see that dark and awful hour,
    The cup received as given,
The deathly strife, the Conqueror's power,
    The angel help from heaven.

While direful hues my sin assumes,
    My soul condemned and lost,

The way of life that scene illumes,
  And shows the ransom cost.

Gethsemane, thy hallowed shade,
  Thy tender memories dear,
That day of days, can never fade,
  And Jesus still is near.      1882

---

[MAR. 25.]   Call ye upon him while he is near.  ISA. lv. 6.
   Thou art not far from the kingdom of God.  MARK xii. 34.

## THE KINGDOM NEAR.

NOT far from the kingdom—so near to the gate
Where pardon and hope for the penitent wait,
Where life from the dead and salvation from sin
Are blessings made certain by entering in.

That kingdom all glorious is not of this clime,
Its realm is celestial, immortal, sublime;
Its subjects are angels, the sinless and just,
And all who make Jesus their Saviour and trust.

The truth and the Spirit bring multitudes near,
The call of its King in the gospel they hear,
A glimpse of its beauty is flashed on their sight
While thinking of loved ones now saints in its light.

What glories are thine, blesséd kingdom of heaven!
What radiant crowns to the saved shall be given,
What rivers of pleasure shall flow thro' their souls,
What raptures of bliss while eternity rolls!

O kingdom of Jesus! shall mortals come nigh,
And stop at the threshold, and linger and die?
Stand close to the Ark with its beckoning door,
And wait till it closes, and hope comes no more    1882

[MAR. 26.] The angels of God met him. And Jacob said when he saw them, This is God's host. GEN. xxxii. 1, 2.

In the resurrection they neither marry nor are given in marriage, but are as angels in heaven. MATT. xxii. 30.

## AS THE ANGELS.

As THE angels—blesséd story!
　Holy, like their loving Lord,
Saints shall be when raised to glory,
　Sharing in their rich reward;
Safe within the pearly portal,
　Free from shadowing cloud or night,
Dwellers in the land immortal,
　Peace and joy their full delight.

As the angels—life's fruition!
　Messengers of Love divine,
Trusted with a glorious mission,
　Serving still in deeds benign;
To the loved of earth descending,
　All unseen but sweetly nigh,
Guardian helpers, souls befriending,
　Waiting for their call on high.

As the angels—Jesus praising
　For his victories of grace,
Filled with rapture deep, amazing,
　As they see him face to face!
Blesséd home of rest supernal,
　No more sorrow, death, or sin;
Oh, the bliss of Life Eternal!
　Oh, the joy of entering in!

1882

[MAR. 27.]   Tabor and Hermon rejoice in thy name.  Ps. lxxxix. 12.
     And he was transfigured before them.  MATT. xvii. 2.

## MOUNT TABOR.

A HIGH mountain apart, that adorns Galilee,
Speaks sweetly of Jesus and heaven to me.
To climb the steep sides of dear Tabor I love,
And think of the glory that hovered above.

'Tis not that the Lake of Gennesareth fair,
Enraptured I see from the high summit there,
Nor landscapes enchanting on every hand met—
Views sacred and lovely I ne'er can forget.

Not Jordan's deep vale, nor Megiddo's so green,
Nor Hermon, Gilboa, and Carmel, there seen;
Not Bashan's dark wall with the light on its crest,
Nor the Great Sea of blue in soft beauty at rest.

These all, with their memories tender or sad,
Rush into my spirit so buoyant and glad;
But the Transfiguration of Jesus sublime
Is the glory transcending all visions of time!

His meek face in prayer 'neath the star-dome of night
Is changed to a brightness outshining the light;
His travel-worn garments a splendor assumed,
That never the robes of an angel illumed.

Lawgiver and Prophet to Jesus draw nigh,
In glorified forms flashing down from the sky,
And deep was their converse of Calvary near,
While the favored exclaim, "It is good to be here."

In grandeur celestial the glory-cloud came,
Overshadowing all with its marvelous flame,

And through it the voice of the Father broke clear,
"This is my Belovéd, and him shall ye hear."

Ay, beautiful Tabor! thou speakest of heaven,
Of the light and the glory to ransomed ones given,
The King in his beauty, the land that's afar,
When the soul in that heaven shall shine as a star.

1865

[MAR. 28.] Believe in .. God, so shall ye be established. 2 CHR. xx. 20.
The fig tree which thou cursedst is withered away. MARK xi. 21.

## HAVE FAITH IN GOD.

Have faith in God! The withered tree
　　Forecasts the doom of vain pretense;
Thus unbelieving souls shall be,
　　When comes the day of recompense.

Have faith in God! The house of prayer,
　　Where much offends his vision pure,
Shall soon his cleansing process share,
　　And truth restored shall long endure.

Have faith in God! His promised power
　　Shall bid the fiercest foe be gone;
Fear not, but know the darkest hour
　　Precedes the near celestial dawn.

Have faith in God! He loves his own:
　　Is aught too hard for sovereign grace?
Cling to his word, besiege his throne,
　　Mountains shall shake and flee apace.

Have faith in God! Oh, blesséd day,
　　When faith shall reap its last rewards,
The gospel win its destined way,
　　And all the earth shall be the Lord's! 1882

[MAR. 29.] Thou hast no healing medicines. JER. xxx. 13.
Jesus answered and said .. bring him hither to me.   MATT. xvii. 17.

## THE EPILEPTIC BOY.

BRING HIM TO ME.  O pitying Lord!
How sweet thy kind persuasive word,
What sympathies in thee o'erflow,
What love for suffering sons of woe!

*How long?*  In childhood's early day
This evil spirit found its prey,
Baffled all skill of healing sought,
And through the years a blight has wrought.

See now the raging of the storm—
The torn and scarred and wasting form;
His life a scene of peril made;
O Master! canst thou render aid?

*Canst thou believe?*  Find here the test,
The rock of trust where souls may rest,
Where human weakness grasps the might
Of power divine—turns faith to sight.

*Lord, I believe.*  Thy help impart,
That confidence inspire my heart:
Thou art the Christ, God's only Son,
At thy command the work is done.

*Come out of him!*  At Jesus' beck,
The demon leaves the shattered wreck;
The healing touch, the gracious word—
The boy stands forth, erect, restored!

O Saviour! when we cry in grief,
Dispel all lingering unbelief;

Let the soul-healing work divine
Make those we love forever thine!        1882

[Mar. 30.] In that day. .the eyes of the blind shall see. Isa. xxix. 18.
He said, Lord, that I may receive my sight. Luke xviii. 41.

### BARTIMÆUS.

Waiting at the city gate,
Blind and poor—ah, wretched state!
Who will bring the craved relief?
Who dispel the cloud of grief?
Oh, that Christ, the Man of might,
Here would come, and give me sight!

Hark! what throng is on the street?
Passes Jesus thou wouldst meet!
Son of David, Master dear,
Mercy show a sufferer here!
Hold my peace? I'll louder cry—
Mercy, Saviour, or I die!

Rise, he calls!—What accents sweet
Greet me at the Master's feet!
Do for me? Thou Lord of light,
Sight restore—oh, give me sight?
As thou wilt, for faith like thine
Brings the boon, the work divine.

Oh, what wonders, strange but true,
Burst upon my raptured view!
Best of all to see thee, Lord,
Hear thy kind assuring word;
Glorious is thy grace to me—
Saviour, I must follow thee.        1882

[MAR. 31.]   The Lord God said, It is not good that the man should be alone; I will make an help meet for him. GEN. II. 18.

What therefore God hath joined together, let not man put asunder. MATT. xix. 6.

## THE SANCTITY OF HOME.

In creation's fair beginning,
     In the bloom of Eden's smile,
Ere the blight of human sinning,
     Ere the darkening taint of guile,
See the plan of God's designing
     For the homes of all our race—
Two in one through love combining,
     One in heart, in flesh, in place.

Blest the home of God's ordaining,
     Manly bridegroom, worthy bride,
Mutual love supremely reigning,
     Joyous helpers side by side;
Full affection sweetly sharing,
     As the life-years sweep along,
Each for each all burdens bearing,
     Turning sorrow into song.

Children dear, the Lord's bestowing,
     Bringing music, adding love,
Trained in truth, and Christlike growing,
     Home suggesting heaven above;
Peace and gladness, fond caressing,
     Serving well and living right;
Church and state and world all blessing,
     Bringing on millennial light.

Let no faithless vandal plunder
    Home's sweet ties and sacred rights;
Let no statute put asunder
    Whom the Lord for life unites.
Truth divine regard and cherish,
    Shun the sins defying God,
Lest our homes and nation perish,
    Whelmed in guilt's polluting flood.    1882

[APRIL 1.] Return unto me, and I will return unto you, saith the Lord of hosts. MAL. iii. 7.
   Returned unto the Shepherd and Bishop of your souls. 1 PET. ii. 25.

### THE WANDERER.

PILGRIM! hast thou far departed
    From the Saviour's loving arms?
Dost thou wander, fickle-hearted,
    Mid the world's alluring charms?

Dost thou cherish fleeting pleasures
    More than joys of Jesus' love,
Mindless of the heavenly treasures
    Which he bade thee place above?

Hearken to the Saviour speaking,
    Turn your steps to him again;
Long for you has he been seeking,
    Shall he call and seek in vain?

Vagrant ways are sad and dreary,
    Fading are earth's hopes at best;
Haste to Jesus! there the weary
    Find secure and blessèd rest.    1840

[APRIL 2.]   Behold, thy King cometh unto thee. ZEC. ix. 9.

They that went before, and they that followed, cried, Hosanna; Blessed is he that cometh in the name of the Lord.   MARK xi. 9.

## HOSANNA!

LET the shout of triumph, pealing,
   Sound o'er Olives' sacred brow;
'Tis the prophet's burst of feeling
   In a blest fulfillment now.
         With hosannas,
   To thy King, O Zion, bow!

Garments lay in paths before him,
   Strew the leaves of victor-palm,
Let the throngs, as they adore him,
   Chant their old triumphal psalm:
         Loud hosannas
   Shall his mighty name embalm.

Onward, Prince!  With exultation
   We the Son of David see!
Blessèd kingdom of salvation,
   Come, and make thy subjects free!
         Glad hosannas
   Ring their welcomes now to thee!

Children in the temple singing,
   Catch the strains and swell the tides,
Their hosannas grateful bringing,
   As to Zion's gates he rides—
         Sweet hosannas
   To the Lord who saves and guides.

Saviour! slain and risen to glory,
   Still ride on as Zion's King;

And fulfill the prophets' story—
  To thy feet all nations bring:
    Then hosannas
From a ransomed world shall ring!    1882

————◄◆►————

[APRIL 3.]  Behold, to obey is better than sacrifice.  1 SAM. xv. 22.
If ye love me, ye will keep my commandments.  JOHN xiv. 15.

## LOVING OBEDIENCE.

KEEP my commands, the Saviour said,
  If me ye love, believing;
And loving, loyal hearts obeyed,
  To his example cleaving.

I'll follow, then, my glorious Lord,
  Whate'er the ties I sever;
He saved my soul, and left his Word
  To guide me now and ever.

For me the cross and shame to bear,
  Dear Saviour, thou wast willing,
Nor would I shrink thy yoke to wear,
  All righteousness fulfilling.

Jesus, to thee, I yield my all,
  In thy kind arms enfold me;
My heart is fixed, no fears appall,
  Thy gracious power shall hold me.

How sweet the way divine to take,
  So clear in Gospel story:
On souls that follow Christ shall break
  The Spirit's beam of glory.    1863

[APRIL 4.] Many daughters have done worthily, but thou excellest them all. PROV. xxxi. 29.

She hath done what she could: she hath anointed my body afore-hand for the burying. MK. xiv. 8.

## MARY ANOINTING HER LORD.

THE feast went on, the last dear entertainment
  True friends might give the precious Son of God;
The hour was nearing for his forced arraignment
  By hating souls that thirsted for his blood.

Impelled by love undying, sweet, spontaneous,
  Mary with grateful feeling as was meet,
Regardless of the crowd or things extraneous,
  Poured the rich nard on Jesus' head and feet.

Fragrant the odor, all the senses calming,
  A sacrifice that only love would crave:
She saw with him alone the sad embalming
  Of that dear form so soon to reach the grave.

The tenderest memories to her soul come thronging,
  When in the way of truth her feet he led,
And that dread time of dark suspense and longing
  Till he returned and raised the precious dead.

She could not feast, but must by some expression
  Forecast near scenes of mingled hope and gloom:
The choicest, costliest thing of her possession
  Is love's discernment of the cross and tomb!

The Saviour saw it, gave his commendation,
  Rebuked the selfish spirit that opposed,
Sent down the ages to each land and nation
  The glorious deed this loving act disclosed.

She hath done what she could: a grand memorial,
   An everlasting word for earth and heaven!
Better than fame in bronze or art pictorial—
   The high approval of her Saviour given.

Ye humble ones that long to serve the Master,
   Obey the impulse of a loving soul;
Give him your cherished nard in alabaster,
   And find a record on the eternal roll.     1882

---

[APRIL 5.] She reacheth forth her hands to the needy. PROV. xxxi.
20.
   She hath wrought a good work upon me. MATT. xxvi. 10.

## THE BEST COMMENDATION.

LIVES whose eulogy is written
   In a blessing on the heart,
Wrought through love and self-denial,
   Ne'er from memory shall depart.

Graved upon the soul's bright tablet,
   Wasting time can ne'er efface,
Heaven shall keep the cherished record
   In its own eternal place.

When the light of mortal being
   Darkens in the shadowy vale,
When all scenes of earthly beauty
   From the fading vision fail,

Oh, what peace shall fill the spirit,
   Conscious of a life for good;
Oh, how rich the Saviour's blessing—
   *She hath done whate'er she could.*     1849

[APRIL 6.]   Mine own familiar friend, in whom I trusted, which did eat of my bread, hath lifted up his heel against me. Ps. xli. 9.

They began to be sorrowful, and to say unto him one by one, Is it I? Mk. xiv. 19.

## IS IT I?

WHILE they feasted paschal day,
Heard the twelve their Master say,
"One of you shall me betray."   *Is it I?*

As the startling sentence fell,
Who the pain it gave could tell?
One its import knew full well.   *Is it I?*

Forth with purpose dark and dread,
From that tender scene he fled,
False and heartless as he said,   *Is it I?*

Thus the Son of God to scorn,
Better had he ne'er been born,
Ne'er had seen life's rosy morn.   *Is it I?*

Are there no betrayers now?
None who break their solemn vow,
Made when burdened spirits bow?   *Is it I?*

With the chosen here enrolled,
Bearing trusts within the fold,
Yet in heart unchanged and cold:   *Is it I?*

Find we not through guises thin,
Souls that would, for gain or sin,
Sell their Lord such price to win?   *Is it I?*

Jesus, with omniscient ken,
Reads the inmost hearts of men,
Knows the traitor now as then.   *Is it I?*   1882

[APRIL 7.] If ye think good, give me my hire. . . So they weighed for my hire thirty pieces of silver. ZEC. xi. 12.

Woe unto that man through whom the Son of man is betrayed!—MATT. XXVI. 24.

## THE BETRAYAL.

AH, what a night of woe!
 The garden sorrow past,
Beneath the traitor's blow
 The Master falls at last:
Betrayal dark with friendly kiss—
Is any act more foul than this?

How e'en could ruffian bands,
 On him, so loving, meek,
Lay their unholy hands,
 Or words of insult speak?
While angel legions hovering near
Would glad in his defense appear!

The Son of God is bound,
 And rudely borne away;
The night is dark around—
 Can it be ever day?
Is judgment coming, slow or swift?
Can clouds so dense e'er show a rift?

O Jesus! oft betrayed,
 My Saviour and my Lord,
On thee my faith is stayed,
 And on thy blessèd word:
Rest here, my soul, and serve and wait,
Nor e'er betray a trust so great! 1882

[April 8.] Ye shall keep it a feast to the Lord. Ex. xii. 14.
As often as ye eat this bread, and drink the cup, ye proclaim the
Lord's death till he come.  1 Cor. xi. 26.

### THE LORD'S SUPPER.

How sweet the scene. how blest the hour,
　　With Jesus at this feast divine;
His prayers are here, his words of power—
　　Deep meanings thro' these symbols shine.

He gave the bread—the grain was crushed
　　To make the food that life sustains;
Thro' his dear form the death-throes rushed,
　　He saved our souls by mortal pains.

He gave the cup—the grapes were pressed
　　To bring the purpling boon supplied;
Our souls nor earth nor heaven give rest
　　Till bathed in Calvary's crimson tide.

To us what matchless mercy flows—
　　Redemption's everlasting prize—
Through agonies none ever knows,
　　Save him who made the sacrifice.

Remember Me.　O Saviour dear,
　　Can we thy work or words forget?
The cross, or thorns, or nails, or spear,
　　Thy boundless love, our boundless debt?

These sacred thoughts and memories deep
　　Forbid that aught our love should dim;
With grateful hearts the feast we keep,
　　And sing the tender parting hymn.　　1882

[APRIL 9.]  The good land which the Lord giveth you.  DEUT. xi. 17.
There followed him great multitudes from Galilee and Decapolis and Jerusalem and Judea and from beyond Jordan.  MATT. iv. 25.

## LEAVING THE HOLY LAND.

O PALESTINE! sacred, beloved of our God!
I tread where the prophets and patriarchs trod,
Where footsteps of angels have hallowed the sod.

I enter thy gates, O Jerusalem dear!
I walk about Zion, her towers I revere;
Look down o'er Moriah, the Temple was here.

I go where the Saviour, by mountain and shore,
With twelve he had chosen, oft journeyed before,
Relieved the sad-hearted and preached to the poor.

I gaze on sweet scenes that his eye had surveyed,
I trace his dear steps to Gethsemane's shade,
I weep where he wept, and I pray where he prayed.

I stand by the hall where false judgment was given,
I go to the hill where the Cross-nails were driven,
I enter the tomb of the loved One of Heaven.

I pass o'er the Kidron to Olivet nigh,
Where Bethany nestles so sweet 'neath the eye,
Where the risen Redeemer ascended on high.

O Land of the holiest memories, adieu!
My wanderings in thee I shall often renew;
Thy beautiful landscapes are ever in view.

O desolate Land! 'neath a blight to remain,
Till thy children, long scattered, are gathered again,
And Christ, once rejected, shall over thee reign. 1861

[APRIL 10.] It was thou, a man mine equal, my companion and my familiar friend.  Ps. lv. 13.

Wilt thou lay down thy life for me? .. The cock shall not crow, till thou hast denied me thrice.  John xiii. 38.

## PETER'S DENIAL.

READY for war,
He must not fight for Jesus taken;
Yet he, while faith and hope are shaken,
Followed afar.

He sees his Lord
Borne helpless to the high priest's palace,
The victim of relentless malice,
And sheathed his sword.

Is all now lost?
Ah, whither is the kingdom drifting?
Satan the Apostle's soul is sifting
At fearful cost.

While at the fire
His chilled and weary body warming,
Unknown temptations, fierce, alarming,
Repress desire.

There in the hall
Proceeds the mockery of trial;
And here a craven thrice denial
In Peter's fall.

At the shrill sign
Sad memories are o'er him sweeping,
And oh, what bitterness of weeping
'Neath eyes divine!

With broken heart,
Forgiven, and free from self-assertion,
Apostle now by new conversion,
    To do his part.

From censure keep:
His lapse ere sun arose was ended;
Are your denials less extended?—
    No cause to weep?                   1882

———————◆———————

[APRIL 11.]  Awake, O sword...smite the shepherd, and the sheep
  shall be scattered.  ZEC. xiii. 7.
  Ye shall be scattered, every man to his own, and leave me alone.—
JOHN xvi. 32.

### SMITTEN—SCATTERED.

O'ERWHELMED at his arrest
    By foes the traitor led,
Apostles, dazed, distressed,
    Forsook their Lord and fled!

O sad and scattered flock,
    Your smitten Shepherd view!
Can faith survive the shock?
    What now remains for you?

Darker than night profound
    Their sinking hopes appear;
Not one faint ray is found,
    No day, nor sun, is near!

Ah! yield not thus your faith;
    Hold fast! and soon shall shine,
Through all this gloom and death,
    What light and love divine!         1889

[APRIL 12.] Thou scarest me with dreams, and terrifiest me through visions. JOB vii. 14.

Have thou nothing to do with that righteous man : for I have suffered many things this day in a dream because of him. MAT. xxvii. 19.

## PLEA OF PILATE'S WIFE.

PILATE, on the judgment-seat,
With the Prisoner at his feet,
Feels the conflict stir his soul,
Self and conscience seek control:
Will he now the Christ release?
Or shall right and justice cease?

O my love!—his wife's appeal—
Think with whom you have to deal!
Yield not to his cruel foes,
Nor this righteous Man oppose;
I have suffered with affright,
Dreaming of him through the night.

He appeared as one from heaven,
Friend of man divinely given,
Teaching, healing, none refused,
Blessing still, though oft abused;
Then I seemed to hear the cry,
Jesus, Jesus, crucify!

Oh, that cross! Beyond, I saw
Scenes that filled my soul with awe—
Jesus on his throne of light,
Crowned with glory and with might;
All the world were at his feet:
Thou wast there that Judge to meet! 1882

[APRIL 13.] He was wounded for our transgressions, he was bruised for our iniquities. ISA. liii. 5.

He humbled himself, becoming obedient even unto death; yea, the death of the cross. PHIL. ii. 8.

## CHRIST ON THE CROSS.

THE cross, the cross! nailed to the cross,
 My soul, thy Saviour see!
Behold his agony and blood—
 The price that ransoms thee!

The shame, the shame! the scorn and shame,
 The crowd of mockers, see!
For me the Sufferer bore it all—
 He gave himself for me.

The wounds, the wounds! those painful wounds,
 Oh, they were made for me!
His hands and feet, his holy head,
 All pierced and torn I see!

The death, the death! the awful death,
 That Jesus died for me!
I hear his cries, his prayer, "Forgive,"
 His bleeding side I see!

The love, the love! the matchless love,
 That bled upon the tree!
It moves my tears, it melts my heart,
 It brings me, Lord, to thee.

The grace, the grace! such wondrous grace,
 For sinners lost, so free!
Dear dying Lamb! how can a soul
 Refuse to come to thee!

1871

[APRIL 14.] He poured out his soul unto death. ISA. liii. 12.
He said, It is finished. and he bowed his head, and gave up his spirit. JOHN xix. 30.

## THE DEAD CHRIST.

THE mighty scene is past,
The day unparalleled in time,
The utmost reach of human crime;
   Christ dying—dead at last!

Earth's ancient mountains quake,
All nature feels the dreadful shock,
Forces unseen death's gates unlock,
   And saints in tombs awake!

Hushed is the crowd with fear;
Enters the mother's heart the sword;
Conviction thrills the Roman's word—
   The Son of God is here!

Tender and loving hands
That precious mangled form take down,
Remove blood stains, the piercing crown,
   And wrap in linen bands.

Laid in the new rock-tomb,
The stone they roll against its door:
Ah! hearts of sadness, tears that pour,
   And unexampled gloom!

Sweet is the Saviour's rest,
Beyond all burdens of the day,
From man's relentless scorn away,
   Serene, alone, and blest.

O Jesus! for me slain,
Make in my rocky heart a place

Where thou shalt come with dying grace,
　　To rest, and rise, and reign. 1882

[APRIL 15.] How is the strong staff broken, the beautiful rod! JER.
xlviii. 17
Of them that had been slain for the word of God, and for the testi-
mony which they held. REV. vi. 9.

## THE MARTYR PRESIDENT.

How is the strong staff broken,
　　And rent the beauteous rod!
How strangely hast thou spoken,
　　O sovereign, righteous God!
Like startling volleyed thunder,
　　Dashed from a cloudless sky,
All horror-struck, we wonder,
　　And trembling ask, oh, why?
Our Father! we adore thee,
　　We know thy reign is just;
Smitten, we bow before thee,
　　Our place is in the dust.

How is the strong staff broken!—
　　The Nation mourns its Chief,
And showering tears betoken
　　Its mighty loss and grief!
The tide of triumph swelling,
　　Confounded, staggers back:
From mast and hall and dwelling,
　　The banner droops in black!
Hark! Freedom's bells are tolling,
　　Her solemn cannons roar,
And Sorrow's billows rolling,
　　Break mournful on the shore!

How is the strong staff broken,
　That held us mid the storm!
Our safety's cherished token,
　We clung around his form,
Till, Moses-like, he renders—
　Near through the exodus—
His soul where Nebo-splendors
　Beamed bright for him and us!
Through all the strife remaining,
　Be thou, O God, our Guide,
Freedom and Right maintaining,
　For which our Lincoln died!　　1865

---

[APRIL 16.]　I will give peace in the land. LEV. xxvi. 6.
　Be comforted; be of the same mind; live in peace. 2 COR. xiii. 11.

## NATIONAL PEACE.

THE day of joy has come!
Let bugle blast and drum
　Sound now for Peace!
O'er all the Union free,
From lake to Southern sea.
Swells the glad jubilee
　For war's release!

The banner of the brave
Who sought the land to save,
　And gained the prize,
Now flutters where it fell,
Awakes the ancient spell,
Triumphs anew to tell
　To wondering eyes!

No more the call to arms,
No longer dread alarms
　　Where warriors tramp;
The deadly strife is o'er,
Stayed the red tide of gore,
Hushed the loud cannon's roar,
　　In field and camp!

Rest o'er the land shall fall,
And liberty for all
　　The song shall be!
The power of bondage broke,
Removed its galling yoke,
God hath the fiat spoke—
　　The country free!

Great was the sacrifice,
Great was the offered price—
　　Treasure and blood;
But greater is the gain—
Preserved our vast domain,
Without its guilty stain,
　　And curse of God! 　　　1865

---

[APRIL 17.] As the appearance of the bow that is in the cloud in the day of rain, so was the appearance of the brightness. EZE. i. 28. The rainbow was upon his head. REV. x. 1.

## THE BOW ON THE CLOUD.

SEE! on the passing tempest, wild and grand,
As wrought and rounded by a seraph's hand,
The blending lines in wondrous beauty glow,
Span the dark cloud and touch the earth below.

So to the world o'erswept with sin-brought wrath,
Sweet Mercy comes, and bright along its path
Hangs her blest bow, as hope to lost ones given,
That looms from earth and culminates in heaven.

1846

[APRIL 18.]   Thou hast led thy captivity captive.   Ps. lxviii. 18.
Now when he was risen early on the first day of the week, he appear-
ed first to Mary Magdalene.   MARK xvi. 9.

## CHRIST'S RESURRECTION.

THROUGH the saddened night of weeping,
    All the mournful Sabbath day,
Ah! what lonely vigils keeping,
    What shall chase the gloom away?
Comes at last a joyous morning,
    Beams of glory bathe the earth,
Never time knew such adorning
    Since creation's Eden birth.

Ere the sun in splendor rising
    Touched the hills with golden breath,
Jesus, foe and friend surprising,
    Burst the rocky bars of death!
Angels saw the glorious capture,
    Crowning miracle of time,
Women caught the news with rapture,
    Told it in their joy sublime!

How that sweet bewildering gladness,
    When disciples saw their Lord,
Banished all their heavy sadness,
    Tuned anew faith's drooping chord!

Higher now their sweep of vision,
  Rent the veil that made it dim;
Theirs the broad, the great commision—
  Bring the whole wide world to him! 1882

---

[APRIL 19.] Who is the King of glory? The Lord strong and mighty.
Ps. xxiv. 8.
I was dead, and behold, I am alive forevermore, and I have the keys
of death and of Hades. REV. i. 18.

## JESUS LIVES!

JESUS lives! the King of glory,
  Tastes no more of mortal strife;
Hear, O earth! the wondrous story—
  Gift of God, Eternal Life!

Jesus and the Resurrection!—
  Sound it to the world's far bound;
Oh, the blesséd, grand reflection—
  Dead may live and lost be found!

Risen Saviour! ours for ever,
  Thou the life, the truth, the way;
Grace and strength shall fail us never,
  Heaven and earth are in thy sway!

Thou wilt rend our tombs' dark portal,
  Coming from thy gracious throne;
Thou wilt make our forms immortal,
  Glorified and like thine own!

Death's Despoiler! thou wilt take us
  To thy royal realm above;
More than conquerors thou wilt make us
  Through the mightiness of love! 1882

[APRIL 20.] Now shall he be great unto the ends of the earth. MIC. v. 4.

Go tell my brethren that they depart into Galilee, and there shall they see me. MATT. xxviii. 10.

## AFTER THE RESURRECTION.

Past sad hours of separation,
   Many a heart a joyful fount,
Gathering now with gratulation
   On a Galilæan mount.
Glad disciples! as they meet him—
   See their Master—as he said;
Deep the wonder as they greet him,
   Jesus, risen from the dead!

Came the quickened recollection
   Of the words he often spoke:
Cross and death and resurrection
   Like a sunburst o'er them broke.
Glorious is the message given
   In that kingly last command,
All of power in earth and heaven
   Wielded by his mighty hand!

Go ye then and teach all nations,
   True believers be the prize;
Them confessed in new relations,
   In the triune Name baptize.
All things I command, observing,
   Ever kept in closest view,
Teach to those their Master serving,
   So shall they be faithful, true.

So shall I be with you ever,
  Whatsoe'er your paths betide:
Always with you, leaving never
  Souls that in my word confide;
With you all, my name confessing,
  Though ye toil in every clime;
With you always, cheering, blessing,
  To the end of earth and time.          1880

[APRIL 21.]  It is the blood that maketh atonement.  LEV. xvii. 11.
He ever liveth to make intercession for them.  HEB. vii. 25.

## DID JESUS DIE FOR ME?

DID Jesus die for me?
  Give up his life for mine;
Thy blood, O Christ! brings me to thee,
  Cleansed in the fount divine.

Does Jesus live for me,
  An endless life of love?
Then I shall live, his glory see,
  And dwell with him above.

Does Jesus plead for me,
  My Priest before the throne?
He will my blesséd Surety be,
  His ransomed he will own.

Did Jesus rise for me,
  Victor of death and tomb?
His power shall set my body free,
  Clothed in immortal bloom.          1889

[APRIL 22.] The heart also of the rash shall understand. Is. xxxii. 4.
Because thou hast seen me, thou hast believed : blessed are they that
have not seen, and yet have believed.  JOHN xx. 29.

## THOMAS CONVINCED.

THE same bright day the Saviour rose,
    Apostles meet in evening's calm—
The day that will, till time shall close,
    The resurrection scenes embalm.

What strange events the hours have brought,
    Amazing joys, with hopes and fears:
While thus absorbed in deepest thought,
    Lo! in their midst the Lord appears!

He comes in love his own to greet,
    His presence gives them rapt delight,
His "Peace to you" is heavenly sweet,
    His hands, his side, oh, wondrous sight!

Desponding Thomas was not there,
    To have his feeble faith made strong:
To miss the hour and place of prayer,
    How much is lost by such a wrong!

A lonely week of gloom and grief,
    The doubting one then hither trod:
How Jesus helps his unbelief—
    How Faith exclaims, "My Lord, my God!"

Oh, they with untold joys are blest,
    Who have not seen but yet believe,
And, leaning on their Saviour's breast,
    The fullness of his love receive.

Their life the feet so torn have sought,
  The hands so scarred have clasped their own,
The heart so pierced their souls has bought—
  They shall be his before the throne.    1874

---

[APRIL 23.]  Lord, thou hast been our dwelling place in all genera-
tions.  Ps. xc. 1.
God is love : and he that abideth in love abideth in God.  1 JN. iv. 16.

## THE LORD OUR HOME.

O LORD, in whom are all my springs,
  Joyful to thee I come;
My grateful heart exultant sings
  To know thou art its home.

The shelter of thy glorious arms,
  How strong and safe and sweet!
From sense and sin, from all alarms,
  I fly to this retreat.

There is my sure and tranquil rest,
  In every troubled hour;
Weary, I lean upon thy breast,
  And feel its soothing power.

In that dear place of purest love,
  What wings encircle me!
Naught in the world can ever move
  My trusting soul from thee.

My Lord! if now I find in thee
  So blest and sweet a home,
What shall the heavenly mansion be,
  When to its door I come?    1875

[APRIL 24.] Lift up your heads, O ye gates; yea, lift them up, ye everlasting doors: and the King of glory shall come in. Ps. xxiv. 9.

While he blessed them, he parted from them, and was carried up into heaven. LUKE xxiv. 51.

## CHRIST'S ASCENSION.

Joyous was the angel song
    At the Saviour's lowly birth,
Glorious is the angel throng
    Come to see him leave the earth;
        O'er the mount on cloudy wing
        Wait the chariots of the King.

Finished all his mission vast,
    Truth unveiled, redemption wrought,
Death and grave triumphant passed,
    Life and light to mortals brought:
        Never more shall grief or pain
        Break his loving heart again.

With his chosen now he stands,
    Richest blessings on them pours,
O'er them spreads his gracious hands,
    Then above them, lo, he soars!
        Higher, grander, heavenward flight,
        Till a cloud obscures the sight.

Hark! the song of triumph rolls,
    As he sweeps the gates above;
Angel hosts and ransomed souls
    Welcome home the Lord they love:
        King of glory! take thy throne,
        Wield the scepter, wear the crown!

Church of God! the gospel spread,
  Bring the world to Jesus' feet:
He shall come, judge quick and dead,
  Claim his own, all things complete.
    Send the Spirit, mighty Lord,
    Give the victory to thy Word!     1882

---

[APRIL 25.]  He brought me to the banqueting house, and his banner over me was love.  CANT. ii. 4.

Behold, I stand at the door and knock: if any man hear my voice, and open the door, I will come in to him, and will sup with him, and he with me.  REV. iii. 20.

## THE SOUL'S FEAST.

ONCE I heard a sound at my heart's dark door,
  And was roused from the slumber of sin;
It was Jesus knocked, he had knocked before,
  Now I said, Blesséd Master, come in!

Then he spread the feast of redeeming love,
  And he made me his own happy guest;
In my joy I thought that the saints above
  Could be hardly more favored or blest.

In the holy war with the foes of truth,
  He's my shield, he my table prepares,
He restores my soul, he renews my youth,
  And gives triumph in answer to prayers.

He will feast me still with his presence dear,
  And the love he so freely hath given,
While his promise tells, as I serve him here,
  Of the banquet of glory in Heaven.     1860

[April. 26.] Whatsoever thy hand findeth to do, do it with thy might.
Eccl. ix. 10.

Son, go work to-day in the vineyard. MATT. xxi. 28.

## CHRISTIAN SERVICE.

Go work to-day!  Thy gracious Lord commands it,
　All heaven would leap at once to obey his voice:
Sublime the call, and he who understands it
　　Makes this high work of love his happy choice.
　　　　　Haste, work!
　That thou art summoned to it, soul, rejoice!

Go work to-day!  What waiting fields invite thee!
　The Church, the widening vineyard of the Lord,
What beauty there, what clusters rich incite thee,
　　And then at last the glorious reward!
　　　　　Haste, work!
　Nor ever deem thy Master's service hard.

Go work to-day!  Behold the world around thee,
　Where myriads to the verge of ruin sweep;
Does not the peril of their souls astound thee,
　　And loudly summon thee to wake from sleep?
　　　　　Haste, work!
　Thrust in thy sickle and rich harvests reap!

Go work to-day!  Put forth a strong endeavor
　To do through every hour thy Saviour's will;
'Tis work he wants, true earnest hearts that never,
　　In labors he appoints, grow faint or chill.
　　　　　Haste, work!
　A cause so blest an angel's heart might fill.

Go work to-day! The Saviour's love impelling,
  Think how he wrought, and gave himself for thee!
That love, so wonderful, to others telling,
  Shall fire thy soul, and thou their faith may see.
      Haste, work!
And thy reward a starry crown shall be.

Go work to-day! This day—wait not another!
  Thou knowest not what it may bring to light;
Life, hope, are found to-day—wait not, O brother!
  Lest o'er the field shall fall a deadening blight.
      Haste, work!
The day is passing, soon will come the night! 1872

---

[APRIL 27.]  As for me and my house, we will serve the Lord. JOSH. xxiv. 15.

Not forsaking the assembling of ourselves together, as the custom of some is. HEB. x. 25.

### HOME AND LORD'S DAY WORSHIP.

SWEET is the cheerful voice of prayer and praise,
That love-bound hearts at holy altars raise,
As early sunbeams round the dwelling shine,
Bright with a glory and a care divine;
As evening twilight with her lingering smiles,
To heavenly thoughts the grateful heart beguiles:

As comes that day, the holiest of the seven,
When rests o'er earth the sacredness of heaven,
And with meek worshipers are gladly trod
The hallowed courts of our benignant God,
Where dews of grace on waiting hearts are shed,
And with the Word receptive souls are fed. 1846

[April 28.] They joy before thee according to the joy in harvest.—
Isa. ix. 3.

And they went forth and preached everywhere, the Lord working
with them, and confirming the word by the signs that followed. Mark
xvi. 20.

## CHRIST'S LABORERS.

Blest laborers in the kingdom
    And patience of our Lord,
Ye only heard his summons,
    Nor thought of earth's reward.
Ye saw the whitening harvest,
    Ye longed to reap and save,
And, loyal to your Master,
    Your life and vigor gave.

He owned the precious offering,
    He crowned the earnest toil,
And clustering sheaves well garnered
    Display the heavenly spoil.
Blest fields that bear your footprints!
    Glad souls to Jesus won!
They mid the darkness brighten,
    To glory these march on.

Courage! ye patient toilers,
    The silver lining grows;
The clouds themselves are drifting,
    The bow of promise glows.
Hark! thrilling shouts of triumph!
    The mighty swell of songs!
Ride on, thou conquering Saviour!
    To thee the world belongs.

1870

[April 29.] They that be wise shall shine as the brightness of the firmament; and they that turn many to righteousness as the stars for ever and ever. DAN. xii. 3.

One star differeth from another star in glory. 1 COR. xv. 41.

## THE SHINING THRONG.

As THE stars in yonder sky
Fill their varied spheres on high,
  So to ransomed souls are given,
  When they pass life's tranquil even,
  Blest abodes prepared in Heaven.

As the stars are fixed in light,
Through the ages beaming bright,
  So when saints their home attain,
  Ne'er shall they go out again,
  But with Christ for ever reign.

As the stars at morning's blaze,
Only seem to lose their rays,
  So the called we mourn and miss,
  Live and shine in worlds of bliss,
  Far from clouds that darken this.

As the stars with constant glow,
Charm and guide what throngs below,
  So the blest, admired above,
  With us in example move,
  Helping still through deeds of love.

As the stars that small appear
Would be wondrous great if near,
  So to feeblest saints in Heaven,
  Once by doubts and trials driven,
  Glories wonderful are given.

1875

[APRIL 30.]　The king was a leper unto the day of his death. 2 CHRO.
xxvi. 21.

　Lord, if thou wilt, thou canst make me clean. And he..touched
him, saying, I will; be thou made clean. MATT. viii. 2, 3.

## THE LEPER CLEANSED.

OUTSIDE the crowd that Jesus taught,
As wondrous words with wisdom fraught
Fell from his lips, a heavenly fount,
In the glad Sermon from the Mount,
A loathsome leper there was found,
Attentive to the gospel sound.

Enchained, enwrapt, deep through his soul
The rising tides of feeling roll,
While the Discourse in grandeur grows,
And thoughts so solemn mark its close;
Then, as the Teacher rose, withdrew,
He and the wondering throng pursue.

"Though all unclean and cast aside,
And every sacred boon denied,
Oh, will not this Great Prophet give
The favor wished and bid me live?
May I not fall before his face,
Confess his power and trust his grace?"

What conflict raged within his heart!
To Christ would go—then feared to start:
But more and more his need was felt,
Till forth he rushed, and humbly knelt,
And prayed to him of heavenly mien,
"Lord, if thou wilt, canst make me clean."

"I will—be clean!" the Saviour said,
And touched the lowly leper's head:
Quick through his wan and wasting frame
A thrill of strangest rapture came;
Disease and pain—each vestige gone,
He hailed a new creation's dawn!

Jesus divine! what wondrous power
Attends thy word in mercy's hour!
O trembling sinner, Christ believe,
And his recovering grace receive;
Then, cleansed of guilt, and all forgiven,
Thou 'lt live renewed, an heir of Heaven.    1851

---

[MAY 1.]   Thou renewest the face of the ground.  PS. civ. 30.
  Consider the lilies of the field, how they grow.  MATT. vi. 28.

### BEAUTIFUL MAY.

Now we sing you a lay
For the beautiful May,
So charmingly sweet in its floral display.

Brightly green is the earth
In its vernal re-birth,
And the birds in the tree-tops make merriest mirth.

God is seen every hour,
For he smiles in each flower,
And earth's resurrection discloses his power.

But, receiving his grace,
And the love in his face,
In the brighter New Heaven he'll give us a place.    1879

[MAY 2.] Then shall mine enemies turn back in the day that I call: this I know, that God is for me. Ps. lvi. 9.

If God is for us, who is against us? Rom. viii. 31.

## HYMN OF TRUST.

God is for me! oh, how glorious!
　Who the weakest saint can harm?
He will make that saint victorious,
　Held and sheltered by his arm:
　　God is for me—
　Nothing shall my soul alarm.

Wonderful the gift he gave me,
　Lost, without a hope or claim;
Matchless mercy, when to save me
　Christ the Lord of glory came!
　　God is for me,
　Thanks eternal to his name!

Promises how great and precious
　Cheer and gladden all my way;
Peace and comfort, sweet and gracious,
　Keep me in their blesséd sway.
　　God is for me,
　Guides and guards me day by day.

Every scene his goodness brightens,
　His enfolding love I share;
Present help each burden lightens,
　Never fails his tender care:
　　God is for me,
　Nothing shall my trust impair.

All my heart this truth shall cherish,
  All my life, dear Lord, be thine;
Then were earthly good to perish,
  Thy blest smile would on me shine.
      God is for me,
  I am his and he is mine.

When shall close this mortal being,
  When I reach the other side,
Oh, the joy, the bliss of seeing
  Jesus and the white-robed bride!
      God is for me,
  Safe he 'll bring me o'er the tide.  1875

---

[MAY 3.]  At evening time there shall be light.  ZEC. xiv. 7.
  In all these things we are more than conquerors through him that
loved us.  ROM. viii. 37.

## A VESPER LAY.

WHAT though our years touch eventide,
Where strength and toil are laid aside,
Eternal truth and right remain,
Warfares to wage and victories gain.

All foes outlived, a coming day
Shall hail their blessèd world-wide sway:
So faith be firm and patience wait,
Hands ever strong and hearts elate.

O'er conquests grand we now rejoice,
With hope inspiring soul and voice;
Onward we look to clearer light,
And Christ triumphant sing to-night.  1889

[MAY 4.]  Remember the days of old, consider the years of many generations.  DEUT. xxxii. 7.

Others have labored, and ye are entered into their labor.  JOHN iv. 38.

## THE PAST'S BOUNTY.

THE past, by progress and decay,
Has made us what we are to-day;
Whate'er we prize and hold in store
We have from those who lived before.

On rugged fields they wrought with care,
We enter in, the fruits to share:
Scorn not this wealth in trust bestowed,
Nor lose the source from whence it flowed.

We are not shadows, vapors dim,
Nor dying strains of vesper hymn;
Our work abides when we are gone,
Our footprints crystallize in stone.

We have no past, the boon's not ours,
Till pale and drop the first fair flowers:
Our minds take not life's deep intent
Till well we scan its history spent.

The problem's solved in care and toil;
These are our teachers, thence our spoil:
Time gone, the bliss and pain it brings,
Come back in deeper, nobler things.

Grand heritage! and naught can wrest
This glorious past when once possessed;
Its lessons true, affections pure,
Will changeless ever more endure.

1870

[MAY 5.] What manner of house will ye build unto me? Isa. lxvi. 1.
Know ye not that ye are a temple of God ? 1 Cor. iii. 16.

## BUILDING A TEMPLE.

Mark the cathedral, grand and vast,
Slowly to rise, but long to last ;
Builders, that lay foundations deep,
Cease from their toil, and sink to sleep.

The generations go, and come,
Ere walls are crowned with lofty dome ;
But worshipers are found the while
'Neath sheltering arch of nave or aisle.

They hear the word, the prayer, the hymn,
Though walls are rude and windows dim :
The workmen plod—toil ceases not,
But shows each year some finished spot.

At last, far down the track of time,
The temple stands complete, sublime ;
What fair proportions, lofty height,
What wondrous blending shade and light!

Each gothic arch, of point so true,
Windows to let the glory through !
Art. beauty, taste, and grandeur given,
Symbol of worship, type of heaven.

The noblest life that charms our own,
From youth's true dawn has upward grown ;
In worthiest deeds, in knowledge meet,
The temple rises, stands complete.

1878

[MAY 6.] Run, speak to this young man. ZEC. ii. 4.

I have written unto you, young men, because ye are strong, and the word of God abideth in you, and ye have overcome the evil one. 1 JOHN ii. 14.

## A YOUNG MEN'S INSTITUTE.

HERE opens Art her wealth refined,
    To all who hither hie;
That wealth shall bless the earnest mind,
    And charm the eager eye.
      Thus lovely landscapes spreading nigh
        Shall lure the vagrant hours
      To scenes where smiles a favoring sky,
        And bloom the purest flowers.

Here, at the close of toiling day,
    Let throngs of youth repair,
In Learning's fruitful gardens stray,
    And lose their sordid care.
      So shall the mind grow large and fair,
        The heart be blithe and pure,
      And treasured wisdom each shall share,
        From every loss secure.

Here, with the great of ages fled,
    In grandest scenes of yore,
Young willing feet may gladly tread,
    Among these tomes of lore.
      Thus wandering oft those regions o'er,
        Sweet gales shall greet the soul,
      And pearls be found on many a shore
        Where crystal waters roll.

Here, too, sweeps by the living world—
  The thoughts that now bear sway;
And on the latest scroll unfurled
  Is mapped the great To-Day!
So, ere the vision fades away,
    The mind its good may woo,
And feel its pulses stronger play,
    Life's earnest work to do.     1860

---

[MAY 7.] If I forget thee, O Jerusalem, let my right hand forget her cunning. Ps. cxxxvii. 5.

Love the brotherhood. 1 PET. ii. 17.

## LOVE FOR THE CHURCH.

THE saints of old their Zion loved,
Trials their strong attachment proved,
Would not forget, were harps unstrung,
Jerusalem they oft had sung.

So ye, renewed by gospel grace,
Should find the Church a heavenly place,
Love it above all earthly joy,
For it your noblest powers employ.

Deep mother love she gives to you;
To her be loving, loyal, true;
Waste never what to her belongs—
Your service best, your sweetest songs.

As thrives the Church all good shall thrive;
She 's God's, to make the dead alive,
Lift up the fallen, souls prepare
In Heaven's eternal bliss to share.     1868

[MAY 8.]　In this mountain shall the Lord of hosts make unto all peoples a feast of fat things. ISA. xxv. 6.

When the king came in to behold the guests, he saw there a man which had not on a wedding-garment. MATT. xxii. 11.

## THE MARRIAGE FEAST.

THE gracious King of heaven,
　The majestic holy One,
Hath invitations given
　To the marriage of his Son.
Oh, strange that mortals bidden,
　Should reject the loving speech,
And let the feast be hidden
　Evermore beyond their reach!

The love that makes the wedding,
　Will not fail its urgent quests;
So, through the highways treading,
　Servants find the needed guests.
Oh, blesséd grace and glory,
　Freely offered to the poor—
Salvation's festal story,
　Winning souls forevermore.

When comes the King supernal,
　And is calling for each guest
To share the feast eternal
　In the mansions of the blest,
O garment of redemption!
　Be enwrapt　my soul about,
Or there is no exemption
　From the doom of those without.　1880

[MAY 9.]   Unto you that fear my name shall the sun of righteousness arise with healing in his wings.   MAL. iv. 2.

He that followeth me shall not walk in darkness, but shall have the light of life.   JOHN viii. 12.

## THE SUN OF RIGHTEOUSNESS.

WHEN first upon me broke,
    Thy beams, O Sun!
To a new day I woke,
    New race to run.
Subdued the power of sin,
Nature has fairer been,
Thy light and glory e'en
    As Heaven begun.

Wide the horizon grew,
    And grows to-day;
Things beautiful and new
    Rise 'neath thy ray.
Self loathed and left behind,
Life lost a life to find,
To thee drawn heart and mind,
    How blest my way!

Should clouds o'erhang my path,
    Veiling the sky,
Tempests break forth in wrath,
    Billows roll high;
Still shines thy matchless light,
Outlives the darkest night,
Brings morning calm and bright,
    Is always nigh.

1889

[MAY 10.]　The maiden was fair and beautiful.　ESTHER ii. 7.

He said, Weep not; for she is not dead, but sleepeth. LUKE viii. 52.

## SHE SLEEPS IN BEAUTY.

SHE sleeps in beauty—heavenly fair,
　Her little form seemed not as dead;
As though an angel slumbered there,
　I gazed upon that cradle bed.
Death's hand had touched the silver strings
　Which bound the spirit to its clay,
And as it soared on seraph wings,
　She slept—how beautiful she lay!

She sleeps in silence—oh, how still
　And soft her peaceful slumbers are!
No thunder sound, nor clarion shrill,
　Can wake that gentle sleeper there.
The voice of friends she heeds no more,
　Nor lists, as near her grave they tread;
Nor will that dreamless sleep be o'er,
　Till Christ shall call the silent dead.

She lives with Jesus—not a tear
　Shall ever dim her spirit's eye;
For in that bright celestial sphere,
　No grief is found, nor danger nigh.
Safe, in the Saviour's gentle arms,
　Which once the little children pressed,
And clothed in purest, loveliest charms,
　She finds a sweet and peaceful rest.

She lives in Heaven—oh, who would call
　　Her radiant spirit from its home,
And cause it here, in mortal thrall,
　　This sad and sinful earth to roam.
Unfading bliss is hers above,
　　And happier far that blest abode,
Where all her endless life is love,
　　Resplendent with the smile of God.　　1846

---

[MAY 11.]　The days of our years are threescore years and ten.—
Ps. xc. 10.
Being such a one as Paul the aged. PHILEM. 9.

## A PASTOR'S SEVENTIETH BIRTHDAY.

THREESCORE and ten! bright, grand birthday!
　　Heart thanks for him who sees this hour,
Still young and strong our souls to sway
　　With poet touch and pulpit power.

Hail! faithful servant, who has reached
　　The honored bound that now appears,
And best of all who Christ has preached
　　For more than half a hundred years.

What souls, from ways of sin and earth,
　　Have thro' his work to Christ been given!
What pilgrims of immortal birth
　　Have thus been led and trained for Heaven!

The lingering years be rich and calm,
　　Till life's long-shining sun goes down,
Where victory blooms in glory's palm,
　　And Pastor wears his fadeless crown.　　1883

[MAY 12.] The righteous shall flourish like the palm tree. Ps. xcii. 12.

I saw, and behold, a great multitude which no man could number, out of every nation, and of all tribes and peoples and tongues, standing before the throne, and before the Lamb, arrayed in white robes, and palms in their hands. REV. vii. 9.

## FLOURISHING LIKE THE PALM.

PLANTED in thy house, O Lord,
　Mid the trees of righteousness,
Watered by thy sacred Word,
　Beautified with precious grace,
　　Ransomed child of thine I am,
　　Make me flourish like the palm.

Let me leave the world below,
　Rise above its sordid strife,
Daily like my Saviour grow,
　Robed in his undying life.
　　Cleanse my soul, O healing Balm!
　　It will flourish like the palm.

Let my wings of faith be spread,
　Bear me to the mercy-seat,
Blend my spirit with its Head,
　Make me thus in Christ complete;
　　So my heart, pure, firm and calm,
　　Lives to flourish like the palm.

Let my leaves be green and fair,
　Clustering fruits in me abound,
All my deeds thy love declare,
　All my hopes in thee be found;
　　Life shall be a joyous psalm,
　　Graceful, useful, like the palm.

When full age at last has come,
　　When beyond the Jordan-tide,
Garnered to my heavenly home,
　　Let me with the glorified,
　　　　Sing the triumphs of the Lamb,
　　　　Bear a conqueror's fadeless palm.　　1864

---

[MAY 13.] The Lord shall arise upon thee, and his glory shall be seen upon thee. And nations shall come to thy light. IS. lx. 2, 3.

They departed, and went throughout the villages, preaching the gospel. LUKE ix. 6.

## HOME MISSIONS.

Go FORTH, ye heralds, true and wise,
　　Lift up the voice that saves and cheers,
Where humble homes and hamlets rise,
　　Along our country's far frontiers:
There, at the first. Christ's reign begin;
Bar out dark unbelief and sin.

See homes increase and hamlets spread,
　　Great cities rise with wealth and power;
Oh, if by truth their hosts be led,
　　We hail the Gospel's triumph hour!
Bright, glorious day that shall record
Our millions won to Christ the Lord!

From frozen climes to sunny plains,
　　From stormy coast to calmer sea,
Are heard the sweet immortal strains
　　Of God's salvation, pure and free:
O'er regions vast toward either pole,
The tidal waves of mercy roll!　　1889

[MAY 14.]  He shall grow like a cedar in Lebanon. **Ps. xcii. 12.**

Speaking truth in love, may grow up in all things into him, which is the head, even Christ. **Eph. iv. 15.**

## GROWING LIKE A CEDAR.

THE righteous, regaled at the grace-opened fountain,
  And, feasting each day on divine living bread,
Grows strong like a cedar on Lebanon's mountain,
  The Rock underneath and the Heaven overhead.

His influence widens like boughs far extending,
  To cover broad spaces with hallowing shade;
The tender and weak he gives bulwarks defending,
  And leads them to strength by his sheltering aid.

Cold storms and wild tempests assail him with rigor,
  He stands, he endures, he enlarges with time;
His life hid with Christ—immortality's vigor
  Pervades it with freshness and glory sublime.

Material meet for the wonderful building,
  Our God is erecting on Zion's glad hill,
The Saviour its corner, redemption its gilding,
  Its vastness and splendor the universe fill.

His life has a fragrance of sweetness and beauty,
  The smell of a field that Jehovah hath blest;
On scenes of his prayers and spheres of his duty
  The holiest memories shall linger and rest.

O God! let me not, to the dark tents of Kedar,
  Depart from thy Spirit, from Jesus my Guide:
But grow in thy courts like a Lebanon cedar,
  Rejoice in thy love, in thy service abide.      1864

[MAY 15.]   I will declare thy name unto my brethren : in the midst of the congregation will I praise thee.  Ps. xxii. 22.

For the love of Christ constraineth us.  2 COR. v. 14.

## SOMETHING FOR THEE.

SAVIOUR ! thy dying love
    Thou gavest me,
Nor should I aught withhold,
    Dear Lord, from thee.
In love my soul would bow,
My heart fulfill its vow,
Some offering bring thee now,
    Something for thee.

O'er the blest mercy-seat
    Pleading for me,
Upward in faith I look,
    Jesus, to thee :
Help me the cross to bear,
Thy wondrous love declare,
Some song to raise, or prayer,
    Something for thee.

Give me a faithful heart—
    Likeness to thee,
That each departing day
    Henceforth may see
Some work of love begun,
Some deed of kindness done,
Some wanderer sought and won,
    Something for thee.

All that I am and have—
    Thy gifts so free—
Ever, in joy or grief,
    My Lord, for thee :
And when thy face I see,
My ransomed soul shall be,
Through all eternity,
    Something for thee.

1862

---

[MAY 16.] They pierced my hands and my feet. Ps. xxii. 16.

Far be it from me to glory, save in the cross of our Lord Jesus Christ. GAL. vi. 14.

## THE CROSS OF CHRIST.

FROM the cross of Calvary's mountain
    Flows for sin the cleansing flood;
Bathe me, Jesus, in that fountain—
    Fountain of thy precious blood.

There my faith and hope are centered,
    All my burdens there I lay;
There salvation's gate I entered—
    Entered on the living way.

Dying Lamb, and Prince of glory,
    Oh, what fullness dwells in thee!
Wondrous cross! how sweet the story—
    Story wondrous sweet to me.

Living Saviour! guide me ever,
    I have placed my hand in thine;
Loving Shepherd! let me never—
    Never leave the fold divine.

1858

[MAY 17.] All thy waves and thy billows are gone over me. Ps. xlii. 7.

O my Father, if this cannot pass away, except I drink it, thy will be done. MATT. xxvi. 42.

## A WONDROUS GARDEN.

THERE is a wondrous Garden yet,
  Beyond the Kidron's murmuring flow,
On the low slope of Olivet,
  Where ancient trees so grandly grow.

Midnight closed o'er that olive shade,
  Sad moon and stars looked down to see
The Saviour's conflict as he prayed
  The cup might pass, if that could be.

How deep the anguish of that hour!
  What waves of sorrow o'er him roll!
'T was hell's malignant, awful power
  Assailed his true and holy soul.

Christ conquered there!—for baffled foe
  An angel came how strong and bright;
But ah, what finite mind may know
  The death-like struggle of that night?

What Eden lost, O Garden dear!
  In thee thro' him was more than found;
His sorrow and his triumph here
  Forever consecrate this ground.

O lesson-fraught Gethsemane!
  Thy Sufferer fills my heart and song;
All blood-bought souls oft think of thee
  With deeper love and faith more strong. 1880

[MAY 18.] Ethiopia shall haste to stretch out her hands unto God.
Ps. lxviii. 31.

I am debtor both to Greeks and Barbarians, both to the wise and to
the foolish. Rom. i. 14.

## THE CONGO MISSION.

WHERE rolls the Congo river,
 In soft, majestic flow,
Or where its waters quiver
 In foaming falls below;
O'er all its fertile borders,
 Where millions live and die,
Oppressed by sin's disorders—
 "Come, help us!" is the cry.

Shall commerce track the region,
 And lead an eager train?
Shall traffic with its legion
 Brave death itself for gain?
And shall the Lord's anointed,
 Who know the truth and life,
To save the world appointed,
 Be backward in the strife?

Awake, ye hosts of Zion!
 Behold the favored hour;
Your Captain's word rely on—
 His strength shall be your power.
Forth to the field before you,
 His harbingers have gone;
And now, his banner o'er you,
 He calls, "Come on, come on!"

Give, saints! as God hath given,
　　And see as your reward
Dense pagan darkness riven,
　　And Christ received as Lord.
While you the work engages,
　　A continent in gloom
Shall burst the chains of ages,
　　And rise in light to bloom.　　1885

———————◆———————

[MAY 19.]　He is the messenger of the Lord of hosts.　MAL. ii. 7.
　Tend the flock of God which is among you, exercising the oversight.
1 PET. v. 2.

## THE CHRISTIAN SHEPHERD.

THE shepherd true is like his Lord,
His life with His in sweet accord;
He walks the path the saints have trod,
And those astray leads back to God.

By sick and dying bows in prayer,
Brings words of peace and comfort there;
The mourning soul of sorrow heals,
With weeping weeps, their sadness feels.

He joys to fight the hosts of sin,
New triumphs for the cross to win;
To roll from earth the tides of woe,
And make celestial fountains flow.

In Christ alone he finds the grace
To reach and save our sinful race;
The flock he leads in useful ways,
The world to bless and God to praise.　　1853

[MAY 20.] Art not thou from everlasting, O Lord my God, mine Holy
One? we shall not die. HAB. i. 12.

That they may lay hold on the life which is life indeed. 1 TIM. vi. 19.

## SONG FOR THE SOUL.

MORTAL, wake! the spell is broken!
　God hath made thy spirit free;
On it he hath stamped the token
　　Of thy being yet to be!
　　　In the future, far outstretching,
　　　See the picture thou art sketching!

Life is not thy earthly staying,
　Death is not to breathe thy last;
Souls can not be here delaying,
　　Spirits live not in the past:
　　　Destiny is all before thee—
　　　Lo, its star is beaming o'er thee!

Art thou faithful, upward tending?
　Glory waiteth for thee there;
Art thou faithless? life's dark ending
　　Sinks thee downward to despair:
　　　Ask thy spirit where it goeth—
　　　Question closely—for it knoweth!

Mark the path thy feet are treading—
　See thy footprints left behind;
What the influence thou art spreading
　　In the commonwealth of Mind?
　　　Raiseth it toward Heaven's portal,
　　　Longings of thy brother mortal?

Look upon the boundless acres,
  Where the whitening harvest stands;
Hear the mandate—'t is thy Maker's—
  There employ thy heart and hands:
    Reap! and all-enriching wages
    Shall be thine through coming ages!

Give thy life to earnest duty,
  Give the energy of youth;
Then shall scenes of glorious beauty
  Crown fidelity to truth:
    Earth shall bless thee for thy living—
    Heaven shall ring with thy thanksgiving! 1846

[MAY 21.]  They shall behold a far stretching land.  ISA. xxxiii. 17.
And there shall be night no more.  REV. xxii. 5.

## VISION OF THE LAND OF LIGHT.

SOME hallowed moment, how the soul serene
Peers through the veil of this terrestrial scene,
Ascends the loftiest steeps of heavenly thought,
Takes in the outlook to that vision brought.

There wondrous realms to sight illumined rise,
Bathed in the splendor of celestial skies;
There stretch away in endless lines of light,
Vistas of beauty never marred by blight.

All charms, all grandeurs, and all glories blend
In the broad landscape where no nights descend;
And there what myriad beings dwell and shine,
In joy as rapturous as in form divine!      1857

[MAY 22.]   Let us go up to the mountain of the Lord.   MIC. iv. 2.

As he was praying, the fashion of his countenance was altered, and his raiment became white and dazzling.   LUKE ix. 29.

## AS JESUS PRAYED.

As JESUS prayed on Tabor's height,
  His face with glory shone;
So, Father, lift on me the light
Of thy dear visage, smiling bright,
  While prostrate at thy throne.

As Jesus prayed, his way-worn dress
  In heavenly whiteness beamed;
So, with thy glorious righteousness,
Saviour, infold, enrobe, and bless
  My soul, thy blood redeemed.

As Jesus prayed, came guests from Heaven,
  And talked of Calvary:
To aid me, oft by trials driven,
Let angel messengers be given,
  And speak thy peace to me.

Where Jesus prayed, th' o'ershadowing cloud,
  The bright Shekinah, came;
So, at thy feet in reverence bowed,
Let thy sweet presence me enshroud,
  My love and zeal inflame.

Where Jesus prayed, the Father's word
  In love declared his Son:
Oh, ever in my heart be heard
The voice of my approving Lord—
  Claim me in love thine own.

Where Jesus prayed—like Heaven the scene,
  A glory hallowed place:
I'll pray till on God's mount serene,
Christ bids me with his saints convene,
  Transfigured by his grace.          1863

---

[MAY 23.] My word .. shall accomplish that which I please. ISA. lv. 11.
  Taught in him, even as truth is in Jesus. EPH. iv. 21.

## GOSPEL TRUTH.

TRUTH is glorious, truth will conquer,
  'T is the Spirit's piercing blade,
Cleaving sin and soul asunder,
  While it heals the wound it made.

Truth shall reach the mind in darkness,
  Even move the iron heart,
Guilt disclose, and bring repentance,
  Bidding tears of sorrow start.

Marvelous the melting story
  Calvary's bloody cross reveals;
Wondrously the voice of mercy
  Through the broken spirit peals.

Great the triumphs of the Gospel,
  Grand the victories of love;
Oh, the mightiness of weapons
  From the armory above!

Not the force of human valor,
  Not the warrior's steel and mail,
Not all art of man's invention,
  Siege the soul and thus prevail.          1849

[MAY 24.]   Thou makest the outgoings of the morning and evening to rejoice.  Ps. lxv. 8.

When day was now breaking, Jesus stood on the beach.  JOHN xxi. iv.

## MORNING IN PALESTINE.

THE brightening beams of early day
Are melting night's last gloom away;
The stars, retreating one by one,
Pale in the glory of the sun.

The mystic meteors of the sky
Cease to attract the watcher's eye;
The specter shadows in the vales
Trip off along their morning trails.

The dreamy stillness of the hour
Is broke by life's awaking power;
In leafy bough or on the wing,
The merry birds their matins sing.

Adown the hillsides slanting creep
Soft waves of light to valleys deep;
A thousand dew-drops, turned to gems,
Give floral heads their diadems.

The crystal lakelets doubly show
All things that on their margins grow;
And light is gleaming, Galilee,
Upon thy pure and hallowed sea.

Gilboa's top's no longer dim,
Nor Ebal dark, nor Gerizim:
God's tints of beauty o'er thee shine,
O lovely land of Palestine!

1854

[MAY 25.] I shall be satisfied, when I awake, with thy likeness. Ps. xvii. 15.

The hour cometh, in which all that are in the tombs shall hear his voice, and shall come forth. JOHN V. 28.

## THE RESURRECTION.

THE Lord descends! the trumpet peals!
  The sound the vast creation shakes;
The trembling earth his presence feels,
  And every tomb responsive breaks!

The saints come forth their Lord to greet,
  And Heaven's bright throng as angels fair;
The parted long with rapture meet,
  And songs of joy fill all the air.

Like Christ's all-glorious form divine,
  Their own are made in this glad hour;
Henceforth with him to reign and shine,
  Clothed in immortal life and power.

That shining host, as radiant stars,
  Flood all the sky, God's jewels bright;
Blood-washed and crowned, no evil mars
  Their heritage of full delight.

What beauty gleams on every brow
  Of all that countless ransomed train!
They shout the last grand triumph now
  O'er death's dread power and dark domain.

Inspiring hope! Oh, welcome sight,
  When we our Lord's return shall see,
And through his resurrection might
  Attain our promised destiny!           1879

[MAY 26.]   It shall be a jubilee unto you. LEV. xxv. 10.

Go ye therefore, and make disciples of all the nations. MAT. xxviii. 19.

## A MISSIONARY JUBILEE.

Go PREACH to every creature, said the risen, living
    Lord;
Inspired Apostles listened to th' evangelizing word;
Earth beamed with light and glory as the gracious
    news was heard;
        Our King marched conquering on!

We meet where, fifty years ago, the heavenly germ
    was born;
God's blessing made its promise as the beauty of
    the morn,
And shaketh now like Lebanon that springing grain
    of corn:
        All hail the Jubilee!

With the first few that bore the cross to Burma's
    darkened land,
The fathers, linked in labor here, have met o'er
    Jordan's strand;
Oh, may their mantles wrap their sons, a great and
    growing band,
        As they go marching on!

At this high Jubilee we sing, Behold what God
    hath wrought!
What conquests for Immanuel in many a battle
    fought!

And at the next, God give the boon—the world for
    Jesus sought.
      Oh, let thy kingdom come!

The groaning earth, a suffering race, for Christ's
    redemption waits;
O King of glory, come and reign! be lifted up,
    ye gates!
He shall come in, his scepter sway—the scene our
    souls elates!
      Our God is marching on!      1864

---

[MAY 27.] Incline your ear, and come unto me. ISA. lv. 3.
  Come; for all things are now ready. LUKE xiv. 17.

## SALVATION'S PRINCE.

SALVATION'S Prince is marching on, by loyal hearts
    confessed;
He comes to rescue captive souls, to give the bur-
    dened rest,
And amnesty for sin proclaim—oh, hail the pardon
    blest,
      And to his banner come!

Now rally, all ye soldiers in the army of the Lamb;
Prepare for glorious victories through his almighty
    Name,
And be the watchword, as ye march, your Captain's
    glad acclaim:
      All things are ready, come!      1864

[MAY 28.]   The opening of thy words giveth light.  Ps. cxix. 130.

Lydia .. whose heart the Lord opened, to give heed unto the things spoken by Paul.  ACTS xvi. 14.

## PHILIPPI.

No SYNAGOGUE erected
   Philippi's gate within,
A few devout collected
   Where prayer had often been.
'Twas near the Gangas' waters,
   Low murmuring as they creep,
That Judah's sons and daughters
   Their ancient worship keep.

Responsive to the vision—
   The Macedonian cry—
Paul's prompt and firm decision
   Has brought the Gospel nigh.
The roofless tent received him,
   He spoke of Christ the Lord,
And opened hearts believed him,
   Attending to the Word.

Then, by a good confession,
   The quickened from the dead
Are, in their faith's expression,
   Baptized into their Head.
The Church of Christ is founded,
   The first on Europe's shore,
Which Lydia's faith unbounded
   Embalms for evermore.

From many a distant city,
   From regions dark and broad,
The cry for help and pity
   Should stir the hosts of God,
To preach the great salvation,
   And build the Church divine,
Where souls of every nation
   In sin and error pine.

1884

---

[MAY 29.] Yea, I have a goodly heritage. Ps. xvi. 6.
One soweth, and another reapeth. JOHN iv. 37.

## OUR HERITAGE.

THE saintly souls, so noble, true,
That from the past rise up to view,
Wrought till their day of toil was o'er,
Then joined the faithful gone before.

Their life, so like a tale that's told,
Soon to its measured limit rolled;
Tho' words are gone, and sounds have died,
The story lives—'t will e'er abide.

Still ours, because they're here no more,
But left us mantles once they wore;
Our highest wealth, soul-pulses felt,
Are virtues rare that in them dwelt.

Whate'er adorns and crowns our life,
From suffering, toil, unwearied strife,
Is wrought—the purest robe of love,
Whose warp and woof long years have wove. 1870

[MAY 30.] Precious shall their blood be in his sight. Ps. lxxii. 14.
Waxed mighty in war, turned to flight armies. Heb. xi. 34.

## OUR DEAD HEROES.

Flowers for the missed ones, fresh in their bloom,
Gifts of the grateful brighten their tomb.
Sing the glad anthems loved they so well,
Speak of their loyalty, deeds of theirs tell;
Visit each grave with a floral oblation,
Leave where they slumber love's sweet decoration.

Tears for the brave ones, fallen in strife,
Liberty's martyrs giving their life;
Patriot soldiers, loving their land,
Hasting to battle, heroes so grand;
Honor their memories on history's pages,
Build for them monuments lasting through ages!

Dirges for brothers sleeping in death;
Faced they the cannon's sulphurous breath!
Feared not the foeman, never would yield,
Bled for their country, died on the field!
Precious their offering, let it be cherished!
Gratitude give them, for nobly they perished.

Fame for the true hearts, true to the Flag;
Strong for the Union, firm as the crag;
Fire-blasts of battle, missiles of lead,
Turned them not backward, laying them dead!
Valor like theirs with earth's choicest is blended
Long as the Flag waves, so bravely defended!

Garlands unfading give to our braves;
Flowers immortal bloom on their graves!
Veteran warriors, young hearts and bold,
Foremost in conflict—silent and cold!
Memory keeps and rehearses their story;
Die not their names, star-lighted with glory!

Rest for the martyred, rest in the grave;
Thunders of battle wake not the brave;
War-drum and shouting, musketry's roar,
Rolling loud o'er them, heeded no more!
Peace that they fought for came to us timely,
Freedom they died for triumphed sublimely!   1866

[MAY 31.]   Thy glory, O Israel, is slain upon thy high places. 2 SAM.
i. 19.
   A good soldier of Christ Jesus. 2 TIM. ii. 3.

### HIS COUNTRY CALLED.

His country called! her urgent voice he heard,
And patriot ardor deep his spirit stirred;
Forth to the early field of strife he flew,
Faithful to God, to Freedom's banner true.

In nature gentle, generous, and mild,
Tender as woman, guileless as a child;
As cheerful as the light, serenely grave,
A Christian soldier, bravest of the brave.

His kindly friendship, noble, pure, sincere,
Won kindred hearts and made them ever dear:
At home, in camp and field, 't was e'er the same,
Associates joyed to speak or hear his name.

That awful charge! how gallant and how well
He met the fearful task, and nobly fell!
His comrades mourned a loving brother slain,
And soldiers' tears fell fast like summer rain.  1864

[JUNE 1.]  I see him, but not now: I behold him, but not nigh.—
NUM. xxiv. 17.

Sir, we would see Jesus.  JOHN xii. 21.

## SEEING JESUS.

WE would see the blesséd Jesus,
    Though our sight be poor and dim:
Sinless, perfect, wondrous Being,
    Oh, what beauty shines in him!

We would see the lowly Saviour,
    Who in human pathways trod:
In the Son we see the Father,
    Near to us, a gracious God.

We would see the precious Jesus,
    See him as incarnate Love—
On the cross the sinner's ransom;
    Pleading at the throne above.

We would see the tender Saviour,
    Share his sympathy in grief;
In our dark o'erwhelming sorrows
    His sweet comfort gives relief.

We would see, by faith's clear vision,
    Jesus all our life and peace—
Gaze, we would, till we are like him,
    Till we see him face to face.  1867

[JUNE 2.] Thou rulest the pride of the sea: when the waves thereof arise, thou stillest them. Ps. lxxxix. 9.

He awoke, and rebuked the wind, and said unto the sea, Peace, be still. MARK iv. 39.

## THE SAVIOUR'S VOICE.

THE winds are fierce, the storm is loud,
　The frightful waves roll swift and high;
Above, a dark and threatening cloud
　Obscures the azure vaulted sky.

A bark is on the foaming deep,
　And terror fills the seamen's breast:
Jesus is there, but, wrapped in sleep,
　Seems not to heed their wild unrest.

Vainly they strive against the storm,
　To bring the vessel safe to shore;
In dread of pending fatal harm,
　They wake their Lord and aid implore.

He stands amidst the awful scene—
　The winds, rebuked, obey his will;
The boisterous sea is calm, serene,
　At the blest mandate, "Peace, be still."

Like seamen on the ocean's tide,
　Bound to a far and foreign clime,
O'er life's rough sea we swiftly glide,
　And pass beyond the verge of time.

If storms should rage and hearts be sad,
　And hope give way to grief and fear,
Still this one thought should make us glad,
　The Saviour, though he sleep, is near.

Should even the darkest tempest rise,
　　Presaging gloom and threatening ill,
How soon 't will vanish from our skies
　　When Jesus speaketh, "Peace, be still."

How sweet the comfort of that voice,
　　When to the anxious soul 'tis given!
It bids the troubled heart rejoice,
　　And o'er it sheds the calm of Heaven.　1839

---

[JUNE 3.]　The Lord giveth the word: the women that publish the tidings are a great host. Ps. lxviii. 11.

In due season we shall reap, if we faint not. GAL. vi. 9.

## SUNDAY SCHOOL ANNIVERSARY.

THE Master is present—we meet in his name;
The Spirit will guide us, our spirits inflame
With heavenly wisdom and Pentecost fire,
If we look for his help with strong faith and desire.

The past is assuring! the Lord has come down,
And given us converts, our joy and our crown;
In our work we rejoice, with the angels above,
O'er widening triumphs of Christ's mighty love.

But vast are the fields that still rise to our view,
And blessèd the promise, so cheering and true,
That faithful seed-sowers, in patience and tears,
Shall be laden with sheaves in the glad harvest years.

Then forward! go forward! there's glory before,
A heavenly Leader, a song on the shore!
The Cloud Pillar, beckoning, hangs from the sky,
And beyond every Marah an Elim is nigh.　1874

[JUNE 4.] Woe unto them that call evil good, and good evil; that put darkness for light, and light for darkness. ISA. v. 20.

Beware of false prophets, which come to you in sheep's clothing, but inwardly are ravening wolves. By their fruits ye shall know them.— MATT. vii. 15.

## PILGRIM SONS.

PILGRIM sons! on ground enchanted
    Linger not in soft repose;
'Tis by wolves and sirens haunted,
    Wakeful, wily, scheming foes.

Watchful ever! Arch deceivers
    Would our holiest things displace,
While defiant unbelievers
    Scorn the word of truth and grace.

Look! the Man of Sin approaching,
    Clad in dark and baleful might,
On our dearest hopes encroaching,
    Spreads his desolating blight.

Sons of light! awake from sleeping,
    Give to all the Book divine!
Truth and Liberty are weeping—
    Shall our altar-fires decline?

Breathe upon us, mighty Spirit!
    Arm our Israel for the strife;
Let the Church from thee inherit
    Power prevailing through thy life.

Generous toil and alms bestowing,
    She shall make our broad land bloom,
Whose reflected light, far flowing,
    Shall the wider world illume.

1845

[JUNE 5.]   Ask now of the days that are past.  DEUT. iv. 32.
Christ also loved the church, and gave himself up for it.  EPII. v. 25.

## THE CENTURY CHURCH.

To-DAY thought's current backward rolls,
    Through time's unceasing flow,
And finds a band of faithful souls
    A hundred years ago.
They gathered here and formed the Church
    Mid earnest prayers and tears;
Their work sublime outlived their time—
    It spans a hundred years!

They bore the banner as they might,
    And clung in faith to God;
True to the truth, and strong for right,
    The Church has safely stood.
Faint, yet pursuing, sorely tried,
    Sometimes dark seemed the day,
Then came the light with the Spirit's might,
    And blessings cheered their way.

In humble temples here they reared
    And gave unto the Lord,
His grace and glory oft appeared—
    They feasted on the Word.
So they their generations served,
    Patient mid hopes and fears;
They worked and wept, the true faith kept,
    And live a hundred years!

What faithful watchmen on these walls
    Have sped the gospel sound!

And many a soul, the Christ who calls,
  Has heard and sought and found.
With joy these shepherds of the flock
  Welcomed each ransomed one;
In paths well tried they led the bride
  The way the Lord had gone.

And here when prayers and toils were o'er,
  These hundred years gone by,
How many saints have reached the shore
  That holds their home on high!
From sacred scenes, communions sweet,
  And Zion's songs divine,
They soared above to realms of love,
  And there in glory shine.                    1873

---

[JUNE 6.]  He that is wise winneth souls.  PROV. xi. 30.
  As the Father hath sent me, even so send I you.  JOHN xx. 21.

## PIONEER PASTORS.

CHRIST's chosen! well their work was done,
Who, with the souls they sought and won,
Built up, through willing hearts and hands,
The Shepherd's few and scattered bands.

The flocks they fed, the folds prepared,
Toils and privations freely shared,
Sowed the good seed in tears and cares,
Nor failed their faith, nor ceased their prayers.

Foundations wisely laid in hope,
Plans well devised for breadth and scope,
Brought blest returns, if scant in store,
Enriched their souls, and ours the more.       1875

[JUNE 7.]   The voice of weeping shall no more be heard in her, nor
the voice of crying.  ISA. lxv. 19.

And God shall wipe away every tear from their eyes.  REV. vii. 17.

## THE TEARLESS LAND.

No TEARS in Heaven!  Oh, bléssed thought!
City of God with splendors fraught,
Who can its glorious things unfold—
Harps, robes, and crowns, and bliss untold,
    Where shine the saints in endless day,
    And every tear is wiped away!

How oft is wept by mourners here
The humbling penitential tear!
Angels rejoice when such are shed
By souls that hence are heavenward led;
    When hither called, and entering in,
    They weep no more o'er self and sin.

By deep bereavement sorely tried,
How every earthly fount seems dried!
But all the streams of trouble cease,
And souls find sweet, unbroken peace,
    As to their rest they soar on high,
    Where tears are wiped from every eye.

Life seems a wasting scene of care,
To hearts that anxious burdens bear:
Oh, happy change, whene'er 't is given
To pass the opening gate to Heaven!
    No boding thought e'er shades the mind
    Where every tear is left behind.

Nor there those crystal drops that here
Sometimes as tears of joy appear,
For every weeping night is past,
And morning joys shall ever last.
Blest world of love, sweet realm of bliss,
Free from the tears that fall in this!    1875

---

[June 8.] Before they call I will answer; and while they are yet
speaking, I will hear. Isa. lxv. 24.

Looked .. into heaven and saw the glory of God, and Jesus. Acts
vii. 55.

## HER LAST WORDS.

As BEAUTIFUL and angel-like she waited,
  With loving parents anxious by her bed:
She pleasantly looked up, and then related:
"I've tried to pray, and pray again," she said,
  With earnest wish the words of prayer to keep,
"But can not finish, for I fall asleep."

"My dearest daughter," said her tender father,
  "The Lord will hear and bless you all the same;
'Tis not so much the words of prayer, but rather
  Your heart's desire, upborne in his sweet name,
That he beholds with sympathizing love,
And sends the gracious answer from above."

This gave her comfort, and on Jesus' bosom
  She seemed most calmly, sweetly, to recline.
As to the sunbeams turns the dew-bent blossom,
  She upward gazed toward glories all divine,
As if a loving view of Christ to keep,
When weary nature sank in gentle sleep.    1867

[JUNE 9.]  Behold, he cometh, saith the Lord of hosts.  MAL. iii. 1.

Being found in fashion as a man, he humbled himself, becoming
obedient even unto death.  PHIL. ii. 8.

## CHRIST ON EARTH.

THE King of glory came to earth,
The promised child of heavenly birth,
That children all may know and love
The Saviour from the world above.

In wisdom as in form he grew,
Obedient, faithful, ever true;
A blest example thus to give,
That youth may seek like him to live.

The sinless Man of Nazareth
Still to the weary toilers saith,
That while in labor, pain or grief,
To think of him brings sweet relief.

Temptations fierce and strong and sore,
And all our burdens, Jesus bore;
He knows each weakness, failure, sin,
And shows us how to strive and win.

His works of mercy and of might—
For sickness health, for blindness sight—
Foretold Messiah's brighter day
Under the Spirit's gracious sway.

Ah, more than all, the Son of God
Alone the dreadful wine-press trod:
The Garden woe, the Calvary cross
Bring life to us—to him its loss.

And yet he lives—the risen King!
Graves lose their victory, death its sting,
And all the saints in Christ secure
Salvation free, for ever sure.  1880

---

[JUNE 10.] He shall gather the lambs in his arm, and carry them in
his bosom. ISA. xl. 11.

Suffer the little children, and forbid them not, to come unto me: for
of such is the kingdom of heaven. MATT. xix. 14.

## CHRIST BLESSING LITTLE CHILDREN.

A BEAUTIFUL picture, charmingly grand!
 I gaze with enraptured delight,
And I seem to stand in the far Holy Land,
Beyond the swift Jordan's uneven strand,
 With the real scene in sight.

The holy and bless̀ed Saviour I see,
 With love and rebuke in his eye:
Let them come to me, little children to me,
Of such shall the kingdom of heaven be—
 Mothers, bring your darlings nigh.

They lovingly come before Jesus there,
 Or nestle close up to his breast,
While with tenderest care and holiest prayer
His hands softly press o'er their golden hair,
 Where his benedictions rest.

Oh, sweestest of scenes! how its beauties shine
 Beyond all attraction of art!
Dearest Shepherd divine, let th' children be thine,
Put thy bless̀ed hands on the heads of mine,
 And thy love within each heart.  1862

[JUNE 11.] Remember also thy Creator, in the days of thy youth.—
ECCL. xii. 1.

Now is the acceptable time; behold, now is the day of salvation.—
2 COR. vi.2.

## YOUTHFUL PIETY.

How TENDER the message, how golden the truth,
Oh, listen, dear children! attend, precious youth!
'T is the voice of the Spirit, the heavenly Dove,
Your Creator remember, remember and love.

In life's early morning, so beauteous and fair,
Ere the burden of sorrow or pressure of care
Shall a dread unbelief to your spirits impart,
Oh, think of the Saviour and give him your heart!

The world, were it yours, it could never bestow
The robe of salvation that's whiter than snow;
Ah! the loss that awaits you, the painful regret,
If for pleasure you live—your Creator forget.

Remember him now! it is wisdom's sweet voice;
Turn, turn from all sin, make a heavenly choice;
Wait not for the morrow, the call is to-day—
The best of all blessings is lost by delay.

Oh, think of the sad and the desolate lot
Of the man in old age who his God has forgot;
Evil days are upon him, no soul-peace is given,
No Saviour's support, and no treasure in Heaven!

If the Lord you remember to love and obey,
Your pathway shall brighten till life's closing day,
And then through the gate of the City of God
Your souls shall ascend to that glorious abode.   1876

[JUNE 12.] Come, ye children, hearken unto me; I will teach you the fear of the Lord. Ps. xxxiv. 11.

Consider the lilies of the field, how they grow. MATT. vi. 28.

## CHILDREN'S DAY.

GLAD earth her wealth discloses,
　　And shines in bright array,
As June's sweet month of roses
　　Brings round the Children's Day.

Each grateful heart now raises
　　Its thanks to God above,
And in his temple praises
　　The Saviour's wondrous love.

Of lilies once he told us,
　　That we might trust the Lord;
His hand will lead and hold us,
　　If we obey his word.

Dear children, think about him,
　　And hear his voice to-day;
You can not do without him
　　As life shall pass away.　　　　1877

---

[JUNE 13.] The merciful man doeth good to his own soul: but he that is cruel troubleth his own flesh. PROV. xi. 17.

Be tenderly affectioned one to another. ROM. xii. 10.

## BE KIND AT HOME.

BE kind in thy household,
　　Be cheery and bright;
There's a beauty in kindness
　　That beams like the light.

Be patient and loving,
　　Whatever may come;
For the sake of the dear ones
　　Be kind in thy home.

To the wife of thy bosom,
　　Oft cumbered with care,
Be tender and thoughtful
　　Each burden to share;
Be generous and noble,
　　With sympathy meet,
And hallow with kindness
　　A union so sweet.

Be kind to the children,
　　Nor check the fresh love
That would make them as angels,
　　Glad gifts from above.
Their young hearts are tender,
　　Sad tears may quick come;
Provoke not, by ill tempers,
　　The dear ones at home.

To all in the household,
　　To greatest and least,
To persons that serve thee,
　　To toil-weary beast,
Be forbearing and gentle,
　　Be cheery and bright;
There's a beauty in kindness
　　That beams like the light.

1877

[JUNE 14.] The heart of the prudent getteth knowledge; and the ear
of the wise seeketh knowledge. PROV. xviii. 15.

In your faith supply virtue; and in your virtue knowledge. 2 PET. i. 5.

## THE REALM OF KNOWLEDGE.

THE realm of knowledge widely spreads,
    All boundless are its vast domains;
Majestic mountains lift their heads,
    And smile upon the beauteous plains.

Deep winding vales, with verdure crowned,
    Extend through all this blooming land;
Here silvery lakes and streams abound,
    And breezy forests old and grand.

Exhaustless mines of glittering gold
    Beneath the flowery surface lie;
Above is gloriously unrolled
    The star-bright banner of the sky.

How beautiful this widening world,
    What lovely scenes are here enshrined,
What radiant splendors are unfurled,
    To glad the eye and feast the mind!

Ho! come, and climb its peerless hills,
    Range by its pearly-margined tides,
While deepening joy thy spirit thrills,
    And wisdom every footstep guides.

Turn from the cares of sordid strife,
    Let nobler ends thy labor claim;
Here consecrate the powers of life,
    And reach the goal of heavenly fame. 1852

[JUNE 15.] Can thine heart endure, or can thine hands be strong, in the days that I shall deal with thee?  EZE. xxii. 14.

He that endureth to the end, the same shall be saved. MARK xiii. 13.

## ENDURANCE.

THE gospel message taught me
    The gloom of nature's night;
From this the Spirit brought me
    To new-born life and light.
Within this world of beauty
    I longed to walk secure,
Pursue each path of duty,
    And to the end endure.

Unfailing grace preserved me
    In every threatening hour,
While truth and hope have nerved me
    With more than mortal power.
How blest in every station
    To feel one's footing sure,
Stand strong amidst temptation,
    And to the end endure.

But weak is man's endeavor,
    With human strength alone;
His soul is needing ever
    A girding from the Throne.
An unseen force must hold him
    From every sinful lure;
If Jesus' arms enfold him
    He'll to the end endure.

This humble way pursuing,
  Each truly faithful soul,
All foes and fears subduing,
  Shall reach the promised goal.
There, in exalted station,
  Now glorified and pure,
He'll share the great salvation
  With all who thus endure.    1882

---

[JUNE 16.] O Lord, our Lord, how excellent is thy name in all the earth! Ps. viii. 9.

My fellow-workers, whose names are in the book of life. PHIL. iv. 3.

### AUTOGRAPHS.

BRIGHT stars along the heaven,
  Sweet flowers in fields below,
Grand mountains in their ranges,
  Clear rivers as they flow,
As lessons of their Maker,
  His love and power declare;
In sacred letters written,
  His autograph is there.

A world of kindly friendship
  In beauty round us lies;
How lovely are its landscapes,
  How pure its beaming skies!
The names of those who form it
  Will ever cherished be,
And pleasant memories waken
  Their autographs to see.    1874

[JUNE 17.] Thine eyes shall see the king in his beauty. ISA. xxxiii.17.

We shall be like him; for we shall see him even as he is. 1 JOHN iii. 2.

## SEEING THE KING IN HIS BEAUTY.

I SHALL see him in his beauty,
  When I reach the heavenly shore,
See him, altogether lovely—
    King and Lord whom I adore:
      With saints and angels praising,
      In open vision gazing,
    See my Saviour evermore.

In his glory I shall see him,
  As he shone on Tabor's height,
In celestial vestment splendors,
    And the Cloud-Shekinah bright,
      When prophets high in heaven
      Return to earth were given,
    To confer with him that night.

Not as when among the lowly,
  Sick he healed, the hungry fed,
Bearing insults from the scornful,
    By man's hate to Calvary led—
      My eyes shall then behold him,
      Where glorious scenes enfold him,
    Many crowns upon his head.

I shall see him in his beauty,
  Shall be with him—so he prayed—
And transfigured shall be like him,
    By his grace in me displayed:

My King! for thy salvation,
In grateful adoration,
At thy feet my all be laid.      1889

---

[JUNE 18.] The latter glory of this house shall be greater than the former, saith the Lord of hosts. HAG. ii. 9.

Go ye, and stand and speak in the temple to the people all the words of this life. ACTS v. 20.

## THE LORD'S HOUSE REBUILT.

WE thank thee, Lord, for memories sweet,
    That cluster round our former home;
And now, as here we joyful meet,
    Oh, with thy richer mercies come.

This latter house, of ampler space
    And fairer form, we give to thee;
Thy presence ever fill the place,
    The Spirit's power thy servants see.

Thy Word of Life, unfolded here,
    As food to hungry souls be given;
Prayer earnest reach thy bending ear,
    And heartfelt praise rise sweet to Heaven.

Here throngs of precious souls believe
    The gracious message from above,
The birth divine with joy receive,
    The new life crown with works of love.

Here converts oft their Saviour own,
    And well-tried saints rejoice anew,
All join to make his kingdom known,
    Till they its heavenly glories view.      1871

[JUNE 19.] Ye shall call upon me, and ye shall go and pray unto me and I will hearken unto you. JER. xxix. 12.

Whensoever ye stand praying, forgive, if ye have aught against any one. MARK xi. 25.

## PRAYER AND FORGIVENESS.

STRENGTH to prevail, O Lord,
　　Must come from thee alone—
Faith's grasp upon thy word,
　　Its hold upon thy throne,
Its strong, persistent, deathless pleading,
That brings the blessings we are needing.

Anoint us from above,
　　Create the deep desire,
Constrain with Christ's own love,
　　Touch all our hearts with fire,
And make our wills with thine agreeing,
That prayer may go from faith to seeing.

Thanks for the pledge so sure,
　　The range so large and free,
Full answers to secure,
　　When faith bears up the plea.
Amid what treasures souls are basking,
That know this privilege of asking.

Whene'er we stand or kneel,
　　To pour our hearts to thee,
Forgiveness may we feel—
　　Ourselves forgiven be:
Let not our prayers be unavailing,
Through unbelief or sinful failing.

1882

[JUNE 20.] Thou shalt remember all the way which the Lord thy God hath led thee .. to prove thee. DEUT. viii. 2.

Call to remembrance the former days. HEB. x. 32.

## DIVINE REMEMBRANCE.

O GOD of love and grace,
Thou art our dwelling place,
   Amid the years:
Thy pillared cloud by day,
With night-illuming ray,
Hath guided all our way
   Of hopes and fears.

Our fathers knew thy power
In every trying hour,
   And to thy throne
Their want and weakness brought,
For strength and wisdom sought;
So patiently they wrought
   To make thee known.

Their earnest voice was heard,
As on thy changeless Word
   The Church they built.
How hath it grown and stood,
Its branches fair and good,
Nurtured by Calvary's blood,
   And cleansed from guilt.

Still, Lord, with us abide,
Our labors bless and guide,
   Let grace abound;

Take now thine own great might,
Put all thy foes to flight,
And spread thy truth and light
The world around.                1872

---

[JUNE 21.]  This is my beloved and this is my friend. CANT. v. 16.

Himself hath said, I will in no wise fail thee, neither will I in any wise forsake thee. HEB. xiii. 5.

## THE CHANGELESS ONE.

THERE is a little vine,
That humbly trails along the forest glade,
Whose verdant hues and beauties never fade,
Nor cease for once to shine.

It lives in spring's glad hour,
And is the same 'neath summer's sunny skies;
Sere autumn's frosty fingers it defies,
Nor yields to winter's power.

Such is the changeless love,
The pure affection of that lasting Friend,
Whose smile imparts a joy that ne'er shall end—
A boon from heaven above.

Whatever be our lot,
Sickness or health, or trial's darkest hour;
If friends forsake, and tempests o'er us lower,
That Friend forsaketh not.

Be all our trust in him,
As pilgrims through this sinful world we go;
His quenchless love, a balm for every woe,
Shall ne'er grow cold or dim.                1842

[JUNE 22.]  In the night his song shall be with me.  Ps. xlii. 8.

We look for new heavens and a new earth, wherein dwelleth right-
eousness.  2 Pet. iii. 13.

## A NIGHT SONG.

Night, beautiful Night!
Oh, for gifts divine!
For the pure intellectual light,
For the fire of genius bright,
On my soul to shine!
Then would I sing of thy splendor,
And praise to thy majesty render,
Night, beautiful Night!

Stars, glorious Stars!
Gleaming as of old;
Of the heavenly vault are ye crystal spars?
What things are within your silver bars?
Let the tale be told;
Let my thoughts, so long to you soaring,
Your mysteries deep be exploring,
Stars, glorious Stars!

Earth, wonderful Earth!
Wrapt in alien gloom;
Beauty and blessing marked thy birth;
Error and woe have caused thy dearth;
Truth shall make thee bloom.
Wanes thy night, and the coming morning
Shall bring thee a new and pure adorning,
Earth, wonderful Earth!

Heaven, mysterious Heaven!
Dream of bliss to be;
Not unto flesh and blood are given—
For them thy veil shall ne'er be riven—
Hope and home in thee.
Beyond these stars, thou land immortal,
The pure soul finds thy welcome portal,
Heaven, mysterious Heaven!  1857

---

[JUNE 23.] While I was musing the fire kindled: then spake I with
with my tongue. Ps. xxxix. 3.
They sing as it were a new song. REV. xiv. 3.

## THOUGHT AND SONG.

THOUGHT, all-boundless Thought!
Of the mind thou 'rt born;
Forth into light, as the brain hath wrought,
By toil and pain thy jewels are brought,
Bright as tints of morn.
Throughout the universe thou art sweeping,
Its marvelous treasures are in thy keeping,
Thought, all-boundless Thought!

Song, inspiring Song!
For thy touch of power
Waiteth the singer wistful and long;
Give to him utterance sweet and strong;
Come at this still hour;
Suggest high themes that he should be singing,
Kindle the tones of his harp's glad ringing,
Song, inspiring Song!  1857

[JUNE 24.] Give ear, O Shepherd of Israel, thou that leadest Joseph like a flock. Ps. lxxx. 1.

I am the good shepherd; and I know mine own, and mine own know me. JOHN x. 14.

## MY SHEPHERD—PSALM XXIII.

My Shepherd is the Lord,
　　My want is o'er;
Sheltered in his regard,
　　I stray no more.
By waters calm he leads,
Rests me in verdant meads;
My soul, with all its needs,
　　He doth restore.

Guiding aright my path,
　　His name I love;
Such power his presence hath,
　　All ills above,
Though in death's vale and shade,
I will not be afraid,
His rod and staff shall aid
　　And comfort prove.

A table he hath spread
　　Amidst my foes;
His blessing on my head,
　　My cup o'erflows:
Goodness and mercy sure
Shall follow and endure,
His house my home secure,
　　My heaven's repose.

1889

[JUNE 25.] In thy presence is fullness of joy; in thy right hand are pleasures forevermore. Ps. xvi. 11.

The fashion of this world passeth away. 1 Cor. vii. 31.

## THE CONTRAST.

EARTH's hopes, so bright,
To future good extending,
With scenes of beauty blending,
Sometimes reveal their ending,
    A cheerless blight.

The friends we love,
Whose presence soothes our sadness,
And fills our hearts with gladness—
As if impelled with madness,
    Death bears above.

Though not in this,
Yet, in the world supernal,
Where life is always vernal,
And pleasures are eternal,
    Reigns endless bliss.

Perennial there,
The tearless eye entrancing,
Wherever falls its glancing,
Celestial flowers are dancing
    Mid balmiest air.

And there shall meet,
To part no more for ever,
The friends whom naught can sever,
For death shall enter never
    The golden street.

1844

[JUNE 26.] Arise, go .. and preach .. the preaching that I bid thee. JONAH iii. 2.

They therefore that were scattered abroad went about preaching the word. ACTS viii. 4.

## THE FIRST PREACHERS.

PREACH the word in every nation,
  Gospel truth to all our race;
Let them know the blest salvation,
  Bid them take redeming grace!

Joyful then to distant regions
  Flew the heralds of the cross;
Met and won what hostile legions,
  Oft in peril, pain, and loss.

Theirs the zeal that knew no waning,
  Christ to preach and souls to gain,
Founding churches, converts training,
  Till in each his life should reign.

Earth's vain pleasures left, despising,
  Gloried they in Jesus' name,
Suffered for his kingdom's rising,
  Glad its triumphs to proclaim.

Faithful preachers! blest evangel!
  Gifts the Lord ascending gave;
Work most royal—not an angel
  Could a sinner reach and save!

Crowned at last, a sunlike luster
  Hallows all their home divine;
As the stars, a radiant cluster,
  They in endless glory shine.

1875

[June 27.] Who will go for us? . . Here am I; send me. Isa. vi. 8.
To preach the gospel even unto the parts beyond. 2 Cor. x. 16.

## SAILING OF MISSIONARIES.

Where yonder ship lies waiting by the shore,
See gathering groups at early noontide pour.
Sweetly the voice of praise and prayer ascends,
And faithful hearts to care divine commends.

The last adieu to friends and kindred given,
Moved by selectest gales from favoring heaven,
The freighted vessel from her mooring starts,
And bears away those missionary hearts.

Oh, clap your hands, ye ocean isles afar,
And catch the glimmering of the Morning Star!
Rejoice, ye pagan lands, awake, and sing,
Welcome the heralds of the heavenly King!

Be glad each lowly vale and mountain high,
Morn breaks, and your redeeming hour is nigh.
Oh, soon, from all your gloomy realms shall rise
The soul's pure incense to the upper skies!

Temples of Boodh and Brama shall decay,
Blind, burdening idol-worship pass away,
And the broad banner of the cross, unfurled,
Shall float triumphant o'er a ransomed world.

Meager the prize for which earth's heroes fought,
Placed by the service these disciples sought;
And how shall fade mere worldly great renown
Before the splendor of their heavenly crown! 1846

[JUNE 28.] Incline your ear, and come unto me; hear, and your soul shall live. ISA. lv. 3.

Take my yoke upon you, and learn of me; for I am meek and lowly in heart: and ye shall find rest unto your souls. MATT. xi. 29.

## INVITATION.

YE, who bask in life's fair morning,
　　Hoping for long years of bliss,
Ne'er forget the soul's adorning,
　　Nor the world awaiting this.
Purer joys than earth is giving
　　Flow from Jesus's love and truth;
Find the fount of waters living
　　In the sunny days of youth.

Ye, the paths of wealth pursuing,
　　Mid the bustling cares of life,
Numerous years more golden viewing
　　Past the scenes of present strife;
Pause, and let your thoughts be turning
　　To the treasure Christ bestows;
Grasp it while life's lamp is burning,
　　It alone gives soul repose.

Voyagers, on life's troubled ocean,
　　Would you reach the port of peace?
Turn away from earth's commotion,
　　From its sins and follies cease:
Come ye, now! though long delaying,
　　Heed the invitation blest;
Come, the Saviour still is saying,
　　Take my yoke, 't will bring you rest. 1840

[JUNE 29.] Wherewithal shall a young man cleanse his way? By taking heed thereto according to thy word. Ps. cxix. 9.

Jesus looking upon him loved him, and said unto him, One thing thou lackest. MARK x. 21.

## THE RICH YOUNG MAN.

THE Saviour saw and loved him,
    Urging his eager quest;
But when his word had proved him,
    He would not stand the test.
Not for the wealth supernal
    Would he the earthly leave;
Not glorious life eternal
    From Jesus thus receive.

He went away in sorrow
    From near the Saviour's feet;
What promise gave the morrow?
    What joy could it repeat?
Declined celestial treasure
    That might have been his own—
Better than all earth's pleasure,
    Grander than monarch's throne.

He went away in sadness,
    For in his soul a voice
Hushed every note of gladness
    As it rebuked his choice.
Immortal riches spurning,
    A blissful home above—
To bitterness was turning
    The good that held his love.

O ye! in life's bright morning,
 Who grasp what earth can give,
Find here a sacred warning
 That bids you turn and live.
The soul from Jesus going,
 True peace can never know;
To flesh for ever sowing,
 The harvest must be woe.   1882

———————

[JUNE 30.] Whom have I in heaven but thee? And there is none upon earth that I desire beside thee. Ps. lxxiii. 25.

Lord, to whom shall we go? thou hast the words of eternal life.— JOHN vi. 68.

## NONE BUT CHRIST.

LORD Jesus, should I go from thee,
To whom for refuge could I flee?
In thee, where truth and grace abound,
Alone, is life eternal found.

Unworthy, sinful, though I am,
I come to thee, O dying Lamb!
No sacrifice, no blood but thine,
Avails to cleanse this soul of mine.

Aside from thee, the Life, the Way,
I should for ever go astray;
Oh, keep me, Jesus, near thy heart,
Nor let my love from thee depart.

I know thy name, I trust in thee;
Thou art life's Fountain, full and free;
Me in thy love, O Saviour, bind;
My hope, my all, in thee I find.   1889

[JULY 1.]   I will also give thee for a light to the Gentiles, that thou
mayest be my salvation unto the end of the earth.   ISA. xlix. 6.
Jesus spake .. saying, I am the light of the world.   JOHN viii. 12.

## THE LIGHT OF THE WORLD.

LIGHT of the world! but once of lowly station,
    Born in the stall at Bethlehem;
Now on the throne, supreme in exaltation,
    Wearing the kingly diadem.
Here among mortals, sinless, yet oft sighing,
    Solving the great redeeming plan;
On the uplifted cross in anguish dying,
Mystical power to draw the race supplying,
    Tasting of death for every man.

Light of the world! its sin-strong fetters breaking,
    Staying the fateful tide of wrath;
Mercy disclosing and probation making,
    Opening to all a hopeful path.
So to the race reprieved come life and blessing,
    All the vast benefits of time,
Purpose and act with freedom coälescing,
Every rich gift of mind and heart's possessing,
    Treasures unbounded and sublime.

Light of the world! and, pitying its condition,
    Pierced the dread gloom of its despair;
Set it anear to God and heaven's fruition,
    Souls thus to show the glory there.
So, with a world-encompassing affection,
    Infants of all our smitten race,
Reached by an offering of divine selection,

Clasped in the saving arms of love's protection,
  Share the propitiating grace.

Light of the world!—salvation in abundance,
  Bought at such price, and free to all!
God's gift amazing, life e'en to redundance,
  Urged by the Spirit's silent call.
O ye guilt-stained! in penitence awaken,
  Pardon implead through Jesus' name;
Haste to this Refuge, and by faith unshaken
Walk in the Light! else be in sin o'ertaken
  By its desert of quenchless flame.          1885

---

[JULY 2.]  This is his name whereby he shall be called, The Lord is
our righteousness.  JER. xxiii. 6.
Christ Jesus, who gave himself a ransom for all.  1 TIM. ii. 5, 6.

### THE MEDIATOR'S WORK.

JESUS! when thy vast work I see,
  And think how great its cost
Of sorrow, pain, and death to thee,
  In wonder I am lost.

My grateful heart with love o'erflows,
  Thou precious Son of God,
For having borne my sins and woes,
  And saved me through thy blood.

What thou hast done for all our race
  Should melt e'en hearts of stone,
Rouse a lost world to seek thy grace,
  And thee with glory crown.          1889

[JULY 3.] He hath not dealt so with any nation. Ps. cxlvii. 20.

With freedom did Christ set us free: stand fast therefore, and be not entangled again in a yoke of bondage. GAL. v. 1.

## ANTHEM FOR INDEPENDENCE.

ALL hail to the dawn of the glorious morning,
   Immortal in memories through ages of time;
It looms from the past in a golden adorning,
   Forecasting the future in promise sublime.

O birthday of Freedom!—new star that has guided
   To the Bethlehem gift for the Land of the West;
Thy radiance afar through the nations has glided
   As myriads have hailed thee and hoped to be blest.

We welcome and love thee, bright day of our glory!
   We love the grand history linked with thy rise;
For ever thou tellest the struggle and story
   Of patriots who reared the Republic we prize.

Let bells at the sunrise ring clangorous pealing,
   Let loud booming cannon shake land and the sea;
Let hearts overflow with a deluge of feeling,
   And throb in the thought and the joy of the free.

Let young men and maidens, let children with ban-
   And reverend age, all in unison, raise    [ners,
Their deepest thanksgivings and highest hosannas
   To God our preserver, the Ancient of days.

Let the whole Country join in a true celebration,
   From lakes to the gulf, and from shore unto shore,
And gratefully give a renewed coronation
   To Liberty, Union, and Peace evermore!   1868

[JULY 4.] A land that I had espied for them, flowing with milk and honey, which is the glory of all lands. EZEK. xx. 6.

I will be their God, and they shall be my people. 2 COR. vi. 16.

## CENTENNIAL HYMN.

MORN of a hundred years the crown!
　We hail with joy thy gladdening ray,
Behold our country's vast renown,
　And chant Jehovah's praise to-day.

He gave us at the century's dawn,
　The glorious boon that made us free;
Held by his hand, led safely on,
　His banner o'er us still we see.

When clouds arose and thunders broke
　In fiery storms of dreadful strife,
He touched our hearts and they awoke
　To save the Nation's periled life.

O beauteous land! grown strong and great,
　What varied wealth thy stores display,
From rocky shore to Golden Gate,
　From icy lake to sunny bay!

Great God! who mad'st us truly free,
　And in our conflicts kept us one,
Bind fast in love our hearts to thee
　Till centuries no more shall run.

And make this land, through gifts divine,
　Where myriad souls shall have their birth,
In faith and truth and virtue shine,
　Brightest and best of all the earth. 1876

JULY 5.]  A land of hills and valleys .. which the Lord thy God careth
for.   DEUT. xi. 11, 12.
  Yea, verily, Their sound went out into all the earth.   ROM. x. 18.

## SONG FOR NEW ENGLAND.

I LOVE thee, New England, fair land of my birth,
The home of my fathers, the brave of the earth ;
I love thy bold mountains, thy rivers and vales,
Thy warm summer breezes, thy wild winter gales.

My heart is thine ever, blest land of the free,
Away from thy borders, my thoughts fly to thee ;
The smile of thy daughters sweet pleasure imparts,
The voice of thy sons is the voice of true hearts.

A halo is round thee—I love to recall
The deeds of thy heroes, thy history all ;
What memories linger, my bosom to thrill,
At old Plymouth Rock, over crowned Bunker Hill !

The best of all blessings and treasures are thine—
Thy churches and schools—let them never decline ;
Oh, these are thy guerdon of glory so bright,
Since the May Flower came, a new star in the night.

Blest home of wide culture, souls royal and grand,
As long as thy mountains like battlements stand,
While freely thy rivers shall flow to the main,
May the true Pilgrim spirit the Nation sustain.

God bless thee for ever, my native land dear,
His right arm protect the rich heritage here :
May Liberty's banner, unstained, ever wave
O'er the home of the free and the patriot's grave.  1841

[JULY 6.] His brightness was as the light; he had rays coming forth from his hand. HAB. iii. 4.

I will give him the morning star. REV. ii. 28.

## THE BRIGHTEST GIFT.

WRAPT in the gloom of nature's night,
  Burdened and sad I wandered far,
Nor found a ray of cheering light,
  Till Christ I saw, the Morning Star.

When forth it beamed upon my soul,
  Brighter than gold or radiant spar,
My spirit broke from sin's control,
  And blest the precious Morning Star.

As toward the world unseen, unknown,
  I've passed on time's resistless car,
The darkest clouds have quickly flown
  Before the welcome Morning Star.

If fondest hopes should fade away,
  Or aught life's fairest treasures mar,
While here on earth I lingering stay,
  Oh, give to me the Morning Star.

As through death's cold and fearful stream
  I pass from mortal scenes afar,
Oh, let upon my pathway beam
  The brightness of the Morning Star.

Then, in the regions of the blest,
  Called up where sainted spirits are,
My eye, undimmed, shall ever rest
  Upon the glorious Morning Star.

1847

[JULY 7.]  The man said, This is now bone of my bones, and flesh of
my flesh : she shall be called Woman.  GEN. ii. 23.

So ought husbands also to love their own wives as their own bodies.
EPH. v. 28.

## THE FIRST PAIR.

WAS man a lonely ranger,
  In Eden's paths to roam?
Live there a silent stranger,
  Without a mate or home?
He woke—and saw another,
  One most divinely fair!
Was this a sister? brother?
  No, nor an angel there.

The being sweet was human,
  He loved her as his life,
For God had made the Woman
  To be his loving wife.
Together now they wandered
  The Garden-aisles among,
On all its beauties pondered,
  In floral arbors sung.

Their glances far extending,
  Swept o'er what glories bright,
Till earth and sky were blending
  In tints of heavenly light.
Daily their Maker greeting
  Gave life a blesséd charm,
Until, the tempter meeting,
  They yield with fatal harm!

When, in the calm lake sleeping,
　　A stone is rudely tost,
The circling waves go creeping
　　To all the distant coast.
The curse that Eden blasted,
　　And changed its weal to woe,
Hath through the ages lasted,
　　And we its sorrows know!　　1856

---

[JULY 8.]　Her price is far above rubies. The heart of her husband trusteth in her. PROV. xxxi. 10, 11.

For this cause shall a man leave his father and mother and shall cleave to his wife. EPH. v. 31.

### THE SILVER WEDDING.

THE silver wedding, crown of days!
　　It comes amid the flight of years,
And memory each event surveys
　　Along the track of smiles and tears.

Love linked their hearts, young life was fair,
　　Heaven illumed and blest their way;
Now, clustering round the joyful pair,
　　A happy group we see to-day.

We see not all—dear ones are gone
　　To Jesus' arms, for ever blest;
But till the meeting hour shall dawn
　　Love counts the absent with the rest.

No place like thee, O love-lit home!
　　How dear the treasured past serene!
And may the brighter years to come
　　Include the golden wedding scene.　　1865

[JULY 9.] In the latter time hath he made it glorious, by the way of the sea, beyond Jordan, Galilee of the nations. ISA. ix. 1.

He began to teach by the sea side. And there is gathered unto him a very great multitude. MARK iv. 1.

## A SEASIDE HYMN.

O SAVIOUR! who by Galilee
　　Didst call disciples to thy side,
Come to the margin of this sea,
　　And in our summer home abide.

There, sick and sad who knew thy power,
　　Found health and joy by thee conferred;
Here, Lord, in many a favored hour,
　　Repeat the wonders of thy word.

Once, tossed on wild Gennesareth,
　　Thy mandate stilled the stormy waves;
Here let us feel thy calming breath—
　　The Spirit that subdues and saves.

Along that shore were thousands brought
　　To hear the gospel preached by thee;
May thousands here thy truth be taught,
　　Who throng this temple by the sea.

O Master! who the world to teach,
　　The pebbly coast and dark wave trod,
Walk in thy beauty on our beach,
　　That souls may see the Lamb of God.

To magnify thy love and word,
　　Our service here to thee we bring:
Let saints give praise in heart accord,
　　And children glad hosannas sing.

The seaside throng were richly fed,
  As in thy hands the bounty grew;
So break to us the living bread,
  And oft the gracious gift renew.

May we at last, our night-toil o'er,
  See spread at morn the feast divine,
Greet thee upon the heavenly shore,
  And hear thy welcome, "Come and dine." 1884

———————————⟨◆⟩———————————

[JULY 10.] He hath sent me to bind up the brokenhearted. ISA. lxi. 1.
And he went forth again by the sea side. MARK ii. 13.

## WITH JESUS AT THE SEA.

JESUS, I love to walk with thee
By the dear lake of Galilee,
Hear thy sweet voice and see thy might
To sick and blind give health and sight.

At thy behest the demons fled,
The bruised and wrecked, as from the dead,
Obeyed thy call, so wondrous kind,
Restored in life and healed in mind.

Vast crowds were drawn by thy blest name,
The sorrow-laden with them came;
Won by thy words, the weary breast,
Through faith in thee, found joy and rest.

Thou art the same, O Saviour, still,
And all may come to thee who will;
The sinful soul may pardoned be,
The weary find sweet rest in thee. 1889

[JULY 11.] Enoch walked with God: and he was not; for God took him. GEN. v. 24.

Before his translation he hath had witness borne to him that he had been well pleasing unto God. HEB. xi. 5.

## ENOCH WALKED WITH GOD.

BEST of all companionships,
Highest praise from holiest lips,
Brightest path e'er mortals trod,
Enoch early walked with God.

In a time when sin was rife,
Through far-reaching terms of life,
As the years drew near the Flood,
Enoch ever walked with God.

In his household, day by day,
With his loved ones, or away;
If mid true or vile he stood,
Enoch, faithful, walked with God.

All the long three hundred years,
While they passed in joys and tears,
Onward, upward, as he trod,
Enoch closely walked with God.

'Twas by faith he lived and wrought,
Lessons grand the ages taught;
So with truth his feet e'er shod,
Enoch surely walked with God.

Always pleasing to his Lord,
Glorious came his high reward:
Spared from death and grave's abode,
Enoch walked in heaven with God.   1889

[JULY 12.] The Lord saw that the wickedness of man was great in
the earth. . .And the Lord said, I will destroy man. GEN. vi. 5, 7.

They were eating and drinking, marrying and giving in marriage . .
until the flood came and took them all away. MATT. xxiv. 38, 39.

## THE DELUGE.

AT night's deepest hour, mid the dwellings of sin,
A portent from heaven stayed the revels within;
Thro' festival halls swift the terror-wings brushed,
And songs of the bridal and dancers were hushed.

Wild shrieks of dismay strike the palsiéd air,
And dread premonitions are felt every where;
Death's angel comes forth, on the dissolute hurled,
To tread, in ripe wrath, the wine-press of the world.

Oh, never in time, since its birth-hour so bright,
Shut down upon men such a horrible night;
From black rolling clouds how the fury-winds blow,
While tempest and torrent work ruin and woe.

The thunderbolts plunge from the lightning-rent sky,
The flash and the roar speak the doom-moment nigh,
Ah! broken earth's deeps and full cisterns of heaven,
O'er loftiest mountains great billows are driven.

The moon hid her face as if silent she wept,
While ocean-like floods o'er a guilty race swept,
And stars, in their pathway of beauty serene,
Were veiled in their fear to look down on the scene.

O world, self-destroyed! lo, thy sepulcher's made,
A watery winding-sheet round thee is laid;
The planets, in weeds and processions of gloom,
Now lay thy cold form in a desolate tomb.

Behold! o'er the waste of the far-rolling tides,
How safe the lone Ark in its majesty rides!
God rescues the righteous, unharmed evermore;
A new world awaits them, a heavenly shore.   1887

---

[JULY 13.]  Abram went, as the Lord had spoken unto him.  GEN xii. 4.
  By faith Abraham, when he was called, obeyed.  HEB. xi. S.

## ABRAHAM CALLED.

A VOICE his slumbers broke,
    He hears the call of God;
A mighty faith within him woke—
    Obedient, forth he trod.

He knew not where it led,
    The path his feet must take;
He knew the words Jehovah said,
    And naught his trust could shake.

Old friends, familiar, dear,
    Bright landscapes often traced—
He saw them fade and disappear,
    As untried scenes he faced.

The land of promise fair
    The guided pilgrim found;
For him a tenting sojourn there—
    For his the chosen ground.

For him a name sublime,
    A countless people's head;
Blessings through all the coming time,
    O'er all the nations spread.

His faith, to mortals strange,
　　E'en higher pathways trod;
It swept the Heavenly City's range,
　　Whose architect is God.

How safe to walk by faith—
　　Our sight is short and dim—
To do just what Jehovah saith,
　　And leave the rest to him.　　1887

[JULY 14.] I have made thee a watchman unto the house of Israel.—
EZEK. iii. 17.

They watch in behalf of your souls, as they that shall give account.—
HEB. xiii. 17.

## PASTOR AND PEOPLE.

COME with thy servant, Lord, as here
　　Immortal souls he takes in charge;
Angels a task so great might fear—
　　Be thou his help, his strength enlarge.

As bold he speaks thy word of grace,
　　May it a saving message prove;
So shall the throngs that fill this place
　　Bow to the truth in faith and love.

Blest work! the flock to guide and feed,
　　Sin-burdened souls to Jesus bring,
Converts to faithful service lead,
　　And sorrowing spirits teach to sing.

Pastor and people—one in heart—
　　How sweet the ties and toils thus given,
When each for others bears a part,
　　And all at last shall meet in Heaven.　　1875

[JULY 15.] Lot chose him all the Plain of Jordan. GEN. xiii. 11.
Righteous Lot, sore distressed by the lascivious life of the wicked.—
2 PET. ii. 7.

## LOT'S SAD CHOICE.

FROM the heights above Bethel,
　Down the valley below,
A bright circle of verdure
　Held the Jordan's swift flow.
Lot was charmed with its beauty,
　Like a paradise fair;
On its border was Sodom,
　Still he pitched his tent there.

He removed from the faithful,
　From the pure and the true,
Made his home with the wicked,
　Having wealth in his view:
Ah, the taint of their vileness,
　How it soiled his abode;
And ere long came destruction—
　The ripe judgment of God!

Lot's sad folly in choosing
　Is repeated to-day,
And the riches men covet
　Oft are seeds of decay;
Their grand tent in its splendor
　Of fair promise so bright,
Standeth near to the Sodom
　That may perish to-night.

Oh, beware, ye light-hearted,
　Of the vain giddy throng,

Who are lured from ways righteous
   To low pleasures and song.
Think ye now of the ending
   That most surely will come;
If your tents are at Sodom,
   Ye will share in its doom!

Choose the kingdom of heaven,
   As to you it comes near;
Far surpassing Lot's garden
   Will its treasures appear;
And your tent will be daily
   A pure, blesséd abode,
Till exchanged for a mansion
   In the City of God.       1887

---

[JULY 16.] I will give unto thee, and to thy seed after thee .. all the land of Canaan. GEN. xvii. 8.

Being fully assured that, what he had promised, he was able also to perform. ROM. iv. 21.

### GOD'S GIFT TO ABRAHAM.

FROM Egypt's bordering river,
   That runs along its sands,
To far and great Euphrates,
   Beyond the Jordan lands,
This choice and fertile country,
   'Neath watchful skies benign,
With milk and honey flowing,
Where corn and vine are growing,
   I give to seed of thine.

What fair and blooming valleys,
   Where living springs abound,
Full harvests clothe the hillsides,
   Bright gems beneath the ground,
Clear streams send richest verdure
   The lovely lowlands o'er,
Soft showers supply the fountains,
Sweet lakes reflect the mountains,
   The great sea guards the shore.

Thou goest to thy fathers,
   And thine shall strangers be
In a dark land of bondage,
   Affliction there to see:
But them will I remember—
   Will judge their foes severe—
Bring forth mine own with glory,
To tell their wondrous story,
   That all the world shall hear.

The patriarch's faith unwavering
   Received the promise true;
The darkness o'er him vanished—
   Ages of light in view:
Jerusalem in splendor,
   Sits on her sacred hills;
The land the tribes possessing
Gives all the earth a blessing,
   As God his word fulfills.

1887

[JULY 17.] They that be wise among the people shall instruct many. DAN. xi. 33.

Teachers of that which is good; that they may train the young .. TIT. ii. 3, 4.

## TO A TEACHER.

HAPPY children they must be,
Claiming as their teacher thee;
Daily with thee, see thy face
Bright with every charming grace,
Guiding wisdom, patient love,
They so quickly know or prove.

Angel to them, helpful, kind,
Waking e'en the dullest mind,
Which through all its coming life
Fruit shall bear of noble strife,
While sweet memories oft will spring
From the treasures thou didst bring.

Thus thy work I seem to see,
Best of teachers, all agree.
Favored pupils—surely they
All must love thee, and obey.
Heaven bless thee at thy task;
Highest good for thee I ask.                1888

[JULY 18.] Shall not the Judge of all the earth do right? GEN. xviii. 25.

If the righteous is scarcely saved, where shall the ungodly and sinner appear? 1 PET. iv. 18.

## PLEADING FOR SODOM.

FROM Mamre's vale to Hebron's height,
The patriarch walked by faith and sight,
    The angel Lord was near:

His word, of Sodom's pending doom,
Filled Abraham's tender heart with gloom,
 And woke a shivering fear;
For, though the city reeked with sin,
There might be righteous souls within.

He drew still closer to the Lord,
And forth his burdened spirit poured
 In supplicating plea,
That e'en the guilty he would spare
For sake of others living there—
 Far be it, Lord, from thee,
That servants who thy bidding wait
Should meet, as just, the wicked's fate.

The humble pleader's pitying word
The loving Heart of Mercy heard,
 . And gracious answers gave.
Alas! in all the city's bound
No righteous ten conld e'en be found—
 Not salt enough to save!
Sin's harvest doom awaits the night;
The Judge of all the earth does right.

Sweet picture to the hopeful eye—
The rainbow on the frowning sky,
 The beaming morning star,
Ere sun arise its welcome light,
Day's promise fair ere ends the night,
 Blest earnest from afar:
To pleading hearts assurance given;
The Christ to earth shall come from heaven.   1887

[JULY 19.] Up, get you out of this place; for the Lord will destroy the city. GEN. xix. 14.

Sodom .. set forth as an example, suffering the punishment of eternal fire. JUDE 7.

## SODOM DESTROYED.

FLY from the city! oh, haste from its doom!
Angels entreat thee, its judgment has come;
Hold to our hand, and be led from the ire
Charged to consume it in terrible fire!

Up to high Heaven its iniquities cry;
Warnings unheeded, its guilty must die:
This is the day, its fair morning the hour,
When the fierce storm shall its splendors devour!

Flee for thy life! not a brief moment waste;
Look not behind! to the mountain make haste;
Peril is here, linger not on the Plain,
Else be consumed! Lo, it comes—the red rain!

Ere the full sunburst o'er eastern dark hills,
Jordan's rich vale with blest radiance fills,
Awfully lurid, unearthly their light,
Brimstone and fire bury Sodom from sight!

Oh, the deep anguish and horror of soul,
Over the hopeless the flame-billows roll!
Only one look of despair, and the close—
Folly and vileness reap harvests of woes!

Sudden and sharp retribution flashed down;
Ruin and ashes for pride and renown!
Beauty and wealth, and the pleasures they give,
Ne'er, without God, can long flourish or live.

Scarcely the righteous are saved from the sin
Filling the world, and the evil within.
Keep us, Jehovah, in pureness and love;
Send us thine angels, as guides from above.   1887

---

[JULY 20.] Now I know that thou fearest God, seeing thou hast not
withheld thy son, thine only son, from me.  GEN. xxii. 12.

He that had gladly received the promises, was offering up his only
begotten son.  HEB. xi. 17.

## THE OFFERING OF ISAAC.

Not all the watchful march of time
　　Has witnessed such a soul serene,
A faith so wondrous, strong, sublime,
　　As in the patriarch's offering seen.

No question from his spirit flows,
　　When summoned by his faithful God;
At morning's dawn he calmly rose,
　　In full obedience forth he trod.

We may not ken the surges deep
　　That swept the channels of his mind;
Great souls a reverent silence keep—
　　Thoughts that no language e'er can find.

'Tis reached and climbed, Moriah's slope;
　　The lovely son, the wood, the fire;
But whither shines a ray of hope?
　　What token meets a heart desire?

Unwavering faith brooks no delay;
　　The altar holds what wealth of love;
And naught the father's arm can stay
　　But God's clear mandate from above.

This matchless trust, with Heaven's high seal,
Its dearest jewel freely gives:
What glorious truth these acts reveal,
While Abraham's faith immortal lives!

Another scene, prefigured, see—
God's only Son, in felon guise;
He bears the cross to Calvary;
He is for us the Sacrifice!

1887

---

[JULY 21.] He dreamed, and behold a ladder .. and behold the angels
of God ascending and descending   on it.   GEN. xxviii. 12.
Behold, I bring you good tidings of great joy.   LUKE ii. 10.

### JACOB AT BETHEL.

Lo! A wanderer, sad and weary,
Staff in hand, pursues his way,
Till, upon a hill-top dreary,
Ends the long and lonely day.

Sunset shadows round him closing,
Lies he down to soothing sleep,
While, on stony couch reposing,
Silent stars their vigils keep.

Not alone—pure spirit pinions
O'er the slumbering form expand:
Reaching to God's near dominions,
See the mystic ladder stand!

Softly up, its rounds ascending,
Gently down, these angels go;
Heaven and earth thus interblending,
Balm is brought for human woe.

Sweet the vision o'er him stealing,
　Blest the voice that fills his ear,
Wondrous promises revealing,
　Loving guidance far and near. 　1887

---

[JULY 22.] Jacob awaked out of his sleep, and he said, Surely the
Lord is in this place. GEN. xxviii. 16.
I was not disobedient unto the heavenly vision. ACTS xxvi. 19.

## THE DREAM'S REALITY.

GLORIOUS dream of things so real,
　Spread on life's unfurling scroll,
Waiting here the grand ordeal—
　Dawning birthday of the soul!

From such heavenly slumber waking,
　Comes the sense how deep and clear,
Brighter morn than earth's is breaking—
　This is Bethel, God is here!

Ah! he knew not One so near him,
　When he sought the needed rest;
Now in awe he can but fear him—
　Mingled fear and joy how blest!

House of God and gate of heaven—
　Light transforms the stony place,
When the ladder dream is given,
　And the soul finds saving grace.

Rear we then the grateful altar,
　Sacred consecration give;
Purpose true no more shall falter;
　God with us, for him we live. 　1887

[JULY 23.] Then would I fly away and be at rest. Ps. lv. 6.

I .. will receive you unto myself; that where I am, there ye may be also. JOHN xiv. 3.

## HER HOME OF REST.

SHE hath gone to the home of her rest,
　Where Heaven entrances her sight;
She mingles in joy with the blest,
　Arrayed as an angel of light.

She bears a glad harp in her hand,
　And touches with rapture its strings;
To her voice list the seraphim band,
　For sweet is the song that she sings.

In the garner of glory a sheaf,
　Afar from this sorrowing sphere,
She meets with no sickness or grief,
　Nor falls from her eyelids a tear.

Weep not for the spirit that's fled,
　Nor heave the embittering sigh;
She resteth not now with the dead,
　But dwells with her Saviour on high.　1843

[JULY 24.] He said, I will not let thee go, except thou bless me.—GEN. xxxii. 26.

The supplication of a righteous man availeth much in its working. JAS. v. 16.

## PENIEL.

WHEN in trial's pressing hour,
Oh, for more than mortal power!
God, O God! the spirit cries,
Now for me let help arise!
　Leave me not, I cling to thee;
　Lo! thine arms encircle me.

Worthy not of mercies thine,
Thou might'st hide thy face divine,
Pass me in my sore distress,
Others worthier aid and bless;
 But thy promise, Lord, I plead;
 Save me in this time of need!

Wonderful has been thy care,
Lead me still, thy servant spare;
Clings my hand, my soul, to thee,
Now my refuge thou must be;
 Never will I let thee go,
 Till the blessing thou bestow!

What my name? Thou knowest well;
Bethel's radiant memories tell.
What is thine? 'T is known above,
Here and there—Eternal Love!
 Sweet assurance comes to me,
 Blest and rescued, Lord, by thee.

Jacob's triumph, Israel's name,
From that flaming Presence came;
Lord, he saw thee face to face,
Strong in thy victorious grace;
 Praying, wrestling, through the night—
 Oh, Peniel's morn how bright!

Traveler! as the seasons roll,
Come what crises for thy soul!
Round thee pleads a tempting world,
Shafts of Satan at thee hurled:
 Thou thro' wrestling prayer shalt stand,
 Held by God's sustaining hand. 1887

[JULY 25.] They said one to another, We are verily guilty concerning our brother. GEN. xlii. 21.

The patriarchs, moved with jealousy against Joseph, sold him into Egypt: and God was with him. ACTS vii. 9.

## JOSEPH SOLD INTO EGYPT.

THE God who reigns above
    O'er all the earth presides;
His own are kept in love,
    As each in him abides.
From adverse scenes and hateful things,
Rich gifts of good and grace he brings,
Till the lone heart in gladness sings.

The counsels of the vile,
    The acts of cruel foes,
Reveal their treacherous guile,
    Their wickedness disclose,—
As wheels of Providence slow turn,
And conscience-fires within them burn,
The blackness of their deeds they learn.

In Dothan's plots, devised
    At envy's direful beck,
See murderous forms disguised
    Divinely held in check.
Their worst designs are made to fail;
The guilty doers sure shall quail,
As Egypt hence repeats the tale.

How safe are those who know
    And trust the Father's care;
They find where'er they go,
    His strong protection there.

He watches every step they take,
He never will his own forsake,
Nor e'er his word or promise break.

How sweet to see that ill
    Through him becomes our good,
While trusting to his will
    To lead us as he would.
How blest the end, how grand the goal,
What crowns await the patient soul,
What glories while heaven's ages roll!   1887

---

[JULY 26.]  His enemies will I clothe with shame: but upon himself
shall his crown flourish.  Ps. cxxxii. 18.
He is a chosen vessel unto me.  ACTS ix. 15.

### EXALTED.

SLAVED by guilty brothers' trade,
In the lonely journey made,
Far from tender parent's love,
Kept by sweeter care above,
Prisoner by satanic words,
Joseph, thou art still the Lord's!

Sweetly shines in darkest place
Loving light from God's dear face,
Making e'en the prison bars
Like the glory of the stars,
Gilding shadeful, gloomy days—
Nights with heavenly dreams ablaze.

Scenes of sadness passing through,
Ever faithful, patient, true;
Proved by trial hard and sore,—
All these sorrows now are o'er;

Bitter night of grief is gone
In the morning's joyful dawn.

Faithful yet in every thing,
Stands he now before the king;
Wisdom of surpassing ken
Ranks him o'er the wisest men;
Wondrous knowledge, meekly shown,
Crowns him prince beside the throne.

Royal robes and chains of gold
Speak the sway his virtues hold;
Nobler still, his prudent care
Saves an empire from despair!
Trusting God through each dark hour,
Him He lifts to fame and power.

Let us, Lord, where'er we be,
Cling in loyalty to thee:
In the sunny days of youth
Love and keep thy blessèd truth;
Firm in trial, serving, wait—
Thou thine own wilt vindicate.           1887

[JULY 27.]  God did send me before you to preserve life. GEN. xlv. 5.
Overcome evil with good. ROM. xii. 21.

## MADE KNOWN.

I AM JOSEPH! Words of wonder,
    Tingling what astonished ears;
Fell they like untimely thunder,
    Waking deep and guilty fears.
Lone, with Pharaoh's lord assembled,
Dumb and dazed, his brethren trembled.

I'm your brother! Come ye near me;
  Is my father yet alive?
Come, I pray you, do not fear me,
  I your envious deed survive.
Out of evils, soul-distressing,
God has brought a wondrous blessing.

Be not filled with needless sorrow;
  Wide the famine woes extend,
Many a dark and dread to-morrow
  Ere the scourgeful years shall end.
God hath sent me on before you,
As his saving banner o'er you.

Here in Goshen ye shall flourish,
  Father, brethren, by my side;
I will all the household nourish—
  For your every want provide.
Haste and tell the cheering story;
Tell my father of my glory.

Oh, my longing heart is breaking!
  Floods of tears bedim my eyes:
'Tis my lips to you are speaking—
  Oh, this blessèd, glad surprise!
Benjamin!—love's kiss hath spoken;
Brothers all, receive the token!

Type of Christ! The loving Saviour,
  Sold and slain that we might live,
Makes us feel our sin's behaviour,
  Then so freely doth forgive.

Blesséd Lord! our elder Brother,
More to us than every other!　　　1857

[JULY 28.] Commit thy way unto the Lord; trust also in him, and he
shall bring it to pass. Ps. xxxvii. 5.
Honor thy father and mother .. that it may be well with thee. Eph.
vi. 2, 3.

## BROUGHT TOGETHER.

God reigns in all the worlds on high,
　　O'er every land beneath the sun;
　　Past, present, future, all as one,
In clearest light before him lie.

Events upon his wisdom turn,
　　Unfolding as his will decides:
　　Like movements of vast ocean tides,
Life's mightier flow and ebb we learn.

Kingdoms arise and have their day,
　　Their purpose serve in God's great plan—
　　Some higher hope and good for man—
Abuse their power and fade away.

Always the Lord was Joseph's guide,
　　In joyful scenes or sore distress:
　　He would through him the nations bless—
For grander work designed provide.

The brother sold but went before,
　　For father, brethren, kindred all.
　　Jacob, revived, attends his call—
In Egypt finds abundant store.

The shepherd tribes, the chosen race,
　　For Joseph's sake are welcomed there;

Then lo! a scene as grand as rare—
Jacob and Pharaoh face to face.

The courteous word, the bearing true,
   In friendship king and patriarch meet,
   Good will and blessing to repeat,
While God's all-ruling hand we view.

Help me, dear Lord, to trust thy way,
   Though led in darkness or in light,
   For thou wilt make its ending bright,
If faith, obedient, crown each day.        1887

———————————

[JULY 29.]   There the weary be at rest.  JOB iii. 17.
The trumpet shall sound, and the dead shall be raised. 1 COR. xv. 52.

### EVERGREEN CEMETERY.

NATURE and art have furnished here
   A home where hallowed dust shall lie;
Around it clustering charms appear,
   And o'er it bends the beaming sky.

Here oft shall come the solemn trains,
   And, gathering by a new-made tomb,
Leave with last rites the dear remains,
   And then return in silent gloom.

Oft, o'er each grave, affection's tears
   Shall, mid the vernal blossoms, fall;
Till, in the flight of wasting years,
   The cherished spot hath garnered all.

Here, on memorial columns reared,
   Strangers shall honored names behold;

And humbler worth, beloved, revered,
   In saintly fame shall be enrolled.

How sweet shall be their slumbers deep,
   Freed from a world of sin and strife;
Till, waked at last from death's long sleep,
   They rise to everlasting life!    1856

---

[JULY 30.] He increased his people greatly, and made them stronger than their adversaries. PS. cv. 24.

Remember them that are in bonds, as bound with them; them that are evil entreated, as being yourselves also in the body. HEB. xiii. 3.

## ISRAEL IN EGYPT.

GOD's thoughts are deep and far,
   Wisely his purpose planned,
As Israel's hope and guiding star
   To Egypt's wonder-land,
Where their astonished eyes
   Saw pyramids sublime,
Vast temples, tombs, and columns rise—
   The marvels of all time!

God e er fulfills his word;
   Nor fails of all a jot.
When Pharaoh's jealousy was stirred
   Who Joseph's work forgot,
Vain were his burdens laid;
   Taskmasters all in vain;
The chosen nation widely spread,
   And grew as fruitful grain.

The stalwart people wrought,
   Amid afflictions sore,

Till cities, to completion brought,
  Held Pharaoh's treasured store.
And we behold to-day,
  How fails the critic's lure,
When bricks they laid come forth to say
  God's record standeth sure.

Lo! Rameses the Great
  Comes from his Luxor cave;
And other kings of high estate
  Rise from their ancient grave!
Th' oppressor's form, well known,
  Hard visage as of old,
Repeat the toil, the tear, the groan,
  The bondage, Moses told.

God leads us as he will;
  Sometimes through sorrows deep,
His gracious purpose to fulfill,
  His own to prove and keep.
By hardships sorely tried,
  Came forth the mighty throng;
Led safely o'er the Red-Sea tide,
  They sang their triumph song!        1857

'JULY 31.] I have graven thee upon the palms of my hands. Is. xlix. 16.
To set you before the presence of his glory. JUDE 24.

### CONFIDENCE.

LORD, my times are in thy hand,
  Thou hast graved me on its palm;
Sheltered there, I safely stand,
  Rough the storm or sweet the calm.        1890

[Aug. 1.] O clap your hands, all ye peoples; shout unto God with the voice of triumph. Ps. xlvii. 1.

Thanks be unto God, which always leadeth us in triumph in Christ. 2 Cor. ii. 14.

## MORAL TRIUMPH.

Fought is the battle! victory won!
Clouds are departing, shineth the sun.
Day of redemption, hail to thy morning!
Glory gleams on thee, brightly adorning!

Gained is the triumph, Right wins the day;
Freedom ascendant, blesséd her sway!
Fling out the banner, wave it in splendor;
Praise for the conquest gratefully render!

Toil is rewarded, prayer hath been heard,
Faith at last conquers, hope's not deferred.
Shout! ye long patient, rise in your gladness,
Welcome the era ending your sadness!

Comes a strong Angel, earthward again,
Binds the old Dragon fast in his chain.
Joy to the freed ones! woe to the oppressor!
Angel of good, henceforth the aggressor!

Courage! ye toilers, onward for right;
Breaketh the dayspring, passeth the night:
Heaven's light gildeth hilltops and mountains,
Drops down the valleys, smiles on the fountains.

Up now, ye crushed ones, fetters throw by;
Death-freighted thunders roll from your sky!
Vanquished the foeman, selfish and stoic;
God, in the battle, crowns the heroic!                1854

[AUG. 2.] A dream, and visions of his head upon his bed: then he wrote the dream and told the sum of the matters. DAN. vii. 1.

Behold, an angel of the Lord stood by him, and a light shined in the cell. ACTS xii. 7.

## BUNYAN IN JAIL.

BUNYAN! how Satan, helped by men,
    With mischievous endeavor,
Put thee in jail, to put out then
    Thy kindled flame forever!

Celestial genius would not die,
    Through years of long confining,
Whilst thou, with comfort from the sky,
    Wert cheerful, unrepining.

Methinks within thy dungeon's gloom
    A light divine had risen,
To make it Glory's ante-room,
    Though still thy Bedford prison.

How clearly there the heavenly path
    Rose on thy spirit's vision,
That, from the City doomed to wrath,
    Leads to the blest Elysian.

Then passed before thee in thy dream,
    A happy band and saintly;
Thy pictures make them real seem,
    Though oft a little quaintly.

I love to trace their pathway o'er,
    And hear their joyful singing,
Till, thro' the stream, they reach the shore
    Where angel harps are ringing.

1859

[AUG. 3.] Because he hath set his love upon me, therefore will I de-
liver him : I will set him on high, because he hath known my name.
Ps. xci. 14.

We speak, not in words which man's wisdom teacheth, but which the
Spirit teacheth ; comparing spiritual things with spiritual. 1 COR. ii. 13.

## AT BUNYAN'S TOMB.

THOU Prince of Dreamers! I have found
 The place of thy last sleeping,
And grateful tread this hallowed ground,
 With minged joy and weeping.

Dear Bunyan! I have loved thy name
 More than my words can measure;
And long shall pilgrims hold thy fame
 A sweet and precious treasure.

Thou wast a burning, shining light,
 Within thy sphere of duty;
Though then unknown a star so bright,
 So rich in heavenly beauty.

God raised thee from thy lowly place,
 Thou plain, untutored thinker,
And gave thee, ah! what gifts of grace,
 O wondrous Elstow tinker!

Thy heart and lips his Spirit fired,
 When from his foe he gained thee:
To preach his truth he called, inspired,
 Commissioned, and ordained thee.

What crowds, beneath thy earnest voice,
 Thy zeal to save them, burning,
Were made to weep, believe, rejoice,
 From ways of error turning!

Keep, Bunhill Fields, his precious dust,
  Housed in thy rare collection:
How fair he'll shine among the just
  In the great resurrection!

Immortal Dreamer! slumbering here,
  How sweet thy Pilgrim's story!
On thy blest tomb I drop a tear,
  And envy thee in glory.

A jewel-studded crown how bright
  To thy dear head is given:
May I be found with thee in light,
  A pilgrim safe in Heaven.     1859

---

[AUG. 4.] The Lord is thy keeper: the Lord is thy shade upon thy
right hand. Ps. cxxi. 5.
What then shall this child be? LUKE i. 66.

## THE CHILD MOSES.

THE loving Hebrew mother
  Beheld, with radiant joy,
A charm beyond all other
  Crowning her beauteous boy.

Has God this darling angel
  Sent down from heaven's gate,
To be the blest evangel
  To those who sorrowing wait?

Ah! now if aught reveal him,
  Such loveliness must die;
O God! help me conceal him
  From Pharaoh's murderous eye.

In tenderest care abiding,
  What vigils, day and night,
To keep her jewel's hiding
  As only in her sight.

Three months—nor can they linger;
  The keen maternal eyes
See fate's most cruel finger
  Out reaching for the prize.

Soft in the ark she'll fold him,
  And haste at early day;
The dense Nile flags shall hold him,
  He must not float away.

Ah! who can tell the feeling
  That swept her anguished soul,
Or know its deep appealing
  For more than man's control?

Sweet Miriam at her station,
  Awaits, with eager look,
The next great revelation
  For God's most wondrous book.

Lo! Pharaoh's daughter, turning,
  Walks by the river tide,
And quick the ark discerning,
  Commands it to her side.

Sweet in the care-wrought casket,
  She sees the cherub lie;
Her heart is in the basket,
  Won by the infant's cry.

What blest relief and pleasure,
    As through love's quenchless flame
The mother's matchless treasure
    Back to her bosom came.

Her love who found and named him
    Shall rear him as her own:
The princess justly claimed him
    As heir to Egypt's throne.

The Christ-Child here was hidden
    From Herod's bloody hand,
Till by God's angel bidden
    To leave dark Egypt's land.    1887

---

[AUG. 5.]   There hath not arisen a prophet since in Israel like unto
Moses, whom the Lord knew face to face.  DEUT. xxxiv. 10.
    A flame of fire in a bush . . and as he drew near to behold, there
came a voice of the Lord.  ACTS vii. 30, 31.

### CALLED FROM THE BURNING BUSH.

In Midian forty years,
The leader of the chosen hosts to be
In deep seclusion lived, a shepherd he,
    While Israel served in tears.

One day the flock he took
The desert o'er to Horeb's verdant side,
And there a thing most wonderful descried,
    That riveted his look.

From out a bush on fire
The Angel of the Lord Almighty came!—
The bush, still bright in the enswathing flame,
    Remained unburnt, entire!

Pressing for view more clear,
Lo! from the glowing tree his own name's sound:
Forbear; thy feet are now on holy ground;
    Put off thy sandals here.

I am thy father's God;
My people's sorrows are beneath my eye;
Their crushing tasks I know, and hear their cry,
    'Neath the oppressors' rod.

From heaven am I come down
To loose them from the hard Egyptian charge,
And bring them to a goodly land and large,
    That milk and honey crown.

Come now, and thee I'll send,
That thou may'st plead with Pharaoh face to face,
Bring forth my people, an enfranchised race,
    Their Egypt trials end.

That this great thing should be,
Ah! who am I? the meek man humbly said.
The God of Abraham, who Israel led,
    Will surely be with thee.

And this thy mission sign:
When thou the people hast from bondage brought,
Ye'll serve the God who all these marvels wrought,
    Upon this mount of mine.

Lord, as we hear thy voice,
May we obey, seek sin-slaved souls for thee,
Thy mighty grace in their redemption see,
    With them in heaven rejoice.    1887

[AUG. 6.] When I see the blood, I will pass over you, and there shall no plague be upon you to destroy you. Ex. xii. 13.

Our passover also hath been sacrificed, even Christ. 1 COR. v. 7.

## THE PASSOVER.

DRAWS near th' eventful hour
    Of Israel's full release,
When Pharaoh's cruel power
    And bondage-tasks shall cease.
The day—the lamb unblemished slain—
Their great memorial shall remain.

On posts and lintel high
    The fresh red blood is spread
For God's inspecting eye,
    As night shall mark his tread,
When every house, all Egypt through,
Shall know the wonders he will do.

By every Hebrew shared,
    Each household met complete,
The new great feast prepared,
    With bitter herbs they eat.
With girded loins, their feet well shod,
And staff in hand, they wait for God!

His patience long abused
    At length must yield to wrath;
This call, by none refused,
    Will open Israel's path.
Ah! what a night of woe forlorn,
When Egypt saw its dead firstborn!

The crimson on each door
  Was mercy's saving law;
God passed his people o'er
  As there the blood he saw.
Deliverance sure they all receive,
Because his word their hearts believe.

Oh, the great sacrifice!
  The far more precious blood—
The Lamb of Calvary dies,
  To bring the world to God!
He sees that blood—my soul there laved
Is cleansed from sin, from death is saved. 1867

---

[AUG. 7.]  As the days of the heavens above the earth. DEUT. xi. 21.
First the blade, then the ear, then the full corn in the ear. MK. iv. 28.

## DAYS OF HEAVEN.

WHAT faith surveys shall meet the sight:
At evening time it shall be light;
When culminates the age of gold,
Come days of heaven on earth foretold.

No dream are they of man's repose,
Nor brilliant hues at daylight's close,
Nor meteor showers in night's advance,
Nor visions of a shadowy trance.

They come by growth of laboring years;
At first the springing blade appears;
Long periods watch the ear mature,
And the full corn at last is sure. 1878

[Aug. 8.] Moses said unto the people, Fear ye not, stand still, and see the salvation of the Lord, which he will work for you to-day. Ex. xiv. 13.

Wherefore take up the whole armor of God, that ye may be able to withstand in the evil day, and, having done all to stand. Eph. vi. 13.

## AT THE RED SEA.

Why should Israel be dismayed?
  Why this sad and mournful cry?
God will give his promised aid,
    He will help when danger's nigh.
      Fear ye not! but trust in Heaven,
      Soon deliverance shall be given.

He, whose marvelous sovereign power
  Made the monarch quail with dread,
When the lonely midnight hour
    Looked on Egypt's firstborn dead,—
      He is still the Hebrews' friend,
      His right arm shall yet defend.

See you Pharaoh's hosts to-day?
  Soon their ranks will fade from view;
God will make for you a way,
    Light and guide you safely through.
      Stand ye still, dismiss your fear,
      His salvation will appear!

Hither by Jehovah brought,
  Surely he for you will fight;
Foes, who have your capture sought,
    He will overwhelm to-night.
      Onward, then, and trust in Heaven,
      Great deliverance shall be given! 1839

[AUG. 9.] The Lord looked forth upon the host of the Egyptians thro'
the pillar of fire and of cloud, and discomfited the host. Ex. xiv. 24.

By faith they passed through the Red sea as by dry land : which the
Egyptians essaying to do were swallowed up. HEB. xi. 29.

## THE PILLAR AND THE PASSAGE.

THAT mysterious column! it hung from the sky,
    The vanguard as Israel the exodus made;
Lo! a wonderful thing to each upward turned eye,
    A Presence divine—the Shekinah displayed!

As it lifted in grandeur, their course was discerned;
    Its shadow, refreshing, soft over them lay;
How resplendent its form as to crimson it turned,
    And night wore a beauty unknown to the day!

They have come to the Sea, by its margin they rest,
    When lo! their oppressors, revengeful, appear;
But by Moses assured, at Jehovah's behest,
    The march is renewed, they advance without fear.

In the midst of the sea, its dark waters rolled back,
    The chosen go forward, walled billows between;
For they find in the depths solid ground for a track,
    The marvelous cloud brooding over the scene.

Still defiant, the foe presses on in their path:
    The pillar, receding, the armies divides;
To Egyptian pursuers 't is darkness and wrath;
    On Israel, beloved, its bright glory abides.

In the watch of the morning the Angel looked out;
    The flash from the cloud was defeat to the foe :
At the leader's waved staff, the sure signal of rout,
    The refluent floods Egypt's pride overflow!

Now the host in their freedom, the transit complete,
　All grateful and safe on the welcoming shore,
Raise their song to Jehovah—its chorus repeat—
　An anthem of triumph that rings evermore!

To the long journey's end, as the chosen of God,
　To desert or mountain or river bank, came;
In the places of rest, in the pathways they trod,
　Their guide was the pillar of cloud and of flame.

If the night-gloom was deepest, it gave them its light;
　To nations opposed, it was darkness severe:
So the light of God shines on the pure in his sight,
　While the faithless grope ever in shadow and fear.

1878

---

[AUG. 10.] He shall blossom as the lily, and cast forth his roots as
Lebanon. HOS. xiv. 5.

He which hath begun a good work in you will perfect it. PHIL. i. 6.

## BUD AND BLOOM.

THE vernal flowers that break the ground,
And, smiling sweet, shed fragrance round,
Are prophecies of fullest blaze
Of summer blooms in sunnier days.

The budding growths, though little things,
Are oft the clear foreshadowings
Of grand events in glorious years,
When earth's ripe harvesting appears.

The ages toil; slow lapses time;
But, with their steady march sublime,
Comes the rich fruitage sought so long
In prophet's voice and poet's song.

1875

[Aug. 11.] I will sing unto the Lord, for he hath triumphed glorious-
ly: the horse and his rider hath he thrown into the sea. Ex. xv. 1.

This man led them forth, having wrought wonders and signs in
Egypt and in the Red sea. Acts vii. 36.

## THE SONG OF MOSES.

Sing, sing to the Lord! most exultingly sing;
All praise to Jehovah! our conquering King;
He's gloriously triumphed, and Israel is free;
The army of Pharaoh is whelmed in the sea!

When trembling with fear as environed by foes,
The waters he sundered—like walls they arose:
His hand held us firmly till danger was o'er,
And foes that enslaved could pursue us no more.

O God! our salvation, we bow at thy throne:
Thy name is exalted, thy majesty known:
Th'oppressor is vanquished, he fell 'neath thy frown
As bolts of thy thunder in terror came down!

From Egypt set free, in dread peril sustained,
God's right hand has saved us, the victory's gained;
The horse and the rider repose in death's sleep,
They sank with the chariots like lead in the deep.

Thou'lt guide us, as onward to Canaan we go,
By cloud pillar's shade or its radiant glow:
The sun scatters gloom from the far-spread expanse,
So foes of thy chosen shall melt at thy glance.

Thou mighty Jehovah! earth quails at thy nod,
No other is like thee, like Israel's God!
Thy reign is for ever, thy glory divine;
How fearful in praises, what wonders are thine! 1839

[Aug. 12.]  I will rain bread from heaven for you; and the people shall go out and gather a day's portion every day.  Ex. xvi. 4.

Jesus said unto them, I am the bread of life: he that cometh to me shall not hunger.  John vi. 35.

## THE MANNA.

March the chosen sons and daughters
　　Where the guiding pillar tells;
On from Marah's sweetened waters,
　　Elim's palms and cooling wells.
Marvelous God's way to lead them,
　　Give them victory and song;
Still as wonderful to feed them,
　　Satisfy the hungry throng.

O'er the desert breaks the morning,
　　Soft its voice from slumber calls;
Lo! the landscape far adorning,
　　White as snow-flakes manna falls.
Precious bread, divinely given,
　　Angels' food for man's supply,
Fresh from harvest-stores of heaven—
　　Oh, the bounty of the sky!

Day by day 't was God's good pleasure
　　Thus to rain his riches down:
Day by day they had their measure,
　　At the morning's golden crown.
Evening came with special blessing
　　For the wants they yet disclose,
Till, for souls their good possessing,
　　Blooms the desert as the rose.

Strange that murmurs oft are rising,
    Hearts unsatisfied repine,
Mid such miracles surprising,
    Love so tender and divine.
May we, gracious, loving Father,
    Be more grateful, firm, and true,
As thy gifts we daily gather,
    And thy richer Manna view.      1887

[AUG. 13.] The Lord spake with you face to face in the mount out of
the midst of the fire. DEUT. v. 4.
Ye are come unto mount Zion .. and to Jesus the mediator of a new
covenant. HEB. xii. 22, 24.

## SINAI AND CALVARY.

O SINAI! when I come to thee,
Jehovah's flaming justice see,
His holiness, majestic, clear,
Condemned, I shrink away with fear.

No word from thee brings conscience peace,
For guilty souls no blest release;
Thy trumpet voice sounds forth the cry:
Keep all the law, or surely die!

With gladness I to Calvary turn,
Abundant mercy there discern.
Oh, wondrous cross—my tearful eyes
Behold the Lamb of sacrifice.

Jesus, the law fulfilled in thee,
Forgiveness, peace, and hope, I see.
O radiant mount! O precious blood!
Thy death gives life, dear Son of God.    1887

[AUG. 14.] When thou passest through the waters, I will be with thee; and through the rivers, they shall not overflow thee. ISA. xliii. 2.

These things were done in Bethany beyond Jordan, where John was baptizing. JOHN i. 28.

## THE RIVER JORDAN.

O JORDAN! swiftly flowing
 Thy verdant banks along,
Immortal wonders knowing—
 Great themes of sacred song,
Light on the ages throwing,
 As truth and faith grow strong.

Now millions at thy border,
 From desert ways appear,
The chosen hosts in order,
 The vast encampment here,
Trusting their mighty Warder,
 Unawed by foe or fear.

Behold! thy swollen waters,
 That filled their bed profound,
With roar like battle slaughters,
 Are parted, piled, and bound,
While Israel's sons and daughters
 March through on solid ground!

God sent his prophets o'er thee—
 The stream divinely cleft—
By chariot flame before thee
 Was earth for Heaven left;
But mantling might he bore thee,
 O lonely one bereft!

The skies above thee riven,
  A grander scene occurred,
When Christ, the Lord from heaven,
  Thy sacred waters stirred,
The dove-like Spirit given,
  The Father's loving word.

Symbol of death, O river!
  Glory the other side!
My Lord! of life the giver,
  The shadowy stream divide,
When to that blest Forever
  Thou art my Saviour-guide.          1888

---

[AUG. 15.]  I have seen an end of all perfection; but thy command-
ment is exceeding broad.  Ps. cxix. 96.

  The law hath been our tutor to bring us unto Christ, that we might
be justified by faith.  GAL. iii. 24.

### GIVING THE LAW.

Moses, on Sinai's brow with awe,
Receives from God his holy Law—
The great 'ten words' that he commands,
On stone engraved by his own hands.

The scene is grand, the truth sublime,
Precepts proclaimed for earth and time,
Searching man's life, without, within;
A perfect guide to keep from sin.

The thunder, lightning, trumpet peal,
The great and righteous God reveal,
While each command proclaims him just,
And humbles sinners in the dust.          1887

[Aug. 16.] The anointed of the God of Jacob, and the sweet psalmist of Israel. 2 Sam. xxiii. 1.

David, after he had in his own generation served the counsel of God, fell on sleep. Acts xiii. 36.

## DAVID.

Sparkling as the morning star,
  Ruddy as the radiant skies,
Orb of promise beaming far,
  See the son of Jesse rise;
    Beauteous boy of Bethlehem,
    Waits for him a diadem.

Shepherd youth among the hills,
  Nature holds in sweet control,
Heavenly fire his spirit fills,
  Songs unsung are in his soul.
    Girt with strength divine he grows,
    Triumphs over giant foes.

Warrior of the grandest gauge
  Judah's armies ever led,
Mighty deeds mark every page
  Where his battle scenes are spread.
    Minstrels sing his martial fame,
    All the nation speak his name.

When Saul's cloud-veiled sun went down,
  David took his waiting throne;
Ne'er had king a brighter crown,
  Nor a loftier wisdom shown.
    Happy land beneath his reign,
    Peace and splendor came again.

But beyond each boon divine,
 Might of arms or kingly dower,
David's lyrics glorious shine,
 Grander than his regal power.
  Souls devout, through earth and time,
  Feel their fire and catch their chime.  1887

---

[AUG. 17.] The battle is the Lord's, and he will give you into our hand. 1 SAM. xvii. 47.

The weapons of our warfare are .. mighty before God to the casting down of strong holds. 2 COR. x. 4.

## BATTLE WITH THE GIANT.

FROM the slopes of Azekah the Philistines surveyed
The fair tents of Israel in Elah arrayed.
To the summits they gather and, gleaming in light,
Each armor-clad host is prepared for the fight.
  In the valley between,
  Vine and olive in green
Wait the tread and the shock of the terrible scene!

They pause, as reluctant, in still, bated breath,
The war-shout to utter, and rush to the death,
When scornfully, proudly, and slowly, alone,
Stalked the giant of Gath, like a king from his throne;
  And enveloped in mail,
  Strutting down through the vale,
He called loud for a champion to meet and assail.

His form was gigantic, his spear like a beam,
Broad shield, and high helmet, and resonant scream,
As for forty long days he came forth in his pride,
And the armies of Israel contemned and defied!

None dared answer his call,
Neither Abner nor Saul,
Lest beneath his vast sword he should merciless fall.

From Bethlehem's hills a fair shepherd boy came,
And heard the Philistine his brethren defame;
He felt in his soul that the might of the Lord
Would give him the conquest, his valor reward:
  So the beautiful lad
  In simplicity said,
I accept the bold challenge the monster has made.

Then David went forth without armor or shield,
Save the sling in his hand and the stone it must wield.
All Israel stood breathless—the Philistines aghast,
As Goliath fell low when the swift missile passed!
  The youth smote off his head;
  The uncircumcised fled;
Israel, shouting, pursued mid the wounded and dead!

Now silent the boasted defiance and wrath,
As prone on the earth lies the giant of Gath;
His sword and his spear and the mail that he wore,
Unwielded and useless, are trusted no more.
  All the valley and hill
  Ring with victory still,
And the white tents of Elah shake under the thrill!

How glorious is faith in the battle for right!
To conquer is easy when God gives the might;
Sublime the achievements his servants may win,
As they meet in his name the mailed giants of sin.

Souls! your heritage guard!
Would you gain its reward?
Come up to the help—to the help of the Lord!  1868

---

[AUG. 18.]  God my Maker, who giveth songs in the night. JOB
xxxv. 10.
   I heard a voice of many angels round about the throne and the
living creatures. REV. v. 11.

## CELESTIAL MINSTRELSIES.

HARK! a strain of music floats
    Softly through the evening air;
Sweet and soothing are its notes,
    Like the cadences of prayer.

These are songs the Lord inspires,
    Which he giveth in the night,
Stealing out from spirit lyres,
    Changing darkness into light.

Lo! a pensive harp I hear;
    Angel fingers touch its chords,
And a chastened heart sincere
    Utters forth its trusting words.

Hopeful is the music's tone,
    Mid the tears of sorrowing grief,
Shed o'er dear ones loved and gone—
    Dear ones nigh to give relief.

Live they still who knew us here—
    Souls in Christ shall never die—
Long they for us, hold us dear,
    Waiting, watching from the sky.  1854

[AUG. 19.]   Give me now wisdom and knowledge.   2 CHRON. i. 10.
  Ask, and it shall be given unto you; seek, and ye shall find.   MAT.
vii. 7.

### SOLOMON'S CHOICE.

FAIR Gibeon's summit, broadly rounded,
    Upheld an altar-shrine,
Where free burnt offerings abounded,
    As worship's act divine.

Here Solomon the king slept, dreaming,
    After his vows were given,
When came the Lord in glory gleaming,
    As from the gate of heaven.

Ask me, proposed the Voice supernal,
    What I to thee shall give.
Then prayed the king to the Eternal,
    For wisdom how to live:

"Thy mercy to my father showing
    Was bounteous and great;
And kindness still thou art bestowing,
    As I before thee wait.

Called as the king of this vast nation,
    And but a child am I;
I can not fill this mighty station,
    Only as thou art nigh.

Oh, give thy servant understanding—
    A wise, discerning heart,
That he, whate'er the task's demanding,
    May act the noblest part."

A choice that met Jehovah's pleasure,
    A prayer that blessing brought

Of wisdom, wealth, gifts without measure,
  Far more than all he sought.

Oh, help me, gracious, blesséd Father,
  E'er thus to pray and live,
Choosing the heavenly wisdom, rather
  Than what this world can give.    1884

---

[AUG. 20.] The Lord is my rock, and my fortress, and my deliverer, even mine. 2 SAM. xxii. 2.

Other foundation can no man lay than that which is laid, which is Jesus Christ. 1 COR. iii. 11.

## THE ROCK FOUNDATION.

Rock eternal! thou shalt be
Building place alone for me;
Blest foundation, sure and strong,
Earth's one hope through ages long;
All who thee for refuge sought
Safe have been to glory brought.

Rock of Israel, smitten, cleft,
Souls, through sin's despair bereft,
See thee rise o'er waves of time,
Heavenly beacon, tower sublime:
Christ our Rock! they fly to thee,
Building place for them and me.

When the testing hour we know,
Floods of grief the soul o'erflow,
Tempests wild our house assail,
Builders on the sand shall fail,
Rock eternal! thou wilt be
Refuge, Home, and Heaven to me.    1887

[AUG. 21.] The Lord loved Israel for ever, therefore made he thee king, to do judgment and justice. 1 KINGS x. 9.

Behold, a greater than Solomon is here. LUKE xi. 31.

## THE QUEEN AND THE KING.

THE Queen in regal glory
    From distant Sheba came,
Drawn by the wondrous story
    Of Israel's sacred fame.
Awed by the matchless splendor—
    The wisdom of the king—
Her praise what words could render,
    Or worthy tribute bring?

"O Solomon! behold me,
    Faint, at the vast array!
The half had ne'er been told me
    Of what my eyes survey!
I could not then believe it,
    And yet 't was all so true;
Scarce now can I receive it—
    'T is marvelous in my view!

Happy are those so near thee,
    Who see thy royal state,
The servants that revere thee,
    And in thy presence wait:
What wisdom ever gaining
    From golden words of thine;
A place so rare obtaining
    Is sure a boon divine.

Blest be the Lord, whose favor,
    To his beloved is shown;
Blest be thy God for ever,
    Who set thee on the throne;
Crowned thee with wealth and station,
    And wisdom's vast increase,
That thou might'st rule the nation
    With justice, truth, and peace."

O King of kings! what glory
    Is thine in worlds above!
Who, who can tell the story
    Of thy redeeming love?
How sweet the peace and pleasure
    Here to thy servants given!
How glorious the treasure
    Reserved for them in Heaven!    1884

---

[AUG. 22.] **Come ye, and let us walk in the light of the Lord.** ISA.
ii. 5.
Jesus himself drew near, and went with them. LUKE xxiv. 15.

### BLESSED COMPANIONSHIP.

DEAR Lord, when in my walks alone,
    How blest are thoughts of thee;
I lift heart-breathings to thy throne,
    And find thou art with me.

Thy nearness brightens all my way;
    Thy works fresh beauties wear;
Thy love breaks o'er me, and the day
    Is bathed in Heaven's own air.    1890

[AUG. 23.]  Entangled like thorns and drunken as with their drink
they are consumed. (Am. Com.)  NAH. i. 10.
  Some save, snatching them out of the fire.  JUDE 23.

## THE MONSTER VICE.

STILL the monster vice is found;
  The old dragon, yet unbound,
With his fallen spirits, rages,
Writes in woe the awful pages
  Where his daily deeds abound.

Widows' weeds are doubly deep,
  Pleading orphans more than weep,
Ruined spirits chafe their prison;
Mind is lost—what bright stars risen
  Madness clouds in gloom to keep!

What the worm to floweret rare,
  What miasma to the air,
What the life-blood, chilled and frozen,
What false Judas to the chosen,
  Is the cup to all that's fair.

Shall the desolation still
  Hearts and homes forever fill?
Shall the monster live, augmenting,
Man's indifference consenting,
  When to slay him is TO WILL?

Oh, ye souls of heavenly birth,
  Heritage of God on earth,
Save the young from fierce temptation,
Save the tainted from damnation;
  In this conflict prove your worth!      1872

[AUG. 24.] A people which shall be created shall praise the Lord.—
Ps. cii. 18.

He that reapeth receiveth wages, and gathereth fruit unto life eter-
nal. JOHN iv. 36.

## FIELD AND REAPERS.

In this world of sin and sorrow,
　　Ah, what scenes of woe abound!
Wide-spread regions thronged with people
　　Wrapt in darkness, sad, profound!

Ignorance, like night's deep shadows,
　　Rests on countless groveling minds;
War, caste, bondage—all the evils,
　　Deathless souls in fetters binds!

But a happier age is coming,
　　Lo! its tinted dawn appears;
Prophets see its glorious advent—
　　Era of the promised years.

Earth shall then, like primal Eden,
　　Filled with truth and virtue, bloom;
Sins and sorrows, darkening o'er it,
　　Shall have found a rayless tomb.

Field inviting for the earnest,
　　Warm with impulse high and pure,
Where all labors, sweet and holy,
　　Present, future good insure!

Look upon the outspread landscape,
　　From its shadows ne'er recoil;
Give, to make it bloom in beauty,
　　Hearts of love and hands of toil.　　1849

[AUG. 25.] There appeared a chariot of fire, and horses of fire, which parted them both asunder; and Elijah went up by a whirlwind into heaven. 2 KINGS ii. 11.

Elijah was a man of like passions with us. JAMES v. 17.

## ELIJAH.

TISHBITE sage, inspired of Heaven,
Burning light to Israel given,
Clad with zeal and might of grace,
Grandest prophet of his race!

True, sublime in earnest life,
Strong and brave in fearful strife,
Boldly speaks the will of God,
Wields the stern reformer's rod.

Glorious triumphs sought and won,
Deeds immortal nobly done,
Rounding out his work-day well,
Till is touched its vesper bell.

Oh, to him how bright the end!
Opening skies a chariot send,
Drawn by steeds of flaming light,
Wondrous to the prophet's sight.

Angel hands now place him there,
Whirlwinds lift him high in air,
Stars his soaring passage wait,
Heaven shouts welcome at its gate.

Not for us the car of light,
Through the shadow is our flight;
Led by faith's illuming ray,
Need we fear to launch away?

1869

[Aug. 26.]  God setteth the solitary in families.  Ps. lxviii. 6.

The mother of Jesus was there : and Jesus also was bidden, and his disciples, to the marriage.  John ii. 1, 2.

## THE MARRIAGE AT CANA.

Sweet Cana! where the Master came
    With followers new from Jordan's shore,
Whose visit made thy humble name
    Remembered hence forevermore.

Jesus no stern ascetic proved;
    The common scenes of life he blest,
Met oft with friends he knew and loved,
    Was welcomed here a wedding guest.

And Mary, careful, quick to lead,
    Bade helpers serve her Son divine,
When lo! to meet the festive need,
    He changed the water into wine!

This first of wonder works he wrought,
    And made his Godlike glory known;
So were his weak disciples taught,
    His word to trust, his power to own.

Blest Saviour! in our times of cheer,
    As in our days or moments sad,
Grant we may ever find thee near,
    To soothe our hearts, or make them glad.

Ourselves, our offerings, brought to thee,
    Canst thou, O Lord, accept, approve?
We feel how poor and vain they be,
    Unless transformed by grace and love.  1886

[AUG. 27.] My God, my God, why hast thou forsaken me? Ps. xxii. 1.

Jesus .. said, It is finished: and he bowed his head, and gave up his spirit. JOHN xix. 30.

## DYING ON THE CROSS.

BEHOLD the Saviour as he hangs
 On Calvary's cross in blood and shame,
Enduring more than mortal pangs,
 While heartless crowds revile and blame.

Traitor and judge and Sanhedrim
 See now the work their hands have done;
Ah! what shall be their sight of him—
 The King at last upon his throne!

The thoughtless jest, while painful hours
 In untold anguish slowly move,—
Oh, how can heaven restrain its powers
 O'er such a scene of dying Love!

It dreads to look, and darkness falls,
 A chilling shade of deathlike gloom:
These mocking souls the scene appalls—
 A trembling world awaits its doom!

Such crisis-hour earth never saw;
 "My God, my God!" is Jesus' plea,
He feels that loving Face withdraw,
 As o'er him rolls sin's awful sea.

He bears the curse, he triumphs there,
 The Lamb divine for us is slain;
"'Tis finished," bursts upon the air,
 The darkness flies, 'tis light again! 1882

[AUG. 28.] Choose you this day whom ye will serve...as for me and my house, we will serve the Lord. Josh. xxiv. 15.

What then shall I do unto Jesus which is called Christ? Mat. xxvii. 22.

## WHAT SHALL I DO WITH JESUS?

What shall I do with Jesus,
The Christ who may be mine?
Accept him as my Saviour,
Or spurn the gift divine?
His only Son God gave me—
I must, I do decide;
And Christ I take to save me,
Or Christ is now denied.

What shall I do with Jesus,
The precious Lamb of God?
I cast my soul upon him—
He bathes it in his blood:
I'll gratefully confess him
Before the vile and just;
My ransomed powers shall bless him,
My sure and only trust.

What shall I do with Jesus?
For him the cross I'll take;
All earthly losses suffer,
Ere I the Lord forsake.
In scenes of joy or sighing,
His love shall be the same;
While living and in dying,
I'll glory in his name.

What now I do with Jesus,
　　When this brief life is past
Will be with me remembered
　　Before his bar at last:
Nor will he then disown me,
　　With those who hate and scoff;
At his right hand he'll crown me—
　　He will not cast me off.　　　　1865

---

[Aug. 28.] Thou shalt guide me with thy counsel, and afterward receive me to glory. Ps. lxxiii. 24.

His servants shall do him service: and they shall see his face. Rev. xxii. 4.

## HEAVEN.

Far, far above this changing world,
　　Beyond its darkest scene,
What light and beauty are unfurled
　　O'er fields of fadeless green!

No parting sad, no sullen blight,
　　Of pain and death no fear,
No gathering storm, nor cheerless night,
　　Shall in that realm appear.

How joyous they who shall at last
　　Its blesséd treasures share!
For sorrow's cloud shall never cast
　　A darksome shadow there.

Amid the glories of the place
　　The saints their Lord shall meet,
In ecstasies behold his face,
　　And worship at his feet.　　　　1840

[AUG. 29.]  God shall bring every work into judgment with every hidden thing, whether it be good or whether it be evil.  ECCL. xii. 14.

That each one may receive the things done in the body, according to what he hath done.  2 COR. v. 10.

## THE JUDGMENT.

THE Judgment comes!—the end of years;
The Son of Man in clouds appears!
The glory bursts on mortal sight,
Enhanced by all the angels bright;
Shepherd and King, he sits enthroned,
While nations all to him respond.

The risen dead, the living changed—
What myriad hosts before him ranged!
He sees all hearts, and so divides
The sheep from goats—their chosen sides:
That throng so vast upon his right—
The blood-redeemed—oh, glorious sight!

"Ye blesséd of my Father, come!
The kingdom take, your heavenly home.
You honored me with loyal love,
From hearts that knew the birth above;
And oft, in ways ye little thought,
Unselfish deeds in kindness wrought."

Ah! trembling souls upon his left
Are now of every hope bereft;
Their sad neglects make his "Depart"
Reveal each sin and selfish heart.
Saviour! thy grace to me be given,
And call me in that day to Heaven.

1880

[AUG. 30.] **For so he giveth unto his beloved sleep.** Ps. cxxvii. 2.

As we have borne the image of the earthy, we shall also bear the image of the heavenly. 1 Cor. xv. 49.

## REQUIEM.

Lowly in the grave reposing,
    Gentle maiden, sweetly sleep,
While its portals o'er thee closing
    Shall their sacred treasure keep,
        Till again, thy youth assuming,
        Thou appear in beauty blooming.

Soft and silent are thy slumbers,
    Dreamless thy long night of rest,
Naught of grief thy spirit cumbers,
    Welcomed now among the blest,
        Where to thee a home is given,
        Mid the blissful bowers of Heaven.

Tears bedew the dust above thee,
    Sacred is thy peaceful tomb;
Planted here by those that love thee,
    Fairest flowers shall brightly bloom,
        Pointing through their beauties vernal
        Up to life and love eternal.

Angel harps and seraph voices
    Strangely charm thy raptured soul,
While in gladness it rejoices,
    Free from aught of earth's control:
        Sorrow there shall enter never,
        Youth and beauty bloom forever. 1845

[Aug. 31.] O sing unto the Lord a new song; for he hath done mar-
velous things. Ps. xcviii. 1.

My soul doth magnify the Lord, and my spirit hath rejoiced in God
my Saviour. Luke i. 46, 47.

## MARY'S SONG.

My soul the Lord doth magnify,
It hath rejoiced in God Most High,
    My Saviour dear.
He hath looked on my low estate,
And crowned with honor true and great
    His handmaid here.

Henceforth shall generations call
Me blessèd through the ages all—
    A sacred fame—
Because the glorious Mighty One
Great things for me hath surely done:
    Holy his name!

On those that fear him everywhere,
Mercy and grace will he declare,
    Through time's long flight.
The proud in heart have feared his frown,
And princes been from thrones cast down
    By his great might.

He lifts the humble ev'n o'er kings,
The hungry feeds with choicest things,
    Sends rich away;
Remembers all his words of old,
And helps the faithful of his fold,
    From Abrah'm's day.

1889

[SEPT. 1.]    Say ye to the daughter of Zion, **Behold**, thy salvation cometh. Isa. lxii. 11.

The angel said unto them..Behold, I bring you good tidings of great joy which shall be to all the people.   Luke ii. 10.

## EARTH'S FAIREST MORN.

ALL hail the day the tidings bringing,
       Earth's fairest morn!
O'er Bethlehem's plains an angel singing,
What glorious words to mortals ringing,
       The Christ is born!
       The Christ is born!

Shepherds, surprised, behold descending,
       From heaven's abode,
A flaming host, their voices blending
In praiseful chorus never ending,
       Glory to God!
       Glory to God!

Ere to celestial heights returning,
       Hear their refrain;
For human hearts what tender yearning,
What love divine for wanderers burning,
       Good will to men!
       Good will to men!

O friend! to-day a joyful greeting
       Let this song be:
In love my heart to thine is beating,
Of all good gifts, its wish repeating,
       The best for thee!
       The best for thee!

1889

[SEPT. 2.] The voice of one that crieth, Prepare ye in the wilderness the way of the Lord. ISA. xl. 3.

He was the lamp that burneth and shineth. JOHN v. 35.

## JOHN THE BAPTIST.

STAR forecasting brighter ray,
Dawn before the Sun-lit day,
 On the ages breaking.
List the longed-for voice sublime,
Hail the fullness of the time,
 Bloom in deserts making!

Messenger by seers foretold,
Prophet of Elijah's mold,
 Herald of the Valley,
Blazing like celestial flame,
Pointing to the mightier **Name**
 Crowds that round him **rally.**

Ruler, Scribe and Pharisee,
Soldier ranks from Galilee,
 Cities throngs deliver,
Hills of Judah lonely left,
Bashan slopes of hosts bereft,—
 All at Jordan's River.

Ye, repent! the Kingdom's near!
Joy! the Christ will soon appear!
 Make a way before him;
Penitents his grace shall share,
Fruits of righteousnes prepare,
 Loyal hearts adore him.

Lo, He comes! and Jordan's stream
Wears a wondrous sacred gleam—
   Spirit soft descending,
Dove-like, on th' obedient Lord,
And the Father's loving word
   His dear Son commending.

Truth he preached with lightning power;
Rage and vengeance had their hour—
   Martyrdom in prison.
Glorious work, most bravely done;
Fades the star, for now the Sun
   On the world is risen!     1887

---

[SEPT. 3.] The Lord thy God will raise up unto thee a Prophet from
the midst of thee, of thy brethren. DEUT. xviii. 15.
The Word became flesh, and dwelt among us. JOHN 1. 14.

## THE WORD INCARNATE.

WITH God in the deep past,
And God, the First, the Last,
   Who all things made:
Oh, mystery of love!
He left the throne above,
Among lost men to move,
   In flesh arrayed.

He came, the world's true Light,
To pierce its rayless night,
   Bring hope and day;
The Life of men to be,
The Lamb of Calvary,—
Behold, O world! how he
   Takes sin away.

Not by his own received,
But all who him believed,
　　The boon were given,
Of sons through Spirit-birth,
The ransomed of the earth,
Souls of immortal worth,
　　And heirs of Heaven.

O thou incarnate One!
Of God and man the Son,
　　Blest Saviour, mine!
In thee all glories meet,
All truth and grace complete,
All love and mercy sweet,—
　　My Lord divine!　　　　1886

[SEPT. 4.]　Thou art fairer than the children of men: grace is poured into thy lips. Ps. xlv. 2.
Behold, the Lamb of God! And .. they followed Jesus. JOHN i. 36,37.

## SEEN AND FOLLOWED.

FULL of a strange unrest,
　　I sought relief in vain;
The world had lost its zest,
　　And pleasure seemed but pain.
　　　　Ah, who would bring release?
　　　　Give heart and conscience peace?

Hast thou not seen the Christ,
　　While others find him near?
A look for them sufficed,
　　Why linger sadly here?
　　　　Come and behold his face,
　　　　It beams with matchless grace.

They brought me to the Lamb;
  Oh, blesséd eyes were mine!
I breathed his saving name,
  And felt his love divine;
    His look was wondrous fair,
    Such kingly meekness there.

His gracious voice I heard,
  In accents sweet and clear;
His kind assuring word
  Dispelled my gloomy fear:
    Thy need I know and see,
    O burdened soul, trust Me!

My heavenly Master thou,
  My all on earth to be;
Accept my sacred vow,
  I can but follow thee:
    Whate'er I have and am
    Are thine, O lovely Lamb!    1886

---

[SEPT. 5.]   The Lord shall count, when he writeth up the peoples,
  This one was born there. Ps. lxxxvii. 6.
  Verily, verily, I say unto thee, Except a man be born anew, he
cannot see the kingdom of God. JOHN iii. 3.

### THE NIGHT INTERVIEW.

DENSE shadows o'er him crept,
  As Nicodemus made his way alone,
While through his soul in searching undertone
  A deep impression swept.

This Man from heaven must be,
A Teacher sent us from the Throne on high ;
His miracles all human work defy,—
    In him God's power I see.

This to the Christ he said,
And heard in wonderment the answer given,
As if a thunder-stroke from the clear heaven
    Had broken o'er his head.

Truly I say to thee,
Unless a man be born again—anew,
God's kingdom surely he can never view,
    Its glory never see.

How can it be?　Behold,
The Spirit, like the searching wind o'er earth,
Gives to receptive souls the heavenly birth,
    And brings them to the fold.

The teacher thou of men!
To thee I bring the truth so long forgot,
The very gate of life—oh, marvel not,
    Ye must be born again!

The words of that still hour,
.Full, for the world, of God's unmeasured love,
Came as a new evangel from above,
    And wrought with saving power.

And solemnly as then,
These words of Christ ring down the ages still,
Men's inmost souls to touch, arouse, and thrill,
    Ye must be born again!

                    1886

[SEPT. 6.]   I that speak in righteousness, mighty to save. IsA. lxiii. 1.
Jesus saith unto her, I that speak unto thee am he.  JOHN iv. 26.

### THE VOICE OF JESUS.

BURDENED spirit! in thy sorrow
    Bowed beneath a sense of sin,
Longing for some glad to-morrow
    That shall bring thee peace within,—
Jesus cometh! thou art near him,
    Bringing pardon full and free,
Blest Messiah! lost one, hear him:
    "I that speak to thee am he."

Fearest thou, O weak believer!
    That thy faith or courage fail?
That the wiles of man's deceiver
    Will against thy life prevail?
Nay! thy Lord o'ercomes the schemer,
    He will strength and refuge be;
Mighty is thy soul's Redeemer—
    "I that speak to thee am he."

When life's trials are abounding,
    Loss and trouble press thee sore,
Hope and confidence confounding,
    Even prayer seems heard no more;
Still he's near, and not to grieve thee,
    Every pledge fulfilled shall be;
Christ who saved will never leave thee,
    "I that speak to thee am he."

Through the shadows o'er thee falling,
    Light and beauty from above

Drive away all gloom appalling,
  Bring the radiant beams of love;
Faith grows strong and burdens lighten,
  Blessèd guidance thou shalt see,
Jesus' voice thy hope shall brighten,
  "I that speak to thee am he."

Passing years serenely gliding,
  Heavenly light is on thy way,
Comfort knowing, peace abiding,
  Dawns at last Eternal Day.
Jesus kept and led and proved thee,
  Now his grace triumphant see;
Having loved he always loved thee,—
  "I that speak to thee am he."         1886

---

[SEPT. 7.]  O Lord, my strength, and my strong hold, and my refuge in the day of affliction.  JER. xvi. 19.

Jesus saith unto him, Go thy way, thy son liveth.  JOHN iv. 50

## THE NOBLEMAN'S SON.

WEALTH could not now its wish fulfill,
Nor patient use of highest skill,
  Nor tender love and care:
The fever, with augmented power,
And tightened grasp each passing hour,
  Changed hope to sad despair.

The pallid face, the shortened breath,
Foretold the near approach of death!
  Ah, who the lad can save?

The father thought of Jesus then—
Who had to Cana come again—
   And would his mercy crave.

At early morn he hastes away,
With anxious heart through all the day,
   And found at eve the Lord.
"Oh, come, my dying son to heal,
In his behalf thy power reveal,"
   Was his beseeching word.

His poor weak faith not yet divined
The glorious work his Lord designed,
   And so "Come down," he plead.
He did not deem that then and there
The Master's word the child could spare,
   Or raise him up if dead!

But Christ to faith its victory gives;
"Go homeward thou, thy dear one lives!"
   He trusts the promise sure.
From death's dark door the helpless son,
At once to health and vigor won,
   Confirmed the perfect cure!

O Great Physician! how thy power
Avails at any point or hour,
   And heeds nor time nor space!
Oh, happy home! where all believe,
And health and life and heaven receive
   Through Christ's recovering grace.      1886

[SEPT. 8.] My mouth shall speak the praise of the Lord. Ps. cxlv. 21.
Many of the Samaritans believed on him because of the word of the
woman who testified, He told me all things that ever I did. JOHN iv. 39.

## EFFECTIVE TESTIMONY.

SHE saw and drank the living water,
    And went at once to tell
The glorious truths the Saviour taught her,
And how from sin to faith he brought her,
    While talking at the Well.

She hastes with joyous feet and willing,
    The city streets around,
And tells the story new and thrilling,
All ears and hearts with wonder filling,
    Of Christ whom she had found.

Some souls believed, for pardon yearning,
    And others sought and heard
The Man their inmost hearts discerning;
And, truth and life from Jesus learning,
    Received the gracious word.

'Tis sweet for those the Saviour knowing,
    To speak his blesséd name,
To waiting fields with gladness going,
Seed of the kingdom broadcast sowing,
    And erelong reap the same.

Oh, whitening harvest! matchless wages!
    Treasures without alloy:
All whom this grateful work engages,
Win souls to Christ for endless ages,
    Eternal life and joy!

1886

[SEPT. 9.] In that day there shall be a fountain opened to the house of David and to the inhabitants of Jerusalem, for sin and for uncleanness. ZECH. xiii. 1.

I have no man, when the water is troubled, to put me into the pool. JOHN v. 7.

## THE CRIPPLE AT BETHESDA.

O POOL of Bethesda! thy marvelous power
    Invited the suffering throngs to thy side,
To wait in thy porches the favoring hour
    That promised a cure in the health-laden tide.

Ah! helpless and sad, who for thirty-eight years
    Was bowed under poverty, sorrow, and pain,
Now friendless, forlorn, left alone in his tears,
    While earth rolled along in its pleasure and gain.

Dim hope in his soul but just flickered, ne'er flamed,
    A gleam in the night on a dark frowning sky,
If he to that Pool of Bethesda, far-famed,
    Might only be carried, if there he should die!

The boon was bestowed—on the margin of life,
    He saw the infirm to the troubled fount led;
But no friendly hand, in the rush and the strife,
    Led him to the bath from his suffering bed.

"Wilt thou be made whole?" As if music from heaven
    The voice, with the look, went direct to his heart:
Ah, the pitiful tale! Then the mandate was given:
    "Rise up from thy pallet and with it depart!"

O Saviour all-powerful! and Healer benign,
    How blest are thy visits of mercy and might!
Thy words of sweet comfort are agents divine
    To waken true faith, and put hindrance to flight.

No longer, Bethesda, thy healing springs flow—
  The Pool is not there, the five porches are gone;
But thou art the same, Blessèd Jesus, we know,
  Thy wells of salvation still freely flow on!    1886

[SEPT. 10.]  It is the bread which the Lord hath given you to eat.—
Ex. xvi. 15.
I am the living bread which came down out of heaven.  JOHN vi. 51.

## THE BREAD OF LIFE.

FATHER! thy love in Christ we see
    To sinful mortals given;
He came in love our life to be—
    The Bread of God from heaven.

In him we find what rich supply!
    We feast, and never more
Shall thirst or hunger lift their cry;
    Our souls have boundless store.

And faith brings near, in vision sweet,
    The banquet-house above,
Where saints of all the ages meet,
    And feast on Jesus' love.

O famished one! Christ calls for thee,
    Homeless and tossed about;
Hear what he saith: "Who comes to me
    I will not cast him out."

With such assurance, who can wait
    In unbelief and sin?
The Bread of Heaven is at the gate,
    Oh, haste to enter in!    1886

[SEPT. 11.]　He bringeth them unto the haven where they would be.
Ps. cvii. 30.

They were willing therefore to receive him into the boat : and
straightway the boat was at the land whither they were going. JOHN
vi. 21.

## ON THE SEA—AT THE LAND.

DARK the night on Galilee,
Wild the wind and rough the sea;
While the chosen ply the oar,
Vainly striving for the shore,
　　Jesus nears them on the wave,
　　Sees their peril, comes to save.

Full of dread, he calms their fear,
Words of hope they gladly hear;
Joyous welcome him they give,
To the boat their Lord receive;
　　Then at once, oh, work so grand,
　　Boat and they were at the land!

Voyagers o'er life's sea we sail,
In the breeze, or in the gale;
Christ beholds us, comes anear,
Speaks sweet words of love and cheer.
　　Him received, our present aid,
　　Storm or calm, we're not afraid.

Souls in unbelief we see,
Drifting to eternity!
Find they neither hope nor peace,
Naught to give their fears release.
　　Know, ye wndering ones unblest,
　　Christ received brings instant rest!

Who the Saviour sought and found,
Resting on faith's solid ground,
Why have ye forsaken him,
Till your love and hope are dim?
    Lo, he comes to break your night;
    Christ received, at once 'tis light!

God's longsuffering grace abused,
Time and talents all misused;
Roused, your sin and guilt to see,
Where can you for refuge flee?
    Sinking souls, there's help at hand,
    Christ received, you're safe at land!

When our fleeting voyage shall end,
Sea and shore at last shall blend,
Jesus sure will meet us there,
To their home our spirits bear.
    Oh, how blest with him to be
    In the land beyond the sea! .    1886

---

[SEPT. 12.] I the Lord speak righteousness, I declare things that
are right. ISA. xlv. 19.

The words that I have spoken unto you are spirit, and are life.—
JOHN vi. 63.

## THE WORDS OF JESUS.

SINCE stars their chorus sang,
    And morning first awoke,
In mortal ears ne'er rang
    Such words as Jesus spoke:
Fresh truths they brought, pure light they shed,
Great marvels wrought, ev'n raised the dead.

None ever spake as he—
　　To troubled souls what peace!
Pardon so full and free;
　　Bade tears and sorrows cease.
The penitent beheld his face,
And homeward went, renewed by grace.

Bereaved and burdened hearts
　　Hang on his soothing voice;
Sweet comfort he imparts,
　　And they in hope rejoice.
Their load he bears of pain and woe;
He takes their cares, his love they know.

Should darkness intervene,
　　His loving face to hide,
Through mists his form is seen—
　　They hear their blesséd Guide:
I am the Life, the Truth, the Way;—
They cease from strife, they walk in day.

He brings the distant near,
　　He speaks of rest above;
The City shines how clear,—
　　The mansions of his love:
Ye who believe, again I come
You to receive to that blest home.　　1886

---

[SEPT. 13.]　I cleave unto thy testimonies. PSA. cxix. 31.
Know the truth, and the truth shall make you free. JOHN viii. 32.

### MADE TRULY FREE.

JESUS! I would abide
　　In thy sure word,

Close clinging to thy side,
    Thou gracious Lord.
'Tis my sincerest plea—
Always thine own to be,
My heart and life with thee
    In full accord.

So shall I keep the way
    Thou dost approve;
Thy smile cheer every day,
    Bright with thy love.
Thy truth my nature woke,
My fear and thralldom broke,
Brought me, beneath thy yoke,
    Rest from above.

Oh, glorious Son of God!
    The world's one need;
'Tis thy redeeming blood
    Makes free indeed!
Sin's servant wears its chain,
In bondage must remain,
And every hope be vain
    Till he is freed.

Made by the Saviour free—
    Oh, blessèd state!
Then death we never see,
    Nor feel its weight:
'Tis victory over sin,
'Tis God's own peace within,
'Tis Christ himself to win,
    And Heaven's estate!

1886

[SEPT. 14.]  Her sun is gone down while it was yet day.  JER. xv. 9.

The Master is here, and calleth thee.  And she, when she heard it, arose quickly, and went unto him.  JOHN xi. 28, 29.

## A BEAUTIFUL LIFE.

BRIEF seem the years, abrupt the call,
That end a life, but not its all:
These short decades, so quickly gone,
An earthly close, a heavenly dawn,
And yet how much in these few years
To round a human life appears;
For not in length of days we live,
Nor what this passing world can give.

From childhood, bright and sweet and good,
To fair and lovely womanhood,
Earnest and true, the years all tell
Of living right, maturing well.
Early her trusting heart was given
To Christ, the way to life and heaven.
Full of good deeds and graces sweet,
So short a life, yet how complete!

How much she was comes oft to mind
By what a void is left behind!
How large a place on earth was filled
By this dear life so strangely stilled;
Ask parents, all who held her dear,
How much she's missed, so lately here:
Can sorrow, tears, or mourning show
How great the loss their spirits know?

A life so full and precious here,
Transferred to a celestial sphere,
How fitted for its crown above,
Its range of joy, or work of love.
The dear Lord gave, he claimed his own,
The time, the way were wisely known;
How rich the treasure waiting there,
Till friends the blest reünion share!     1888

---

[SEPT. 15.]  Instead of thy fathers shall be thy children. I's. xlv. 16.

God having provided some better thing concerning us, that apart from us they should not be made perfect. HEB. xi. 40.

## MEMORIAL HYMN.

SWEET, holy memories throng to-day
    The place where we rejoicing stand,
Where scenes of beauty stretch away
    O'er hill and vale on every hand.

Not such in olden time the view,
    When first God's servants gathered here,
The field and forest to subdue,
    The home and church and school to rear.

Blest was their early, earnest toil;
    Blest is the memory of the just;
Let sculptured columns crown the soil
    Where sleeps serene their honored dust.

Virtue and faith survive the dead,
    Their fruits to wide results expand;
Sons of the sires have risen and spread
    Their leavening power thro' all the land.

Hither to-day these children come,
　To greet the scenes of other years;
To taste again the joys of home—
　At loved ones' graves to drop their tears.

O God! from thee our treasures flow,
　From thee the present and the past;
A parting blessing now bestow,
　And may we meet in Heaven at last.　　1858

---

[SEPT. 16.]　Her children rise up and call her blessed; her husband also, and he praiseth her.　PROV. xxxi. 28.

The brother whose praise in the gospel is spread through all the churches.　2 COR. viii. 18.

## A POET'S GOLDEN WEDDING.

THESE fifty years of wedded love,
Replete with blessings from above,
Through brightening eras by the way,
Crown here with joy the Golden Day.

No home can sweeter be than this,
Center of pure domestic bliss,
Where gifts and grace divine abound,
And shed their fragrance earth around.

By joyous voices, old and young,
A Christian lyric oft is sung
O'er our domain from sea to sea,
And sure, "My country, 'tis of thee."

In mission lands this home has power,
And gives its largess every hour;
The sad night wanes, the dawn is fair,
"The morning light is breaking" there.　　1884

[SEPT. 17.] I will bring the blind by a way that they know not.—
Isa. xlii. 16.

One thing I know, that, whereas I was blind, now I see. John ix.
25.

## BORN BLIND.

By the waysides daily sitting,
    Asking alms without the gates,
Footsteps of the passers, flitting,
    Hears he, but in darkness waits.

Blind from birth—no face, love-beaming,
    Ever met an answering gaze;
Earth and sky, with beauty teeming,
    Hid from all his doleful days.

Jesus, passing where he lingers,
    Moved with pity for his woe,
Touched his eyes with clay-moist fingers,
    Bade him to Siloam go.

Kind the voice, and faith-inspiring,
    To a quick obedience led.
Oh, the change! he comes admiring
    Worlds of glory round him spread!

Blesséd Saviour! still thou'rt healing
    Souls that will thy word believe;
Wonders of thy grace revealing,
    They a heavenly sight receive.

Vast the numbers, e'er increasing,
    Who have found true light in thee;
Sweet their song, and never ceasing—
    "I was blind, but now I see."

1886

[SEPT. 18.] They all shall have one shepherd. EZEK. xxxvii. 24.
He goeth before them, and the sheep follow him. JOHN x. 4.

## SHEPHERD AND FLOCK.

O Christ of God! thou art the Door,
    And those who enter in
Find pastures sweet for evermore,
    Free from the blight of sin :
Their borders touch the Elysian shore,
    Where Glory's realms begin.

Lord, thou the blessèd Shepherd art
    Of all the flock, well known ;
Their names are written on thy heart—
    Thou dost so love thine own ;
No power their souls from thee can part,
    They share thy royal throne.

For these, thy dear and folded sheep,
    Thou didst thy life-blood give :
No wolf can e'er the wall o'erleap,
    Or enter where they live ;
Almighty hands in safety keep
    Those who thy grace receive.

Dear Shepherd! thou dost go before
    The flock of thine own choice,
Their Leader till the journey's o'er,
    They hear and heed thy voice ;
The wandering ones thou dost restore,
    The faithful e'er rejoice.

And countless other sheep are thine,
    The Father's love has given ;

Hast thou not said, They shall be mine,
　　Though far and lone and riven?
Oh, bring them to the fold divine,
　　The flock select for Heaven.

Ah! when that solemn scene at last,
　　The testing day, has come,
As on thy right the sheep stand fast—
　　The faithless find their doom—
Lord, grant my lot with thine be cast,
　　Thy flock safe gathered home.　　1886

---

[SEPT. 10.] I shall not die, but live, and declare the works of the
Lord. Ps. cxviii. 17.
Fallen asleep; but I go, that I may awake him. JOHN xi. 11.

## LAZARUS DEAD.

LAZARUS sick and lying
Helpless on his couch of pain;
Yet the Master doth remain,
Comes not at the sad refrain—
　　Whom thou lov'st is dying!

Ah, the days so weary!
For in death the brother sleeps;
Sister now with sister weeps,
Silent tomb their treasure keeps;
　　All the world is dreary!

Jesus knows their sorrow,
All their deep and lonely grief,
Was not to their message deaf,
Might have given a quick relief,
　　Waits for a to-morrow.

He will show his glory,
Wake to life his slumbering friend;
Tears and mourning soon shall end;
Down the ages shall extend
    Hope from this sweet story.

Is our Lord withholding
Good for which we, restless, long?
He would make our faith grow strong;
By delay our joy and song
    Grand in their unfolding!

Restful is their sleeping
Who in Christ their Lord have died,
Now their souls with him abide,
And, till earth's great eventide,
    He their dust is keeping!            1886

---

[SEPT. 20.]   I will ransom them from the power of the grave.  HOS.
xiii. 14.
I am the resurrection and the life.  JOHN xi. 25.

## LAZARUS RAISED TO LIFE.

THEY heard of Jesus' coming,
    And hastened to his side:
Hadst thou been here, O Master!
    Our brother had not died.
With tenderness and pity,
    He shared the sisters' pain,
And said, their hearts to comfort,
    Your brother 'll rise again.

We know, O blesséd Jesus!
    What thou shalt ask from heaven,

Of God the mighty Father,
    It shall to thee be given.
We know our buried brother,
    When time's last hour is fled,
Shall, in the resurrection,
    Arise with all the dead.

I am the Resurrection,
    And Life is mine to give;
He who in me believeth,
    Ev'n though he die, shall live;
And whosoever liveth—
    For Life itself am I—
And truly me believeth,
    Shall never, never die!

Around the tomb they gathered,
    Where the belovéd slept,
A tearful throng of mourners,
    And with them Jesus wept.
He called—the dead forthcoming,
    The living man they see!
So Life and Resurrection
    The Lord is known to be!

Thou hast the power, O Jesus!
    Our precious dead to raise;
Thou mightest now restore them,
    Were it for God's high praise.
But they in thee are sleeping,
    Their spirits with the just,
And, at thy glorious coming,
    These graves shall yield their trust. 1886

[SEPT. 21.] I am the woman that stood by thee here. 1 SAM. i. 26.
The house was filled with the odor of the ointment. JOHN xii. 3.

## LOVE'S COMMENDATION.

THE festal scene would soon be past;
The awful cloud was gathering fast,
    To break on Jesus' head;
For waving palm, hosanna cry,
Would louder sound the "Crucify,"
    As foes, malignant, led.

So Mary brings the costly nard,
Pours it upon her blessèd Lord,
    And bowing at his feet,
She wipes them with her flowing hair,
While through the room the odors rare
    Love's precious gift repeat.

She looked beyond the passing hour,
To hate of men, satanic power,
    The cross and all its gloom,
The Lamb of God for sinners slain,
The burial sad, the weeping train,
    The unction for the tomb.

Her work, approved, as Jesus said,
Hath gone where gospel truth has spread,
    And still it tells her love;
Angels have caught the fragrant song,
And saints memorial notes prolong
    Through earth and realms above.

O Saviour! thou wilt surely see
Whate'er is done in love for thee

Shall never fail its end;
The sweet aroma shall not die,
But fill the earth and reach the sky,
And thy blest reign extend.     1886

[SEPT. 22.]  Every one that is bitten, when he seeth it, shall live.—
NUM. xxi. 8.
How sayest thou, The Son of man must be lifted up? JOHN xii. 34.

## THE UPLIFTED CHRIST.

UPLIFTED Son of man!
Thy word that ne'er is broken
Unfolds the heavenly plan,
That from the cross is spoken—
The matchless mystery of grace
To save a lost and guilty race!

O loving Son of God!
So gentle, true and tender;
To shield us from the rod,
Must thou such offering render?
Upon the painful cross expire,
By ingrate man's most strange desire?

Ah! think, my soul, of this:
Thy life that now is given,
The hope of future bliss,
With all the wealth of heaven,
To thee, most undeserving, flow
Through Jesus' death of shame and woe!

The love the cross reveals
Has drawn me to him dying;
That love my pardon seals,

To this dear refuge flying:
O Jesus! for this love divine,
My heart, my life, my all are thine!

The cross, of meaning vast,
Unparalleled oblation!
Oh, may it draw at last
The world to thy salvation!
All ransomed souls to endless days
Shall sing their blest Redeemer's praise.    1886

[SEPT. 23.]  I drew them .. with bands of love. Hos. xi. 4.
Having loved his own which were in the world, he loved them unto
the end.  JOHN xiii. 1.

## LOVED TO THE END.

O SAVIOUR! as the moment neared,
    When thou must leave on earth thine own,
    And by the cross regain thy throne,
Thy tenderest love to them appeared.

'T was love at first that called them thine,
    Won from the world their hearts to thee,
    Made them responsive, strong, and free,
Believers in their Lord divine.

Thy changeless love upon them wrought,
    To mould their souls for service true,
    Their tasks to know, their spheres to view,
From truths thou hadst in patience taught.

Thy love ne'er lost its radiant flame,
    In their expanding hearts it rose;
    In brightening hopes or darkening woes
It was a tower of strength the same.

Unto the end in thee they found
　What heights of joy, what depths of peace,
　Of soul communion what increase,
For love and trust what solid ground.

Gracious the act with love replete,
　That lowly work of thy dear hand,
　As thou didst with thy chosen stand,
And kindly wash their weary feet.

Oh, precious lesson then—to-day!
　May we its purpose know and prove,
　Live in the sweetness of thy love,
And let it all our being sway!　　　　1886

---

[SEPT. 24.]　Come ye, and let us go up to the mountain of the Lord.
ISA. ii. 3.
　They heard a great voice from heaven saying unto them, Come up
hither.　REV. xi. 12.

## VOICES FROM HEAVEN.

Lo, FROM heaven a voice is falling,
　Wandering souls, attentive be;
'Tis your loving Father calling,
　"Hither come!—return to me."

Louder yet the voice is sounding,
　Jesus speaks, how clear and true,
By his cross and grace abounding,
　"Hither come! there's room for you."

In your heart the voice is pleading,
　Through the Spirit, tender, sweet,
"Hither come!" And, upward leading,
　Friends in heaven the call repeat.　　　1890

[SEPT. 25.]  With lovingkindness have I drawn thee.  JER. xxxi. 3.
Let not your heart be troubled, neither let it be fearful.  JOHN xiv. 27.

## JESUS TO HIS DISCIPLES.

FROM troubled hearts be free,
  In God believe;
Have confidence in me—
  My word receive.

Up in my Father's home
  Mansions abound;
For all his children room
  Will there be found.

Were this not clearly so,
  A truth divine,
I should have let you know,
  O friends of mine!

Mourn not I go, for there
  I have in view,
And will myself prepare,
  A place for you.

Surely again I come,
  As you shall see,
And bring you to that home
  In Heaven with me.

For where I am above
  Shall be my own,
For ever crowned with love,
  And near my throne.

Though for a while we part,
  My peace I leave;

Be troubled not in heart—
My peace receive.

1886

[SEPT. 26.]   The vineyard of the Lord of hosts is the house of Israel.
ISA. v. 7.
I am the vine, ye are the branches. JOHN xv. 5.

## VINE AND BRANCHES.

CHRIST is the true and living Vine,
  Of all the trees the crown;
In him what radiant beauties shine—
  The Plant of great renown.

This matchless Vine, how strong and fair,
  Rooted in earthly ground,
And rising through celestial air,
  Its head in Heaven is found.

Immortal branches, numberless,
  Spring from the parent stem,
And clinging there in loveliness,
  Each sparkles as a gem.

The Vine, thus vital evermore,
  Each pendent branch supplies,
Gives life and vigor, boundless store,
  From fountains in the skies.

The branches live in union sweet,
  In oneness, with the Vine;
There blending grace and glory meet—
  The human and divine.

Naught can we do, O Saviour dear,
  Nothing from thee apart;

A withered branch would each appear,
  With neither life nor heart.

But clusters rich the branches show
  That in the Vine abide:
Abundant fruit they bear, and so
  The Father's glorified.

And as the Vine to Heaven is gone,
  And lives eternal there,
The branches must with it be one—
  Its royal glory share.                1886

---

[SEPT. 27.] Come in, thou blessed of the Lord; wherefore standest thou without? GEN. xxiv. 31.

First they gave their own selves to the Lord, and to us by the will of God. 2 COR. viii. 5.

### WELCOME TO THE CHURCH.

Won from the world by Jesus' love,
  To him yourselves are given;
Your hearts are placed on things above,
  Your faces set toward Heaven.

Now to the fold, the church redeemed,
  A welcome glad we give;
In mutual love is each esteemed,
  For to the Lord we live.

This bond and service all unite,
  If pain or pleasure come,
Each in his sphere a shining light,
  Till Christ shall call us home.        1890

[SEPT. 28.] In those days will I pour out my spirit. JOEL ii. 29.

When he, the Spirit of truth, is come, he shall guide you into all the truth. JOHN xvi. 13.

## THE SPIRIT'S MISSION.

O COMFORTER! in Jesus' name,
    Sent to his own to take his place,
Thou didst in Pentecostal flame
    Come as a messenger of grace,
    The love and light of his dear face.

Thou didst in wondrous power descend,
    And on the chosen ones abide;
Thou still art here till time shall end,
    Of all the saved the perfect Guide,
    To aid and comfort all the tried.

The glorious truths the Saviour taught,
    By thee are more and more revealed;
Sweet hidden things to light are brought,
    And they who trust and fully yield
    Know their Redeemer's work is sealed.

Spirit of truth, God's work revive!
    Show to the Church thy latent power;
Make all the ransomed hosts alive,
    Their hearts receptive to thy dower,
    In this most needful passing hour!

O mighty Spirit! now convict
    The unbelieving world of sin;
To them their fearful guilt depict,
    The judgment that their souls are in,
    And how salvation they may win!     1886

[SEPT. 29.] He bare the sin of many, and made intercession for the transgressors. ISA. liii. 12.

Holy Father, keep them in thy name which thou hast given me.— JOHN xvii. 11.

## OUR LORD'S PRAYER.

JESUS! Son of God, in prayer
With the souls so long thy care,
Soon to feel and mourn thy loss,
See thee die upon the cross,
Oh, how sweet, in time of need,
Thou for them to intercede!

Precious are those words of thine,
Round their hearts they strongly twine;
Bring them comfort, hope, and peace,
Bid their sad foreboding cease:
Oh, thy benedictions blest
Give their troubled spirits rest!

Thou didst pray: O Father, keep
These my true and loving sheep:
I have kept them in thy name;
Keep thou them from ill and blame;
In the world e'er let them be
Lights to draw that world to me.

Sanctify them through thy word,
Make them like their loving Lord,
All in heart as one to be,
One in us as one are we,
That the world may know thy love
Sent the Saviour from above.

Father, grant that all my own,
Where I am, be near my throne,
That my glory, given of old,
They may evermore behold:
Righteous Father, this shall prove
Depths of thy eternal love!

1886

---

[SEPT. 30.]  I planted me vineyards; I made me gardens. ECCL. ii. 5.
The husbandman waiteth for the precious fruit of the earth. JAS. v. 7.

## FESTIVAL OF POMONA AND FLORA.

FRUITS and flowers, in beauty blending,
　　Bright arrayed by fingers fair,
Fling their fragrance, sweet ascending,
　　On the autumn evening air:
Lovely vision—scene elysian—
　　Golden harvest rare!
Goddess, from whose fields o'erflowing,
　　Tempting treasures freely fall,
Priestess of the garden, glowing
　　With thy leafy coronal,
Greetings glad we give, Pomona, Flora,
　　Gathered at your Festival.

Art and Nature celebrating—
　　Human skill and gifts divine;
God the field and flower creating,
　　Man to make their glories shine:
Thus 't is given, Earth and Heaven
　　Sweet to intertwine.

'T was in nature's earliest garden,
　　That the sacred tie began,
When the great and gracious Warden
　　Gave the purest gift to man—
Loveliest form and bloom, Pomona, Flora,
　　Angel vision there could scan.

Age and Wisdom, Youth and Beauty,
　　Honored heads, and skillful hands,
From the varied walks of duty,
　　Linked by social, sacred bands,
Free from sadness, meet with gladness,
　　At our Hosts' commands—
Pleased to every heart's desiring,
　　With the wealth that here is stored;
All these luscious gems admiring,
　　Bending branch and vine afford;
And our welcome sing, Pomona, Flora,
　　To the dainties of the board.

Oft, amid such charming treasures,
　　Gathered in a joyous throng,
Be renewed this evening's pleasures,
　　Sung again the festal song;
Gladness lightening, Beauty brightening
　　All the years along;
Till, our wintry season closing,
　　Heavenly spring for us shall rise
On the Edens, sweet reposing
　　'Neath the ever-beaming skies,
Bearing trees of life, Pomona; Flora,
　　Fadeless blooms of Paradise.　　1853

[Oct. 1.] They weighed for my hire thirty pieces of silver. ZEC. xi. 12.
Woe unto that man through whom the Son of man is betrayed! good
were it for that man if he had not been born. MARK xiv. 21.

## JESUS BETRAYED.

MID the Garden shades delaying,
Christ in agony was praying,
Where the plot of foes infernal
Baffled was by Love Eternal.

Cometh he, so long receiving
Care divine with the believing,
Agent of each priestly hater?—
Ay, 'tis Judas, heartless traitor!

Basest, meanest, hireling creature,
Sordid guilt in every feature;
Treacherous friend the Victim kissing,
Rather lips with serpent's hissing!

As the unresisting Saviour
Stands in Godlike, meek behavior,
Angel legions hovering o'er him,
Foes, astounded, fall before him.

O Iscariot! midnight torches
Faintly show how conscience scorches:
Foul betrayer! what thy wages?—
Infamy through all the ages!

Saddest night of earth e'er written,
Lo! the Shepherd now is smitten,
And the little flock forsake him,
As the band with weapons take him.

Blesséd Jesus! this enduring
For my periled soul's securing,
Master, let me not, I pray thee,
E'er in act or word betray thee!    1886

———————◆———————

[Oct. 2.]  The assembly of evil-doers have enclosed me. Ps. xxii. 16.
Pilate therefore said unto him, art thou a king then? John xviii. 37.

## CHRIST BEFORE PILATE.

Morn breaks at last o'er Olivet,
    The weary stars withdraw,
The sun sends forth with sad regret
Such mournful day as never yet
    Our burdened planet saw.

The farce before the Sanhedrin
    Ends with the night's deep pall;
High priest and all his hateful kin,
Their hellish aim at once to win,
    Lead Christ to Pilate's hall.

Alone, the Roman magistrate,
    With Jesus face to face,
Sees in his mien a kingly state,
A majesty unearthly great,
    Though his a culprit's place.

A King, but not of mortal cast,
    A scepter from above,
An empire, mighty, glorious, vast,
That shall all human thrones outlast—
    The reign of truth and love.

What is the truth? So Pilate said,
  As Jesus witness bears:
The Roman felt a solemn dread;
No crime in Him, he clearly read,
  Not ev'n a fault he wears.

Shall I release your King? Nay, nay!
  But let Barabbas go!
Alas! how many souls to-day
The robber choose, cast Christ away,
  And take their doom of woe!        1886

---

[OCT. 3.] The rulers take counsel together against the Lord. Ps. ii. 2.
He delivered him unto them to be crucified. JOHN xix. 16.

### PILATE'S DECISION.

I SEE the meek and lowly One,
  The patient Lord of truth and grace,
A kingdom not of earth his own,
  A sad, sweet glory in his face—
As now the cruel scourge is given,
Lash after lash so harshly driven,
That flesh and soul seem almost riven!

I see the plaited crown of thorns
  Placed, piercing, on his holy head;
The purple robe, with mocks and scorns,
  Around the silent Sufferer spread.
Arrayed, insulted, thus he stands,
While Hail, thou king! shout soldier bands,
And seal their taunts with smiting hands!

I see the Roman, pale with fears,
   Reluctant still to crucify,
So innocent the Man appears—
   No crimes or faults against him lie.
Priests cry the more—a very flood
Of clamorous calls demands his blood:
He made himself the Son of God!

I see that Pilate fears the more,
   And trembling starts with boding dread;
A warning fom a mystic shore
   Is couched in words that last were said.
It may be so: his heart thus stirred,
Say, whence art thou? he asks the Lord,
But Jesus now gives not a word.

I see the Judge, whose testing hour
   Brings to the coward naught of peace.
To crucify I have the power,
   And power have I to grant release.
Then Jesus' answers pierce his soul,
Bid thoughts unearthly through it roll,
Suggest high Heaven's supreme control.

I see the Roman yet again
   Contend with conscience, duty, right;
At last he yields, gives crafty men
   The spotless Christ, the world's true Light,
Delivers to the painful cross
The innocent without a cause;
Alas, his guilt, his shame, and loss!    1886

[Oct.4.] The cities that are inhabited shall be laid waste. Eze. xii. 20.
Jesus Christ is the same yesterday and to-day, yea and for ever.—
Heb. xiii. 8.

## THE SEA OF GALILEE.

Dear, beautiful sight! Embosomed by hills,
    How calmly reposes the Lake!
I gaze, and my soul with rapture thrills,
As the glorious scene my vision fills,
    And holiest memories wake.
       O lovely Sea of Galilee,
How oft my Redeemer hath looked on thee!

All other lakes, in all lands, are denied
    The honors that thou dost know;
Blossoms as radiant may fringe their side,
Fountains as sparkling may swell their tide,
    But thou hast the Jordan's inflow;
       More sacred yet, Gennesaret,
The sandals of Christ thy waves have wet!

How oft I have come, in wondering thought,
    A pilgrim along thy shore,
Beholding the crowds that Jesus taught,
And the deeds his power and mercy wrought,
    As he walked thy margin o'er.
       O hallowed Sea of Galilee,
The home of Messiah was once by thee!

And now, with thankfulest heart, I stand
    Where Jesus so often stood;
I see the same stream, and rock, and land;
The same sweet Tabor and Hermon grand;
    And look on the same bright flood—

Tiberian Sea, so dear to me,
Because my Saviour saw these and thee.

My feet have pressed the old paths he trod,
    And crossed o'er the same clear rills;
I have sat me down on the grassy sod,
Where rested the weary Son of God,
    Who bore our sorrows and ills.
      In thee I take, Gennesareth Lake,
Unbounded delight for his dear sake.

Nazareth's valley and hills are fair,
    And lovely is Bethlehem;
Mount Olivet's scenes their glories share,
In the Garden shade and Bethany there,
    With precious Jerusalem;
      But, dearest Sea of Galilee,
How the life of my Lord is linked with thee!

No crowds along thy thoroughfares pour;
    Lo, silence and ruin to-day!
White sails on thy waves are seen no more;
The cities that flourished upon thy shore
    Have passed in their guilt away;
      But thou art yet, Gennesaret,
A picture unchanged in thy hill-frame set.

And Christ is the same, tho' ascended on high,
    As when by this water he trod;
With the same tender heart, and pitying eye;
As mighty to save, as lovingly nigh—
    Oh, ever the same Lamb of God.
      Adieu, sweet Sea of Galilee!
Thy image remains, and thy Lord, with me. 1861

[OCT. 5.]   The chastisement of our peace was upon him; and with his stripes we are healed. ISA. liii. 5.

His own self bare our sins in his body upon the tree, that we, having died unto sins, might live unto righteousness. 1 PET. ii. 24.

## JESUS CRUCIFIED.

O JESUS! when I think of thee,
    The anguish of thy dying day
Nailed roughly to the cruel tree,
    My breaking heart to grief gives way.

What patient suffering, Lord, was thine
    Through all the long and direful scene;
Earth shuddered deep, nor sun could shine,
    Nor dead in tombs repose serene!

The world's dread weight of sin to bear,
    The woe of such a death besides,
Travail and pain that none could share,
    How dark were sorrow's whelming tides!

Thou didst not shrink, blest Son of God,
    But bear the burden to the close;
Alone the bloody wine-press trod,
    Triumphant thou o'er all our foes.

'Tis by the cross the sinner lives,
    Thy sacrifice for guilt atones,
Thy death the life eternal gives,
    Thy victory lifts to heavenly thrones.

Dear Saviour! I can ne'er forget
    That thou wast crucified for me;
How can I pay love's mighty debt?
    Oh, help me hence to live for thee.

1886

[OCT. 6.] God is unto us a God of deliverances : and unto Jehovah
the Lord belong the issues from death. Ps. lxviii. 20.

With great power gave the apostles their witness of the resurrection
of the Lord Jesus. ACTS iv. 33.

## THE RISEN SAVIOUR.

HEAVEN's messengers alighted
    At Joseph's new-made tomb;
The Roman guards, affrighted,
    Fled in the twilight gloom.
Softly the angel fingers
    The linen cloths unwind;
The Christ no longer lingers,
    He leaves the tomb behind!

The bands of death he sunders,
    The grave is vanquished now:
Most wonderful of wonders,
    Life's crown is on his brow!
His word, so often spoken,
    Is verified complete ;
The gates of hell are broken,
    They lie beneath his feet.

Astonished friends behold him,
    Their heart-grief disappears,
They would in love enfold him
    Who banishes their tears.
Their great rebound from sadness,
    Who can its thrill record?
What voice proclaim their gladness
    As now they see their Lord?

O Saviour! risen!—living!
　All power we know is thine;
Grace, strength, in richness giving,
　The weak shall not repine.
Our heaviest burdens bearing,
　The King will bring us through,
Till all his own are sharing
　The glory in their view.

The resurrection morning
　Will show thy might divine,
Our bodies readorning,
　Made beautiful like thine,
In full redemption's meetness
　For crowns of life above,
Where Heaven's sublime completeness
　Shall magnify thy love.　　　1886

---

[OCT. 7.] Thou wilt not leave my soul to Sheol; neither wilt thou
suffer thine holy one to see corruption. **Ps. xvi. 10.**

When therefore it was evening .. Jesus came and stood in the midst,
and saith unto them, Peace be unto you. **JOHN xx. 19.**

### THE UPPER ROOM.

THE resurrection morn is past,
　With scenes unknown to time before;
That day of marvels waned at last,
　But left a glory evermore.

With dawning hope, but more of gloom,
　As men bewildered and amazed,
Apostles sought the upper room,
　Where late upon their Lord they gazed.

Since that sweet eve of saddened tone,
   That feast with tender love so fraught,
What pressing woes their hearts had known,
   What tragic scenes the days had brought?

Oh, wondrous news! the rock-tomb prison
   No longer holds the form that died;
The Lord they loved had surely risen;
   He lives again—the Crucified!

Shut were the doors that safe enclosed
   This little band in mazeful mood,
When, full in view at once exposed,
   The Nazarene before them stood!

"Peace be with you!" How sweet the sound
   That every heart so strangely stirred:
It is the Lord! what joy profound,
   As him they saw, and knew, and heard!

He breathed upon their souls anew,
   The spirit of their Lord they caught,
And fuller inspiration drew
   From all the blessèd truth he taught.   1875

---

[OCT. 8.]  Our redeemer, the Lord of hosts is his name, the Holy One
of Israel.  ISA. xlvii. 4.

After these things Jesus manifested himself again to the disciples
at the sea of Tiberias.  JOHN xxi. 1.

### THE MEETING AND THE FEAST.

CALM the morn in Galilee,
Where their Lord disciples see;
O'er the waters floats his voice,
Bids their weary hearts rejoice.

So, upon the heavenly shore,
When life's anxious night is o'er,
We shall see our Saviour stand,
Hear his call to Glory-land.

Sweet the season after toil,
As they bring abundant spoil,
See the feast for them to share,
By the Lord made ready there.
So shall we from labor rest,
Be with Jesus doubly blest,
When he mingles what we bring
With the bounty of the King.

Who can tell the joy and cheer,
As the Master's word they hear,
"Come with me and here recline
At this feast of yours and mine."
But more glorious will it be
When the feast of heaven we see,
Where the saved all eat and live
At the banquet Christ shall give.

Blest the scene around the board;
As it closed, the gracious Lord
Brought from him who had denied,
Love sincere, thrice told and tried.
Oh, when round the board above,
Naught can mar our perfect love;
It will flow a clear full stream,
Christ its everlasting theme.          1886

[Oct. 9.] The Lord shall be unto thee an everlasting light. Isa. lx. 19.

If we walk in the light, as he is in the light, we have fellowship one with another, and the blood of Jesus his Son cleanseth us from all sin. 1 John i. 7.

## WALKING IN THE LIGHT.

Walk with the God of light,
 And joyful we
The heavenly pathway bright
 Shall always see:
With saints in brotherhood,
Shall Jesus' precious blood,
A sin-atoning flood,
 Our cleansing be.

To say we have no sin
 Is to deceive,
To fail of truth within,
 The Spirit grieve:
If we our sins confess,
God will forgive and bless,
Cleanse from unrighteousness,
 From fear relieve,

If sin abuse his love,
 And us appall,
Our Advocate above
 For grace shall call.
Jesus, his righteous Son,
By all that he has done,
A ransom full has won
 For us, and all.

Blest they who keep the Word,
   Their guide each day,
Walk closely with their Lord,
   Know and obey,
Works with true faith combine;
In them the love divine
Shall in perfection shine,
   And ne'er decay.

1886

---

[Oct. 10.] Who is this .. that is glorious in his apparel? Isa. lxiii. 1.
When I saw him, I fell at his feet as one dead. And he laid his
right hand upon me, saying, Fear not, I am the first and the last, and
the Living one. Rev. i. 17.

## JOHN'S VISION OF JESUS.

Christ, ascended, has not vanished,
   Now he greets th' Apostle's view
In the isle of Patmos, banished
   For the Word and witness true.

Ah! the glory of that vision,
   Mid the candlesticks of gold!
'Tis the King from realms Elysian,
   Royal robes his form enfold.

Snowy locks of heavenly whiteness
   On his head majestic shine,
While his eyes with piercing brightness
   Flash in splendor all divine!

Sovereign feet, to earth descended,
   Burn like molten brass refined;
Clasps his strong right hand, extended,
   Stars that sparkle, seven combined.

From his mouth, in keenness gleaming,
 Leaps a burnished two-edged sword,
While his countenance is beaming
 Like the sun in fullness poured.

How that view and voice of thunder
 O'er John's soul sublimely broke,
Filled him with a fearful wonder,
 As, the First and Last, he spoke!

O belovéd, fear thou never!
 I your Lord, who once was dead,
Live again—alive for ever!
 Death no more shall be your dread.

Mine the keys of death and Hades;
 All my own with me shall live;
In the valley where the shade is,
 I the victory will give!    1886

---

[Oct. 11.]  I shall go to him, but he shall not return to me.  2 Sam. xii. 23.

In heaven their angels do always behold the face of my Father.  Mat. xviii. 10.

## LOST AND KEPT.

O mourning mother! the sweet child you gave
So soon to Heaven, so early to the grave,
Is yours, a blooming child for evermore,
Safe with the Saviour on the blesséd shore.

Your child, through earthly and immortal years,
Be comforted, and stay your falling tears;
A parting pang, a past—these are the cost,
By which you keep the precious gem you lost.  1870

[OCT. 12.] They seemed as men that lifted up axes upon a thicket of trees. Ps. lxxiv. 5.

.. That in the ages to come he might show the exceeding riches of his grace in kindness toward us in Christ Jesus. EPH. ii. 7.

## TWO HUNDRED YEARS.

WHERE now a joyous throng we stand,
   And beauties round us glow,
Stood a dense forest, wild and grand,
   Two hundred years ago.
How vast the change, from old to new!
   'T would strike the fathers dumb;
But what shall fill the children's view,
   Two hundred years to come?

What struggles, perils, toils, and fears,
   They had to brave and know,
Ere comforts blessed the pioneers,
   Two hundred years ago.
For varied luxuries we possess,
   They had no thought or room;
But what they'll have, oh, who can guess,
   Two hundred years to come?

The church and school, so simple then,
   Expressed the heart's outflow;
Earnest were those strong, thoughtful men,
   Two hundred years ago.
In grander fane and temple found,
   Refinement's richer home,
Th' old virtues live—will they abound,
   Two hundred years to come?

Through all the past, life's growing tide
 Has met the one grim foe;
Old are the graves of those who died
 Two hundred years ago.
We swell the stream where murmuring rolls
 The cadence of the tomb:
What were our lives, and where our souls,
 Two hundred years to come?   1870

---

[OCT. 13.] The voice of rejoicing and salvation is in the tents of the righteous. Ps. cxviii. 15.

Be .. imitators of them who through faith and patience inherit the promises. HEB. vi. 12.

## PAST AND FUTURE.

FROM the past, with its treasures of honor and story,
 Wrought out by an ancestry noble and true,
O favored descendants! the future's bright glory,
 In promise and hope, is entrusted to you.

E'er may virtue and happiness, sisters of beauty,
 Abide in your homes as their gladness and peace,
And the sons of the fathers, unshrinking in duty,
 Make the fame of their heritage ever increase.

May the blessings of earth in the sunshine of heaven
 On every one here in their plenitude rest;
And the far richer grace of the gospel be given,
 As the guide of the soul to the home of the blest.

In the long line of centuries down to their ending,
 May the earliest memories blend with the last:
Thro' successions of years, benedictions descending,
 Till millennial splendors be over them cast.   1870

[Oct. 14.] Ho, every one that thirsteth, come ye to the waters. Isa.
lv. 1.
And the Spirit and the bride say, Come. And he that heareth, let
him say, Come. And he that is athirst, let him come: he that will, let
him take the water of life freely. Rev. xxii. 17.

## THE GREAT INVITATION.

Oft the Redeemer said,
　To sinful souls unblest,
Come, ye that hunger, here be fed;
　Come, weary ones, and rest.

And now the Spirit takes
　The Saviour's place on earth;
Most lovingly the plea he makes,
　Come, find the heavenly birth.

The bride, the church of God,
　Repeats the gracious call:
Come, wanderers, see what precious blood
　Was shed to save you all!

The wakened soul that hears
　Is guilty now if dumb;
Go then with tenderness and tears,
　And bid the sinner come.

O thirsting, restless heart,
　Come to the Fountain—drink!
Christ will the draught of life impart;
　Why linger at the brink?

And whosoever will—
　So freely grace is given;
Come, dying soul! how canst thou still
　Refuse the call of Heaven?

1886

[Oct. 15.] O sing unto the Lord a new song. Ps. xcviii. 1.

Unto the Lamb, be the blessing, and the honor, and the glory, and the dominion, for ever and ever. Rev. v. 13.

## THE NEW SONG.

They sing a new song in the city above,
The Eden celestial, the birth-place of love,
The home of the pure, never shaded by night,
A temple all glorious, its orchestra light:
Oh, beautiful region, unmeasured by time,
And evermore filled with this anthem sublime!

The Lord of the universe lists to its tone,
'Tis joy to the Lamb in the midst of the throne;
The thousands on thousands of fair angel bands,
The living ones, elders, redeemed of all lands,
The first of the saved, and the latest gone there,
All list to this song floating sweet on the air.

The strain is unique, ne'er before was it heard
Till one, washed in blood, entered striking its chord;
The harmonies grew as the numbers increased,
As saints from all points came and sat at the feast:
Now myriads of voices the music prolong,
But only the ransomed can sing this new song.

Ah, what is that music transcending, we know,
All beautiful sounds where the song-flowers grow?
Caught upward Paul heard it but never could tell
Its sweetness unrivaled, its glorified spell.
Such exquisite harp-tones elude our earth-grasp;
Wait till the book opens, and seals shall unclasp.

The theme of the song ever new, and yet old,
Whose melodies charm the fair city of gold,
Is the loving Redeemer, the Lamb that was slain,
Exalted by saints in their loftiest strain:
To the glorious Saviour, who brings us to heaven,
All honor and blessing and praises be given!  1886

---

[OCT. 16.]  To do justice and judgment is more acceptable to the Lord
than sacrifice. PROV. xxi. 3.

Bear ye one another's burdens, and so fulfill the law of Christ.—
GAL. vi. 2.

## NOBLE VIRTUES.

DEAR is the friendship that through life delights
The kindred minds its sacred bond unites;
More strong the mystic power of human love,
Type of the tie that binds the blest above.

Sweet is the sympathy that shares a part
In sorrow's tear and grief's unsolaced heart;
And high the faith that with unyielding sway
Holds fast to truth when error rules the day.

Grand is the right, unawed by fear or frown,
That stems the tide when wrong usurps the crown;
Duty, that moves straight on, and never swerves
To low ambition's lead, or party curves.

Sublime the patience, that persists and waits
For God to turn time's wheels or lift its gates;
Philanthropy, that spurns the ermined ban
That aims to break the brotherhood of man.  1857

[Oct. 17.] They shall be mine, saith the Lord of hosts, in the day that I do make, even a peculiar treasure. MAL. iii. 17.

Therefore are they before the throne of God; and they serve him day and night in his temple. REV. vii. 15.

## THE SAINTS IN HEAVEN.

OUT of each nation, tongue, and land,
Countless, before the throne they stand,
With victor palms in every hand,
  And robes of spotless white.
They lift their blending voices high,
Salvation to our God they cry,
To him who did for sinners die,
  The Lamb enthroned in light.

Lo, the vast ranks of angels all,
Around these hosts a flaming wall,
Now on their faces lowly fall,
  And worship God their King.
His glorious attributes they praise,
Thanksgiving anthems loudly raise,
Proclaim his might to endless days,
  Their lofty honors bring.

And who are these arrayed in white?
How came they to this world of light?
Ah, these from sin and sorrow's night,
  From tribulation came:
They all have bathed in Calvary's flood,
Washed clean their robes in Jesus' blood,
And now before the throne of God
  They magnify his name.

The Lamb amidst that royal throne
Dwells now forever with his own;
Hunger or thirst shall ne'er be known,
　　Nor aught of pain or fear;
For he shall meet their utmost need,
To living fountains ever lead,
Them at immortal banquets feed,
　　And wipe away each tear.　　1886

---

[Oct. 18.]   I have put my words in thy mouth, and have covered thee in the shadow of mine hand   Isa. li. 16.

Blessed is he that keepeth the words of the prophecy of this book.— Rev. xxii. 7.

## THE BOOK OF REVELATION.

Mine of marvels—Revelation!
　　Realm where mystic voices blend;
Cadences of Inspiration,
　　Murmuring through ages, end!
Paradise its pearly portals,
　　Facing earthward, open swings,
And to weary, suffering mortals
　　Visions of its glory brings.

Precious Book! its pages please us,
　　Though we grasp not all the lines;
Mid its crowning splendors Jesus,
　　Image of the Father, shines.
Oh, the bliss to wait before him!
　　With his ransomed ones to be;
Oh, the rapture to adore him!
　　Charmed his radiant face to see.

Record, full of conflict's rattle,
    Zion oft in travail sore,
Marching on through dust and battle,
    Strong at last and conqueror!
O'er earth's wastes the Spirit hovered,
    Making all things sweet and new;
Lost humanity recovered,
    Grandly fills the widening view.

Blest Apocalypse! unsealing
    Heaven, all glorious to our sight;
New Jerusalem revealing,
    Bathed in everlasting light:
Home of all the saints forever,
    City of the Lamb's abode,
Through it flows life's crystal river,
    Bursting from the throne of God.    1886

---

[OCT. 19.] His name shall be called Wonderful. ISA. ix. 6.

He received him into his arms, and blessed God, and said, Now lettest thou thy servant depart, O Lord, according to thy word, in peace, for mine eyes have seen thy salvation. LUKE ii. 28—30.

### SIMEON.

THE saint breathed forth a joyous song,
    And clasped the Infant to his heart;
He saw the Saviour promised long,
    Was satisfied, would e'en depart.

Jesus, in thee what matchless charms!
    Thou art my song, my hope, my stay;
My faith enfolds thee in its arms,
    And sees salvation's brightening day.    1890

[Oct. 20.] I was a son unto my father..and he taught me. Prv. iv. 3,4.
We dealt with each one of you, as a father with his own children,
exhorting you, and encouraging you. 1 Thess. ii. 11.

## MY FATHER.

A RURAL and sequestered spot was where
　Our pleasant, ample farm-house stood,
　Mid field and mead and mountain wood,
A landscape loved, if not surpassing fair.

My father, at the soft sweet eventide,
　Would often take me on his knee,
　In lessons there to question me,
And mark my progress with a glowing pride.

Clinging with gladness to his sturdy hand,
　Out to the fields with him I went,
　And joyous took some little stent
Of reaping, making hay, or tilling land.

It was a deep delight with him to go,
　On journeys to some town prolonged,
　See sights that on my vision thronged,
And wondrous wise in new-found knowledge grow.

When home of friend or relative was reached,
　He bade me to the group repeat
　Some tiny speech, or poem sweet,
Or tell the text of the last sermon preached.

How well he loved his little bashful boy,
　How glad his opening mind to see:
　Did thoughts of coming years with me,
Fill his large heart with hidden, hopeful joy? 1844

[Oct. 21.]   My father, my father, the chariots of Israel and the horse-
men thereof! And he saw him no more. 2 KINGS ii. 12.
    I will receive you, and be to you a Father. 2 COR. vi. 18.

## FATHERLESS.

"YOUR father's dead!" Ah, how the message chilled
    My heart and dimmed my tearful eye!
    With a cold gloom, and oft-heaved sigh,
My little being was to fullness filled.

I saw him as he lay in death's stern arms;
    His eyes were sealed in dark eclipse,
    But on his pale and speechless lips
A loving smile was wreathed in heavenly charms.

Was it the sweet peace of his dying prayer,
    That lingered with the parting breath?
    Or visions, o'er the vale of death,
That rose upon his ransomed spirit there?

Well I remember the funereal train,
    As solemnly it moved and slow,
    Through the deep banks of drifted snow,
And the dear dust was given to dust again.

I was a boy, when this great grief was borne,
    And years but half a score had known:
    I am a man—long years have flown—
But ne'er have ceased that crushing loss to mourn.

When o'er the young and tender spirit falls
    Some awful shade, with sudden power,
    How long the memory of that hour
Remains, and all its mingled gloom recalls!   1844

[OCT. 22.] **A woman that feareth the Lord, she shall be praised.—**
PROV. xxxi. 30.
Honor thy father and thy mother. MATT. xix. 19.

## MY MOTHER.

MOTHER! 'tis evening now,
And I am far from childhood's home of glee;
But as my hand supports my aching brow,
    My thoughts go forth to thee.

I joy to view the place
Blest by a cherished parent's tenderest care,
While memory loves each early scene to trace,
    And fondly linger there.

I think of those glad days,
When I was but an artless, playful child;
Thy love watched all my little sports and ways,
    And on me sweetly smiled.

Oft at the evening hour,
Thou kindly bad'st me to thy side repair,
To tell me of the Saviour's love and power,
    And teach me some sweet prayer.

Those lessons learned from thee
Were not forgotten then, nor are they yet;
Waymarks they've been in peril hours to me,
    To shun the evil met.

Through all life's gathering cares,
My heart with gratitude shall e'er rejoice,
That God so blest me with a mother's prayers,
    A mother's counsel choice.

1842

[Oct. 23.] Is it well with the child? And she answered, It is well.
2 Kings iv. 26.
And He called to him a little child. Matt. xviii. 2.

## TRANSPLANTED.

Beautiful, the precious treasure,
　　Lovely, darling, only child,
Source of new and varying pleasure,
　　Making joy where'er she smiled.

Budding flower! thou hast not perished,
　　Though withdrawn from mortal eyes;
Dearly loved and fondly cherished,
　　Thou dost bloom in Paradise.

Endless life the Saviour gives thee,
　　And unfading beauty there;
To his sheltering arms receives thee,
　　Far from sorrow, sin, and care.

Ye whose tear-drops flow like water,
　　Let your grief and anguish end;
He who took your angel daughter,
　　Is your Father and your Friend.

Trust him now, amid your sadness,
　　Be his word and grace your stay;
He can change your gloom to gladness,
　　He can turn your night to day.

Mourn ye not, though hopes are blighted,
　　Lift above the tear-dimmed eye;
By celestial radiance lighted,
　　Faith reveals your home on high.　　1848

[Oct. 24.] Deliver him from going down to the pit, I have found a ransom. Job xxxiii. 24.

Blessed is the man that endureth temptation : for when he hath been approved, he shall receive the crown of life. Jas. i. 12.

## CROSS AND CROWN.

I love the Lord who died for me,
On the cross—cruel cross!
Where all my hope of heaven I see,
On the cross—shameful cross.
O Saviour! but for thy shed blood,
My soul had sunk in sin's dark flood;
Thou hast redeemed me unto God,
On the cross—painful cross.

Jesus! I hear thy loving voice,
"Follow me—take the cross."
Thou art my blesséd guide and choice;
Follow thee?—take the cross?
Dear Lord, I will with joy obey,
Serve thee throughout my earthly day,
Till thou shalt come and sweetly say,
"Follow me—leave the cross."

Oh, land of light and bliss above!
To the crown—by the cross.
Oh, heavenly rest and home of love!
Aye the crown—ne'er the cross.
All glory to the Saviour-King!
As saints their endless praises bring,
My soul shall join, its triumph sing,
Welcome, crown!—farewell, cross!

1858

[Oct. 25.] The people that know their God shall be strong, and do exploits. DAN. xi. 32.
To each one his work. MARK xiii. 34.

## THERE'S WORK FOR THEE.

THERE's work for thee! Be faithful and aggressive,
 Seek out the ways and means of doing good;
Stay not, but 'neath the heavenly call impressive,
 Go forth and toil as Christ's disciple should:
 Have you for him yet done the best you could?

There's work for thee! Lo, varied fields are waiting,
 Where homes are sad, and hearts lie desolate:
How should sin's fearful havoc, unabating,
 Urge thee to lift from them their burdens great,
 Lest sink they hopeless 'neath woe's crushing fate.

There's work for thee! Ah, souls of royal brightness
 Sweep toward the verge of ruin's full eclipse!
They court the tempter in unwary lightness,
 And press destruction to their maddened lips:
 Save, ere their sun in death's horizon dips!

There's work for thee! The future opes in splendor,
 God's kingdom triumphs in advancing years;
Unwonted hands and hearts their aid shall render,
 And woman's help shall win by prayers and tears:
 Lift high the banner, cast away your fears!

There's work for thee! Oh, glorious task for mortals,
 How to such work the heavenly hosts would bend!
Methinks I see them, through celestial portals,
 Their glad approvals to the faithful send:
 How sweet their welcome when the day shall end!

1880

[Oct. 26.]   Live joyfully with the wife whom thou lovest all the days of the life .. which he hath given thee.   Eccl. ix. 9.

Both righteous before God, walking in all the commandments and ordinances of the Lord blameless.   Luke i. 6.

## A GOLDEN WEDDING.

With longing look, with welcome sweet,
  The Golden Wedding day we see,
Where scenes of half a century meet,
  To crown love's joyous jubilee.

Though far away, it now seems near,
  So brightly rising into view,—
The blissful hour for ever dear
  That sealed the union sweet and true.

Again transpires the rite, the scene,
  We seem within the room to stand;
But ah, what epochs lie between,
  What freighted years of history grand!

Their blended life, like mingled streams,
  Along time's varying course has flowed,
And o'er each change celestial beams
  A radiant glow and warmth have strowed.

Each cloud has had its silvery sheen,
  Comfort has soothed all trials hard,
And on the roughest waves was seen,
  By day or night, the loving Lord.

Blest in their work with large success,
  They sow and reap in noblest deeds,
And still with earnest zeal they press
  Along the way the Master leads.

Children beloved have grown apace,
  Parental names and worth to bear;
And, clustering here this scene to grace,
  Grandchildren come its joys to share.

What hallowed ties these hearts unite,
  As heaven and earth commingle here,
While faith and hope transcend the sight,
  And joy springs up from sorrow's tear.

O wedded love! O blessèd home!
  Years faded leave your wealth and balm;
Years waiting brighter till shall come
  The marriage supper of the Lamb!  1888

---

[OCT. 27.]  I found him whom my soul loveth.  CANT. iii. 4.
  Therefore will I give praise unto thee .. and sing unto thy name.—
ROM. xv. 9.

## A SONG OF THE SAVIOUR.

I WILL joyfully sing
  Of the Saviour who sought me,
My Redeemer and King—
  By his blood he hath bought me.
Oh, he hung on the tree,
  For my soul's guilt expiring,
And his grace shown to me,
  I can ne'er cease admiring.

Of his wonderful love
  I was once all unknowing;
Far from mansions above
  I in darkness was going.

Oh, how happy the day,
　　When, in infinite kindness,
He my sins washed away,
　　And removed all my blindness.

Then I saw him as mine,
　　To embrace me advancing,
And his beauty divine
　　Was my spirit entrancing.
Of ten thousands the chief,
　　In my heart I enthroned him;
He had borne all my grief,
　　And I gratefully owned him.

While I've journeyed along,
　　As a pilgrim and stranger,
He, my Shepherd and song,
　　Was my refuge in danger.
He will lead me through life,
　　For his pledge he hath given,
And, in death's closing strife,
　　Bear me safely to heaven.

Oh, then join in the song,—
　　'Tis salvation's sweet story;
Let the blood-ransomed throng
　　In the cross ever glory.
Hallelujahs shall ring
　　When we pass o'er the river,
And of Jesus we'll sing
　　In his presence forever.

1859

[OCT. 28.] Thou shalt have olive trees throughout all thy borders.—DEUT. xxviii. 40.

Some of the branches were broken off, and thou, being a wild olive, wast grafted in among them. ROM. xi 17.

## OLIVE TREES OF PALESTINE.

AMONG the gray old rounded hills,
 Through regions fair of Holy Land,
A grateful scene the vision fills,
 Where trees or groves of olive stand.

Where'er we go, o'er ridge or vale,
 They kindly greet the stranger's eye;
In rest at noon their shade we hail,
 Our camp at evening finds them nigh.

Rich on the plains, the slopes they trace,
 And oft the rocky summits crown:
The thrifty saplings grow apace,
 Beside the trees of gnarled renown.

Slowly the grafted stems mature—
 From olives wild no fruit appears—
But long the sturdy plants endure,
 And measure oft a thousand years.

They love the hard and flinty soil,
 Drive down their roots amid the rocks,
Draw out from thence their choicest oil,
 And stand secure from stormy shocks.

Symmetric beauty, humble, calm,
 Their pleasant features clearly mark;
Not like the tall and tufted palm,
 Nor tapering cypress, slender, dark. 1865

[Oct. 29.] The Lord called thy name, A green olive tree, fair with goodly fruit. Jer. xi. 16.

And didst become a partaker with them of the root of the fatness of the olive tree. Rom. xi. 17.

## EVERGREEN AND FRUITFUL.

When vernal airs and skies appear,
   Star-blooms of purest white are seen,
Mid olive leaves that all the year
   Keep an unchanging dusky green.

While blossoms fade, or falling oft
   From arching boughs they lately decked,
That verdant hue of foliage soft
   With deeper emerald gems is flecked.

Through arid heats of summer time,
   When fountains fail and fields are brown,
That fadeless green retains its prime,
   And rounding berries fill its crown.

As autumn days their exit make,
   Ring all the groves in merry gale,
While stalwart hands the branches shake,
   And purple fruit descends like hail.

Their sacks the gleeful maidens fill,
   And bear them on their heads away:
On topmost boughs are berries still,
   To cheer the poor who hither stray.

The richest wealth the people know,
   The largest comforts that they see,
Each daily meal, the lamp's bright glow,
   Attest the value of the tree.

                                        1865

[OCT. 30.]   I am like a green olive tree in the house of God.—
Ps. lii. 8.

And when they had sung a hymn, they went out unto the mount of
Olives.  MARK xiv. 26.

## OLD TREES IN GETHSEMANE.

WHEN sacred hills in mantling snow
    Feel winter storms along them sweep,
And torrents cold through valleys flow,
    Unwithered leaves the olives keep.

Down to their life's remotest stage,
    Tho' trunks decay and boughs are grim,
The reverend forms are green in age,
    And berries hang from every limb.

Such are the grand old hallowed trees
    I saw in sweet Gethsemane,
And thought of Him whose holy knees
    Bowed under burdens there for me.

Along the slope of that dear hill,
    To where he vanished in the sky,
Infrequent stands the olive still,
    To bring the days of Jesus nigh.

And o'er the ridge they cluster sweet,
    Where Bethany, beloved for him,
So oft received his weary feet,
    When day declined to twilight dim.

Emblem of peace! I would like thee
    In living fruitfulness abound:
Oh, let me like the olive tree
    Within the house of God be found.

1865

[OCT. 31.] God .. breathed into his nostrils the breath of life; and man became a living soul. GEN. ii. 7.

The things which are seen are temporal; but the things which are not seen are eternal. 2 COR. iv. 18.

## ETERNITY AND THE SOUL.

ETERNITY—tremendous word!—when first
  Pealed out Jehovah's all-creating voice,
Bidding the light o'er gloom and chaos burst,
  And orbs celestial in their course rejoice,—
Thy years were countless as the stars on high,
And thou wast then, as now, the same—eternity!

When crashing spheres bewail the death of time,
  As if dissolving 'neath their Maker's ire;
When he shall wrap the earth in flames sublime,
  And bid the starry lamps of heaven expire—
Thou, in thy mystic track, shalt tireless run,
Only the childhood of thy endless years begun!

The soul, undying as its glorious Sire,
  Must live like thee in its immortal state;
And joy, that wakes the purest seraph's lyre,
  Will bid it welcome at thy golden gate,
If it hath sought the way of life to know,
And do the will of him who bore our sin and woe.

Eternal destinies the soul await—
  The grand decision trembles on an hour,
And should its vast concern be left too late,
  How shall it fly from sin's recoiling power?
Scan, mortal, well, the path thy feet have trod;
Love's earnest message is, Prepare to meet thy God!

1842

[Nov. 1.]    The day of the Lord cometh, for it is nigh.    JOEL ii. 1.
    Then shall they see the Son of man coming in clouds with great
power and glory.    MARK xiii. 26.

## CHRIST'S SECOND COMING.

SEE at last the signs portending,
Earth's full ripeness for its ending,
Christ the Lord himself descending.

Sun and moon in gloom appalling,
Starry spheres from heaven falling,
Boding fear the world enthralling.

In the clouds with awful splendor,
Dooms to seal, rewards to render,
Comes the saints' beloved Defender.

Scene all other scenes transcending,
Power and glory interblending,
Far beyond our comprehending.

Sight sublime for mortal vision!
Angels from the blest Elysian
Gather for the great decision.

Ah, the shout o'er earth resounding!
The Archangel's voice astounding,
Unbelieving souls confounding.

Day of terror, work of wonder!
Trump of God, like mighty thunder,
Rends all sepulchers asunder!

Dead in Christ with rapture rising,
Living saints, through change surprising,
Now their full hope realizing.

All the saved together meeting,
First and last with joyous greeting,
Sweet redemption's song repeating.

Come, ye blesséd!  Christ the giver
Calls to kingdoms fading never—
Heaven's all-glorious life forever!

Lo, they rise in clouds supernal,
To their homeland, bright and vernal,
Ever with the Lord eternal.

Blesséd hope, that naught can smother,
He shall come, our elder Brother,
Wherefore comfort one another.

While thy triumph, Lord, is nearing,
May I, faithful, nothing fearing,
Love and look for thy appearing.

Oh, this precious great salvation!
Grander in the consummation
Of the new and last creation!          1882

---

Nov. 2.] Sorrow and sighing shall flee away. Isa. li. 11.
Behold, I make all things new. Rev. xxi. 5.

### REALIZATION.

Lo, THE fountains of destruction,
    With their thousand bitter streams,
Flood no more our lovely landscapes;
    Gone are they like vanished dreams.

Where the dark Lethean waters
    Felt the plunge of wasted souls,
Now in bright and crystal clearness
    Life's pure river sweetly rolls.          1886

[Nov. 3.] There is a place by me, and thou shalt stand upon the rock. Ex. xxxiii. 21.

He said, I am the voice of one crying in the wilderness, Make straight the way of the Lord. JOHN i. 23.

### ROGER WILLIAMS ROCK.

Rock by the Seekonk shore,
Where briny billows roar,
 I sing of thee.
Here erst the Indian strayed,
Here once his dwelling made,
And here his children played,
 As wild as free.

Years rolled their circles round,
And here they still were found—
 That red-browed race.
Their hunting grounds were here,
Where dwelt the bounding deer,
Where oft, with bow and spear,
 They joined the chase.

Moved by a deep desire,
Perchance the aged sire,
 With woes opprest,
Came here at eventide,
O'er all his sorrows sighed,
To the Great Spirit cried
 For peace and rest.

Perchance, upon this stone,
The trusting maid, alone,
 Hath placed her feet—

Her lover's form to view,
Gliding the forest through,
Faithful and ever true,
　　His love to meet.

Once passed along this wave
A Pilgrim strong and brave,
　　Who landed here:
'T was Roger Williams then,
As he surveyed this glen,
By wondering forest men
　　Was hailed, "What cheer?"

He met the Indian band,
And took their friendly hand,
　　Upon this stone.
Free from oppression's rod,
This peaceful shore he trod,
With heartfelt praise to God
　　For kindness shown.　　　　　1844

[Nov. 4.] He compassed him about, he cared for him, he kept him
as the apple of his eye. DEUT. xxxii. 10.

Wandering in deserts and mountains and caves, and the holes of
the earth. HEB. xi. 38.

### THE EXILE.

Yon goodly city's name
Still speaks its founder's fame;
　　Ay, Providence
Tells of the guiding Power
That, in dark peril's hour,
Had been the Exile's tower.
　　And strong defense.

The Indian tribes are dead,
Or far away have fled:
　　No sons remain
Of painted chiefs of yore,
Whose warwhoops echoed o'er
Old Narragansett's shore,
　　In Philip's reign.

The Exile, too, is gone,
While years have circled on
　　Their ceaseless round.
The truth for which he fought,
The principles he brought,
As this fair land he sought,
　　Here yet are found.

Not only by this tide
May they in peace abide
　　Till earth's last shock,
But o'er our wide domain
Soul-Freedom hold her reign,
And Christ his sway maintain,
　　Firm as this Rock!　　　1844

---

[Nov. 5.]　I shall be satisfied .. with thy likeness.　Ps. xvii. 15.
　If he shall be manifested, we shall be like him.　1 JOHN iii. 2.

### WE SHALL BE LIKE HIM.

WE shall be like him, like the King immortal,
　　The Lamb enthroned in heaven,
Whene'er, to pass the bright celestial portal,
　　The summons shall be given.

Like Jesus, brightness of the Father's glory,
    And see him as he is!
Oh, who can comprehend the wondrous story,
    Or grasp th' unuttered bliss?

Not like the helpless Child of Bethlehem's manger,
    Denied the village inn;
Not like the Sufferer here, a homeless stranger,
    Mid the abodes of sin.

Not like the Christ betrayed, by friends forsaken,
    By foes condemned to die;
Insulted, mocked, and scourged, to Calvary taken,
    Mid shouts of "Crucify."

But as he is—exalted, crowned for ever,
    In glory none can tell,
With saints and angels, heavenly hosts, that never
    Refrain his praise to swell.

Ah, can it be, we shall our Lord resemble,
    When heavén's gate within,
While here, imperfect souls, we often tremble
    At consciousness of sin?

Oh, promise great! confirmed by words of Jesus,
    That fill with joy our hearts:
From sin his precious blood it is that frees us,
    And purity imparts.

Oh, matchless grace of God! that gives us meetness
    To be like Christ we love;
Pursue thy work in us to grand completeness
    For the bright world above.

                       1890

[Nov. 6.] All kings shall fall down, before him: all nations shall serve him. Ps. lxxii. 11.

For he must reign, till he hath put all his enemies under his feet.—1 Cor. xv. 25.

### CHRIST'S REIGN.

Come, day of Gospel glory,
　To mortals waiting long;
Fulfill prophetic story,
　Bid earth break forth in song.
O'er dark lands still in sadness
　A heavenly radiance fling,
Till all their tribes with gladness
　To Christ true homage bring.

The light upon the mountains
　Foretells the glory near;
Salvation's bursting fountains
　Convey the blessing here.
Of prayers to God long going,
　Full answers now come down;
And fields of toilsome sowing
　The ripened harvests crown.

The strong resistless Angel
　Binds Satan fast in chains,
Proclaims the blest evangel,—
　The Saviour comes and reigns!
All nations bow before him,
　They hail his triumph day,
Earth's myriad souls adore him,
　Rejoicing 'neath his sway.

1890

[Nov. 7.] God said, Let there be light: and there was light. GEN. i. 3.

And the light shineth in the darkness. JOHN i. 5.

## WORLD LIGHT.

On primal forms lay gloom profound,
And o'er the wide creation round
    Hung rayless night,
When God, by whom all worlds were made,
Spake, as his glance the earth surveyed,
    "Let there be light."

Grim darkness rolled in clouds away,
And sweetly dawned the new-born day,
    In gleamings bright.
The sun, unveiled, his course began,
The moon, with all the starry van,
    "And there was light."

From God had wandered all mankind,
In moral darkness deep and blind
    As pulseless night.
No cheerful day on them might rise;
Spake then Jehovah from the skies,
    "Let there be light."

The Sun of Righteousness arose,
The Saviour triumphed o'er his foes,
    In glorious might:
The blesséd Gospel's joyful sound
Echoed Judæa's hills around,
    "And there was light."

1838

[Nov. 8.] The Lord is my light and my salvation. Ps. xxvii. 1.

God .. shined in our hearts, to give the light of the knowledge of the glory of God in the face of Jesus Christ. 2 Cor. iv. 6.

## SOUL LIGHT.

WHILE journeying o'er life's solemn way,
I sought from earth a guiding ray;
   'Twas somber night.
Again I sought and humbly prayed;
The Saviour heard and kindly said,
   "Let there be light."

The clouds that filled my sky were gone,
Fair Bethlehem's Star in beauty shone,—
   How blest the sight!
A love divine entranced my soul,
With faith and hope in sweet control,
   "And there was light."

Illumined souls! with pitying eye,
See the far lands where millions lie
   In pagan night.
Send the blest Word of life abroad,
Till savage men shall worship God;
   "Let there be light."

The standard of the cross, unfurled,
Lift up before a suffering world,
   Till all unite
To sing their great Redeemer's name,
While Heaven shall echo the acclaim,
   "And there was light."

1838

[Nov. 9.]  A friend loveth at all times, and a brother is born for adversity.  PROV. xvii. 17.

Be ye kind one to another, tenderhearted.  EPH. iv. 32.

## BROTHERLY KINDNESS.

JOYFULLY we sing our song,
Grandly its full notes prolong,
As our souls in music swell the mellow strain
Over shadows swept away,
Gloomy midnight turned to day,
Hearts of sadness filled with light and life again.

When a brother's cheek is pale,
Hope and health and vigor fail,
Promptly, tenderly, we're watching at his side,
Through each night of pain and gloom,
Till return his strength and bloom,
Or he leaves us, summoned o'er the parting tide.

As in social union sweet,
Joyful greetings we repeat,
With our beaming eyes and loving hearts aglow,
Then for those not with us found,
Those in bonds of sorrow bound,
Friendly thoughts and helpful deeds shall freely flow.

Hail, then, hail unto the band,
Giving kindness' open hand
To the lonely, suffering, needy, sick, and sad!
While the years shall roll along,
Higher strains inspire the song,
Heaven's blessing crown them all and make them
glad!

1866

[Nov. 10.] Sing unto him, sing praises unto him; talk ye of all his marvelous works. 1 CHRON. xvi. 9.

For of him, and through him, and unto him, are all things. ROM. xi. 36.

## NATURE SONGFUL.

THE poet's ever-varying song,
In sweetest hymn and anthem strong,
    From nature flows;
From all her glorious realms of power,
From scented field, from lowly flower,
    From blushing rose.
It comes from the slopes of grandest mountains,
Its echo is heard in their silver fountains,
    And down the cascade goes:
Out from the crystal spring it gushes,
On through the valley green it rushes,
    Breaking its deep repose.

The forest breathes it from afar,
The heavens inspire it in a star,
    The waterfall,
Sublime, sends forth its earthquake sound,
And sweeter melodies are found
    In tinklings small.
It lives in the vast, majestic ocean,
It swells in its grand and awful motion,
    Heaving the billowy wall;
Sings in the rain-drop descending,
Shouts in the storm-cloud impending,
    As deep to deep doth call.

Its spirit leads the sisterhood
Of seasons, fair, harmonious, good,

Around the year;
Gleams in the mild bright eye of spring,
Glows in the summer's iris ring;
    In autumn sere,
Whose beautiful hues, o'er landscapes flying,
Give heavenly tints to foliage dying;
    Then, in winter drear,
Throned in his palace, cold and hoary,
Wrapt in the robes of icy glory,
    And jewels, radiant, clear.

It lives in all the wondrous forms
That nature carves and being warms
    In earth or air—
The searchless wealth of every sea,
Its swarming life, its coral tree,
    Its pearl so rare;
The birds of bright wing the soft air clipping,
Insects in the golden sunbeams dipping;
    The varied plant-world fair;
And in the ages of mystery,
Writ in the rocks of earth's history,
    God's footprints tracing there.     1857

---

[Nov. 11.] I flee unto thee to hide me. Ps. cxliii. 9.
Your life is hid with Christ in God. Col. iii. 3.

### THE HIDDEN LIFE.

Lord, if my life is hid with thee,
    How safe! companionship how blest!
Then pure and sweet my life should be,
    As here I live, as there I rest.     1889

[Nov 12 ] He shall bathe his flesh in water  LEV xvi. 4.

Having our hearts sprinkled from an evil conscience, and our body washed with pure water  HEB x 22.

## MY MORNING BATH.

As CEASE the stars' sweet chimes,
Up from my couch betimes,
I seek refreshment's glow untold
In the free splash of water cold:
　　Such pleasure hath
　　My morning bath.

If sleep has been disturbed
By care or thought uncurbed,
The pour or plunge makes full amends;
The languid look or feeling ends:
　　Such comfort hath
　　My early bath.

The restless feverish plight,
That lengthens so the night,
At once doth vanish quite away,
Beneath th' enswathing crystal spray:
　　Such healing hath
　　My well tried bath.

This act, I daily hail,
Is like a coat of mail;
In summer cools, in winter warms;
Guards against colds, and other harms:
　　Such virtue hath
　　My morning bath.

1890

[Nov. 13.] Whoso findeth a wife findeth a good thing, and obtaineth
favor of the Lord. PROV xviii 22.
Who giveth us richly all things to enjoy. 1 TIM. vi. 17.

## SIDE BY SIDE.

TEN years! ten years! how quickly past,
With memories bright to live and last!
What great events fill this decade!
What march of nations! histories made!
But with these hearts how tranquil seem
The flowing tides of life's swift stream,
Since that blest day the trusting bride
Her loved and dearest stood beside.

Her hand in his, the token given
Of mutual vows and pledge to Heaven,
Few words were said, a brief heart-prayer
For God's good gifts and constant care:
Thus was the rite so simple past,
So soon performed, so long to last,
And she, the fondly cherished bride,
Was one with him she stood beside.

Ten years have fled but kindly wrought
How many scenes with blessings fraught;
Hallowed by love to them belongs
What treasured good, what grateful songs:
Heaven's favoring smile has crowned the years
With countless joys, and yet some tears.
Stood happy then the groom and bride,
But happier now stand side by side.

The years to come, the decades yet,
While all unknown, in hope are met,
Led by the unseen Hand that guides,
Blest by the love that e'er abides.
Oh, be each period still more blest,
Till comes the last, the brightest, best—
To find a union o'er the tide,
In love immortal, side by side.　1871

---

[Nov 14 ] Who can stand before his cold?  Ps. cxlvii. 17.

They kindled a fire, and received us all .. because of the cold.  Acts xxviii 2.

## THE HOSPICE.

The evening shadows deepen down
　Upon our winding bridle trail,
And mingle with the snow-lit crown
　On rocky brows ice-bound and pale.

We climb the pass, o'er spur, ravine,
　Where Alpine winds sweep roughly through,
Until with joy a light is seen—
　The friendly hospice greets our view.

Welcomed by fire and food and rest,
　Within the cheerful mountain home,
The priests, the monks, the dogs, we blest,
　That bid the grateful wanderer come.

As weary pilgrims found of old,
　The great rock-shade a lodge from heat,
Now Alpine tourists, from the cold,
　Find St. Bernard a refuge sweet.　1859

[Nov 15.] I will bring you out from the peoples, and will gather you out of the countries wherein ye are scattered, with a mighty hand EZEK. xx 34

A hardening in part hath befallen Israel, until the fullness of the Gentiles be come in. ROM xi. 25.

## CONVERSION OF THE JEWS.

SEEK, Lord, thine ancient nation,
  Nor let them wander more;
To Christ and his salvation
  The scattered tribes restore.
Remove the veil of blindness,
  To Calvary turn their eyes,
To see thy lovingkindness
  In Jesus' sacrifice.

On them, for his rejection,
  Guilt's heavy burdens lie;
But through thy love's election
  It brought the Gentiles nigh,
Whose fullness seems appearing,
  As we thy work discern;
Oh, swift the hour be nearing
  When Israel shall return!

Bid rivers of salvation
  To waiting Zion flow;
Her children's restoration
  Let all earth's kingdoms know,
As round the cross they rally,
  With joy to Shiloh come,
And throng each hill and valley
  Throughout their ancient home.    1890

[Nov. 16.] Very pleasant hast thou been unto me. 2 SAM. i. 26.
I hope shortly to see thee, and we shall speak face to face. 3 JOHN 14.

## FRIEND OF MY HEART.

As o'ER the past, the hallowed past, reflection softly
    sweeps,
And quick revives the pleasing scenes that memory
    fondly keeps,
A thrill of joy, in these blest thoughts, steals o'er
    my spirit's chords,
And wakens there a melody too pure for mortal
    words.
    I can not sing that rapturous song—
    The heart alone can still prolong
Its blissful, life-inspiring strains, so sweet, so deep,
    so strong.

How like an angel near to me thy lovely image seems!
It comes to bless my solitude, to beautify my dreams.
I hear again thy pleasing voice, I see thy winning
    smile;
And oh, how favored to commune with one so free
    from guile!
    I would not break the magic spell;
    I would not those emotions quell,
That fill the fountains of the soul as from a crystal
    well.

How sweet the time, how full of joy, how swift it
    rolled away,
When in thy presence I have passed the lingering
    hours of day;

When we have gazed on nature fair, around, be-
  neath, above,
And felt her inspiration deep, and heard her voice
  of love;
    Or, when we sought the place of prayer,
    And paid our souls' devotions there;
Such hallowed hours of pure delight, oh, would we
  oft might share.

Where other scenes shall greet your eye, and other
  friends are found,
And nature in her loveliness smiles gloriously around,
Oh, say, will then, as back you gaze, a thought to
  me be given?
And shall I be remembered in the prayer you
  breathe to Heaven?
    Friend of my heart! where'er I turn,
    Thy lovely image I discern;
With me it dwells, and still shall live in memory's
  sacred urn.                                    1845

———————◆———————

[Nov. 17.]  Light, that shineth more and more unto the perfect day.
PROV. iv. 18.
He may say to thee, Friend, go up higher.  LUKE xiv. 10.

### FRIENDSHIP'S CULMINATION.

We bask in friendship's smile, —
A lovelier world soon rises to our sight,
All blooming in affection's purest light,
And life's extending path grows heavenly bright,
    And beautiful the while,
    Like some celestial aisle.          1845

[Nov. 18.] There touched me again one like the appearance of a man, and he strengthened me. DAN. x. 18.

There appeared unto him an angel of the Lord standing on the right side of the altar of incense. LUKE i. 11.

## ANGEL VISITANTS.

BRIGHT angel forms, on soft and airy pinions,
　　Like carrier birds, the messengers of love,
Leave the fair precincts of the blest dominions,
　　With choicest favors from the world above.

They come and give to solitude its pleasures,
　　And throw a hallowed charm around the heart;
Bear up the thoughts to pure immortal treasures,
　　Where kindred spirits meet no more to part.

They come, from the celestial hills descending,
　　Sent by the bounteous Ruler of the skies;
We feel their presence with our spirits blending,
　　When evening orisons to Heaven arise.

They come when o'er the sorrowing heart is stealing
　　The wasting blight of earth's consuming woe;
They come, sweet rays of heavenly light revealing
　　Amid the darkness of our path below.

Joy for the mission of those guileless creatures,
　　That God to us such guardians should send;
Oh, wear they not the well remembered features
　　Of many an early loved and long lost friend?

Still, still around my checkered pathway hover—
　　'Tis sweet to hold communion with the pure—
And welcome me at last, when life is over,
　　Where love and joy eternal shall endure.　　1842

[Nov. 19.] He shall give his angels charge over thee, to keep thee in all thy ways. Ps. xci. 11.

Are they not all ministering spirits, sent forth to do service for the sake of them that shall inherit salvation? Heb. i. 14.

## MINISTERING SPIRITS.

'Tis sweet to think that spirits pure and holy
  Are often hovering round the pilgrim here,
To banish thoughts of grief and melancholy,
  And bid the trembling heart forget to fear.

They come to dry the mourner's fount of sadness,
  To pour a blessing on the drooping head,
And wake the soul to scenes of hope and gladness,
  Along the vistas of the future spread.

The stricken mother, as her darling slumbers,
  Cold, in the silent chamber of the tomb,
Oft hears its prattling voice like seraph's numbers
  Fall on her ear amid surrounding gloom.

The lonely orphan, by the world forsaken,
  Seems oft the kindness of the dead to share,
And feels a thrill of new-born joy awaken,
  As if embraced by fond parental care.

The saddened lover and the joyless maiden,
  Stript of their cherished ones by death's chill hand,
Commune with their returning spirits, laden
  With love undying from the glorious land.

Ye sainted forms of dearest friends departed,
  Methinks I hear your music in the breeze;
And oft, mid scenes of sadness, lonely-hearted,
  My spirit's eye your joyful presence sees.          1842

[Nov. 20.] He that is wise winneth souls. Prov. xi. 30.
A man full of faith and of the Holy Spirit. Acts vi. 5.

## THE BELOVED PASTOR.

RANGED he grandly realms of science,
    Deep philosophies he knew;
Grasped he well profoundest problems,
    Thence the choicest treasures drew.
Never failed the faith he cherished,
    While the broadest fields he trod;
Firmer grew his trust in Jesus,
    Stronger was his hold of God.

From his lips of inspiration,
    Touched by heavenly fire how oft,
Flowed a strong and sweet persuasion
    Bearing every soul aloft—
Bringing Christ a present Saviour
    To the wakened, anxious, lost;
Giving comfort to the mourning,
    Peace to hearts by trouble tost.

Oh, his love was pure and tender,
    All his nature sweet and mild,
With a sympathy like woman's,
    And as guileless as a child.
How his charity abounded,
    Warming like the sunbright rays;
Who could know him but to love him?
    Who could name him but to praise?

Long on Zion's walls a watchman,
    Soldier valiant for the Lord,

Blesséd victories he witnessed—
    Labor brought a rich reward.
Lustrous name upon our records,
    Lives his influence lingering here,
Still his cheery face is with us,
    Still his voice we seem to hear.

When the time for blest departure
    To his saintly spirit came,
He was on the verge of Heaven,
    Waiting for the steeds of flame.
Linger yet his words triumphant,
    Full of faith and peace and trust,
Blending as a benediction
    With the memory of the just.     1878

---

[Nov. 21.] See if there be any sorrow like unto my sorrow. LAM.
l. 12.

Abide ye here, and watch with me. MATT. xxvi. 38.

### GETHSEMANE.

WITHIN the olive shade
    The Saviour see,
As there he knelt and prayed,
    My soul, for thee;
While cold and damp midnight,
Pale moon and dim starlight,
Beheld thy strange sad sight,
    Gethsemane!

Even the faithful fail
    Vigils to keep;
They sink behind the veil

Of weary sleep.
Jesus is left alone,
Bowed on dank earth and stone,
And thou dost hear his moan,
    Gethsemane!

Why is my Saviour there,
    In sighs and fears,
Under a burdening prayer,
    With cries and tears?
While sorrow's dread control
O'erwhelms his holy soul,
His blood to thee doth roll,
    Gethsemane!

Ah, there he took the cup
    His Father gave;
Resigned, he drank it up,
    My soul to save!
Man's guilt and Satan's hate,
Heart-crushing load so great,
How deathlike was its weight,
    Gethsemane!

Garden of love and woe,
    How dear to me!
I oft in spirit go,
    Jesus to see,
Who gives me heavenly aid
To pray as there he prayed,
Within thy sacred shade,
    Gethsemane!

[Nov. 22.] The Lord loveth the gates of Zion more than all the dwellings of Jacob. Ps. lxxxvii. 2.

They worshiped him . . in the temple, blessing God. Luke xxiv. 52, 53.

## THE SANCTUARY.

King of glory, Lord of light!
From thy heavenly temple's height,
Bow thy presence, with us be,
Bless the house we give to thee.

Thou who Zion's gates dost love
Other dwellings far above,
Here abide, adorn this place
With the beauty of thy grace.

When in worship flows the song,
Be the praise heartfelt and strong;
When in prayer is breathed thy name,
Pleading faith each soul inflame.

Ever here thy holy Word
Be the Spirit's conquering sword;
Sinners yield before its might,
Saints in all its truths delight.

Converts to the fold be brought,
In the way the Saviour taught;
Grateful at his table meet,
Keep his death's memorial sweet.

Here, as years shall pass away,
Lord, thy Gospel's wealth display;
Here, when thou shalt write thine own,
Great the numbers born be known.    1871

[Nov. 23.] Deliver my soul .. from men of the world, whose portion
is in this life. Ps. xvii. 13, 14.

He that loseth his life for my sake shall find it. MATT. x. 39.

## LOSING LIFE TO FIND IT.

LOSE your life, if you would find it,
    End its self-delusive chase;
Break the sin-wrought bars that bind it,
    Rise from nature into grace.

Die to sin!—th' immortal spirit
    Only thus begins to live.
Wealth eternal they inherit
    Who themselves to Jesus give.

To the Lord make full surrender,
    Walk by faith, and do his will; .
Service for thy fellows tender,
    Giving shall thy cup o'erfill.

Lost, but found—oh, glad confession!
    Life abundant thrills the soul;
Now are all things your possession,
    Heir of God while ages roll.

One with Christ, the Spirit in you,
    Joined to all the saved and blest,
Heaven rejoicing thus to win you
    To its love and peace and rest.

What the selfish way forsaken,
    Placed by such a life divine?
Rouse thee, soul! from death awaken!
    Let this Christly life be thine!

1890

[Nov. 24.] Her children rise up, and call her blessed. PROV. xxxi. 28.

Now we see in a mirror, darkly; but then face to face: now I know in part; but then shall I know even as also I have been known. 1 COR. xiii. 12.

## MOTHER IN HEAVEN.

TWENTY years ago to-day,
At Thanksgiving's morning ray,
Mother passed from earth away.

Borne by angels through the sky
To the City built on high,
Oh, what glories met her eye!

Mourned we all her spirit's flight,
Yet she sang, in faith's clear light,
"Heavenly home, how fair and bright."

Through the gate, her bliss complete,
Loved ones, waiting, there to meet—
Face of Jesus, oh, how sweet!

While the years have sped on earth,
With their mingled grief and mirth,
What her life of heavenly birth?

Safe in glory twenty years,
Free from sorrow, pain, and fears,
Wiped away all earth-born tears.

Mother! in that school divine,
Where all truths in clearness shine,
Ah, what knowledge now is thine!

Vast and wondrous fields explored,
With their treasures round thee poured,
Glorious things thy mind has stored.

Thou hast seen the saints of old,
Patriarchs, prophets, martyrs bold;
Listened as their deeds were told.

Thou hast talked with angels sweet,
Trod with them the golden street,
Heard them wondrous things repeat.

Once my precious teacher here,
Now could I to thee come near,
Marvels great would greet my ear.

Chiefly thou wouldst speak to me
Of the beauty thou dost see
In the Lord who ransomed thee.

Twenty years! how peaceful there!
Free from earthly strife and care,
Every scene all pure and fair.

Thrills my heart at every beat,
In the hope, O mother sweet!
We sometime in Heaven shall meet.      1879

---

[Nov. 25.] So he giveth his beloved sleep. Ps. cxxvii. 2.
   Them also that are fallen asleep in Jesus will God bring with him.
1 Thess. iv. 14.

### AN EPITAPH.

Sweet flower of love, though faded here,
And o'er thee falls the sorrowing tear,
Faith sees thy charms in Heaven appear.

The night will end, the morning break,
The cherished dust shall then awake;
Who sleep in Jesus, God will take.      1865

[Nov. 26.] Joy and gladness shall be found therein, thanksgiving, and the voice of melody. IsA. li. 3.

That the grace, being multiplied through the many, may cause the thanksgiving to abound unto the glory of God. 2 COR. iv. 15.

## THANKSGIVING.

DAY of blest anticipation!
Lo, it comes with festal mirth,
Brings the loved with gratulation,
 Thankful for the fruits of earth;
Thankful more, as now returning
Where old hearth-fires still are burning.

Children, long time separated,
 To parental hearts are prest;
Home-bred love has not abated,
 Now it glows with joyous zest.
Praise to God, sincere, outspoken,
For the life-links yet unbroken!

Praise to him, the bounteous Giver,
 For the good that crowns the year;
For the mercies that deliver
 Us from danger, want, and fear;
For the Gift in Gospel story,
For the grace that leads to glory.

Welcome, day of glad thanksgiving!
 Calm for age, and bright for youth,
Proving well the worth of living
 Earnest lives for God and truth:
Joyful day for household meeting,
Feast of Home and Love's sweet greeting. 1886

[Nov. 27.]  Until I came, and mine eyes had seen it : and, behold, the
half was not told me.  1 KINGS x. 7.

It is not yet made manifest (it doth not yet appear A. V.) what we
shall be.  1 JOHN iii. 2.

## IT DOTH NOT YET APPEAR.

FAITH on the word divine relies,
　　And holds each promise true;
Sees hills on heavenly hills arise
　　Beyond th' ethereal blue;
Sees mansions there in splendor bright,
　　Above all beauty here;
But Heaven complete palls on her sight—
　　"It doth not yet appear."

Hope goes behind the mystic veil,
　　And sees where angels dwell;
Where saints, departing, joy to hail
　　Their loved, once known so well;
Where all the saved behold their Lord,
　　In vision close and clear;
Still for Heaven's fullness she's no word—
　　"It doth not yet appear."

We fain would look within the gates,
　　And see the glory there;
Ah, what the ransomed soul awaits
　　We mortals could not bear!
Let faith and hope and peerless love
　　Show us the heavenly sphere;
There's more, far more, beyond, above—
　　"It doth not yet appear."

1890

[Nov. 28.] Mine house shall be called an house of prayer for all peo-
ples. Isa. lvi 7.

Constrain them to come in, that my house may be filled. Luke
xiv. 23.

## THE HOUSE OF PRAYER.

Sweet is the house of prayer,
  Dear, hallowed place;
Oft let me thence repair,
  For heavenly grace.
There Jesus meets his own,
There he makes his glory known,
While saints surround the throne,
  And seek his face.

Lord, in this house of prayer,
  Thy Word be taught;
Here ransomed souls declare
  What grace hath wrought;
Here precious numbers meet,
Sitting at the Saviour's feet,
While living waters sweet
  To them are brought.

Blest be this house of prayer,
  Lord, to thee given;
Here hearts thy mercy share,
  By sorrow riven.
Oh, bless thy people dear,
And to all who gather here,
May this glad place appear
  The gate of heaven.

When in the house of prayer,
   We meet no more;
When all our earthly care
   Is ever o'er;
As we shall hence remove
To our Father's house above,
How blest to meet in love
   Those gone before!    1854

[Nov. 29.] Ask thy father, and he will show thee; thine elders, and they will tell thee. DEUT. xxxii. 7.

Remember therefore how thou hast received. REV. iii. 3.

## STEPS OF PROGRESS.

Our fathers, through persistent toil,
Subdued the tough, reluctant soil:
Have we, on better cultured ground,
Life's ladder climbed to loftier round?

Have we built up, with nicer art,
A grander temple of the heart?
Scorn not the steps, moss-grown and gray,
Nor scaffoldings that fall away.

As well the lake, from full, clear bed,
Disdain the streams by which 'tis fed;
As well the noontide glory scorn
The earlier rays from which 'twas born.

The tree, to large proportions grown,
Was nursed by fallen leaves, its own;
From its decay more verdure springs,
And richer fruit on each bough swings.    1875

[Nov. 30.] I lay in Zion for a foundation a stone, a tried stone, a precious corner stone of sure foundation. Isa. xxviii. 16.

Built upon the foundation of the apostles and prophets, Christ Jesus himself being the chief corner stone. Eph. ii. 20.

## THE CORNER STONE.

O God! for whom, at thy command,
The Temple rose, so fair and grand,
Where thronged the tribes with gift and prayer
Thy face to seek, thy grace to share,—
  Our humbler work we pray thee own,
  And bless to-day its corner-stone.

To honor thee these walls we raise,
Thy great and holy Name to praise,
Thy Law maintain, thy Gospel preach,
And all thy precepts love and teach.
  Our offerings take, our labors crown;
  We lay for thee this corner-stone.

Unless thou build the house, dear Lord,
We toil in vain, without reward;
Deign, then, O Architect divine!
To consecrate our work as thine:
  So lay we, 'neath thy favor shown,
  In faith and hope, this corner-stone.

O Spirit blest! guide us to rear
A home for Jesus' followers here,
Where oft the wandering sons of earth
Shall find the new and heavenly birth:
  With thy indwelling sought and known,
  He is our Life and Corner-Stone.

1869

[Dec. 1.]　Who hath despised the day of small things? Zec. iv. 10.

He that is faithful in a very little is faithful also in much. Luke xvi. 10.

## LITTLE THINGS.

Faithful in least is so in much,
　　The blessèd Master said:
Life's little things—it is through such
　　Our history is read.

What vast results a thought creates;
　　What wrecks, a single sin!
On points of time hang hopes and fates;
　　Battles we lose or win.

The things of faith or unbelief
　　As trifles often seem;
But where they lead in joy or grief,
　　Surpasses ken or dream.

They are like ends of wires we grasp,
　　And right or careless draw;
Eternal things they reach and clasp—
　　A thought of solemn awe.

Within the veil they ring the bells
　　That give supreme delight;
Or those that sound unceasing knells
　　O'er spirits lost in night!

We touch, each one, these wires to-day,
　　In good we do, or not:
Vibrations felt so far away,
　　In heaven or hell, are—what?

1891

[Dec. 2.]  He that dwelleth in the secret place of the Most High shall abide under the shadow of the Almighty.  Ps. xci. 1.

My God shall fulfill every need of yours, according to his riches in glory in Christ Jesus.  Phil. iv. 19.

## THE SECRET PLACE.

Grant me, O Lord, each day to know
  The blessèd secret place of thine;
There shall thy love my soul o'erflow,
My faith to sweet assurance grow,
  My weakness grasp a strength divine.

Beneath thy shadow I'll abide,
  Secure from every threatening ill;
Were thousands falling at my side,
No harm should e'er myself betide,
  With thee my gracious refuge still.

I feel thy soft and sheltering wings,
  As banners o'er me kindly spread;
Their brooding care sweet comfort brings,
Their touch dispels all troublous things,—
  A heavenly peace around they shed.

Should mortal foes steal forth at night,
  And poisoned arrows fly by day,
Thy guardian messengers of light
Will lead me on toward vistas bright,
  And keep me safe through all my way.

Thou dost regard my love for thee,
  The reverence for thy name I bear;
Thou hast an ear for every plea,
Thy gifts through all my life I see,
  Thy full salvation I shall share.          1890

[Dec. 3.]  The Lord Jehovah is my strength and song.  Isa. xii. 2.
  I have fought the good fight, I have finished the course, I have kept the faith.  2 Tim. iv. 7.

## THE VETERAN.

This earthly house forsaking,
  To saintly souls is given
A house of God's own making—
  A blesséd home in heaven.
That mansion bright is grander
  Than palaces of kings,
And there the great Commander
  His faithful soldier brings.

When ceased his soul's resisting
  The Spirit's gracious call,
At once for Christ enlisting,
  He gave his life and all.
Love wrought the deep decision,
  And scattered doubt and fear,
For then, in heavenly vision,
  He saw his Saviour dear.

The true, good fight maintaining,
  How bravely was it fought!
New conquests ever gaining—
  Souls to his Captain brought.
With ardor undiminished,
  Ev'n hardness oft endured,
The Christian course he finished,
  Of help divine assured.

In gladness or temptation,
  Through every path he trod,

He kept the faith's foundation—
　　The blesséd Christ of God.
He knew the truth from error,
　　By franchise of the Son;
And naught could give him terror,
　　For Christ and he were one.

On daily grace depending,
　　Through all life's battle long,
When came at last the ending,
　　'Twas like a triumph-song.
His faith and course victorious,
　　The veteran of time
Has won, in warfare glorious,
　　The peerless prize sublime.

See now the soldier loyal,
　　His armor laid aside
For crown and garland royal,
　　Just o'er the Jordan tide.
The gates of glory greet him,
　　The Master says "Well done,"
His loved ones come to meet him,
　　And so is heaven begun.　　　1878

---

[DEC. 4.]　I will be with thy mouth, and teach thee what thou shalt speak. EX. iv. 12.

When the chief Shepherd shall be manifested, ye shall receive the crown of glory that fadeth not away. 1 PET. v. 4.

## A LONG PASTORATE.

FEW pastors keep their early flocks and places,
　　Till well their fields, successive harvests raise,

See, as the decades pass, the same kind faces,
Marking their souls' advance in Christian graces,
 And so, in wise and long-accustomed ways,
 Increase in strength and influence with the days.

Think of the many good and strong discourses,
 In all these years, the pastor here has preached;
What mental labor, and what heart resources,
What never-ending use of vital forces,
 To do this work up to the point now reached,
 With vigor still that can not be impeached.

While toiling on, nor seeking loud sensation,
 Content with earnest duty sought and done,
What peerless progress marks our wondrous nation;
In other lands what change, transfiguration,
 As light, meantime, has spread and knowledge run
 O'er the wide earth wherever shines the sun.

Their watchful, tender shepherd, parents loved him,
 Through all the years' vicissitudes they share;
Children, to manhood growing, well have proved him,
Grateful to-day that naught away has moved him,
 Who blest their childhood with his love and care,
 And led their later steps in hope and prayer.

All honor to the true and faithful pastor,
 Standing in conscious strength still at his post,
His faith abounding in the faithful Master,
His influence deepening, widening, growing vaster,
 As grows in grace and power the church's host,
 Made their kind shepherd by the Holy Ghost.

1875

[DEC. 5.] Aaron and Hur stayed up his hands, the one on the one side, and the other on the other. EX. xvii. 12.

Esteem them exceeding highly for their work's sake. Be at peace among yourselves. 1 THESS. v. 13.

## WHY THE PASTORATE WAS LONG.

WHAT genial, kind, considerate, helpful deacons—
　　To pastoral flesh not thorns nor shoulders cold,
Not crabbed hindrances, but gladsome beacons,
Leading aright, preventing all that weakens—
　　Have kept the peace in this united fold,
　　By lives so gentle and by faith so bold!

What loving, active, almost faultless members
　　Must form a covenant brotherhood so wise;
No scheming ones to stir strife's smould'ring embers,
To change the sunniest months to bleak Decembers,
　　Or mar and break dear heart-cementing ties:
　　O brethren, sisters, yours th' excelsior prize!

What hallowed scenes have knit your souls' affection,
　　In the long journey to the present stand,
While often penitents have made selection
Of Christ their Saviour, guide, and sure protection,
　　Led through the portal by the pastor's hand,
　　And warmly welcomed by the churchly band.

In times of trial sore and deep affliction,
　　As sorrows come and death's dark shadows lower,
These ties grew stronger as, with faith's conviction,
The pastor's words have been a benediction,
　　A tried support of sympathetic power,
　　A solace sweet in every troubled hour.

Blest tie that binds such hearts, O God, before thee,
　Pastor and flock in love's sweet sacred spell:
Still may he preach to them "the old, old story,"
And sons and daughters bring to Christ and glory,
　Till come as must the parting and farewell,
　In heaven to reünite and ever dwell.　　1875

---

[DEC. 6.] Thou shalt be secure, because there is hope. JOB xi. 18.

　I shall be ready always to put you in remembrance of these things, though ye know them. 2 PET. i. 12.

## HOPE AND MEMORY.

SWEET Hope ne'er fails a cheerful smile to wear,
Her finger pointing to the future fair;
Her voice, as music melting from the sky,
Foretells a brighter day and vision nigh.

She cheers the toiler lone in task sublime,
Bids him be patient and abide his time:
The world may pass by and the haughty frown,
His cross shall blossom to a glorious crown!

Enchanting Memory, from her dear retreats,
Regales the spirit with her choicest sweets,
Brings the loved face and friend of other days,
And lights long faded kindles to a blaze.

She calls, each waymark of our life appears,
Carved on the mile-stones of our early years,
And, far scenes linking to the present hour,
Wakes in the soul a fresh aspiring power.　　1857

[DEC. 7.] Is my hand shortened at all, that it cannot redeem? or have I no power to deliver? Behold, at my rebuke I dry up the sea. Is. l. 2.

The first heaven and the first earth are passed away; and the sea is no more. REV. xxi. 1.

## THE SEA NO MORE.

THE sea no more—its storms are past,
Its raging winds and billows cease;
A sacred calm is reached at last,
A land of light, a port of peace.

The sea no more—life's voyager true
No peril meets or trouble fears;
His bark has found an anchorage new,
Beyond alarms, or ills, or tears.

The sea no more—no wrecks are strown
Along the blissful coast serene;
Sin's awful work is there unknown,
Its blighted forms are never seen.

The sea no more—no anxious thought
For those upon the treacherous deep;
To home's delights in safety brought,
O'er sorrowing scenes none e'er can weep.

The sea no more—for parted souls
Each other greet in holiest love;
No surging flood between them rolls,
One land is theirs, the realm above.

The sea no more—the Angel's feet
Touch ocean wave and earthy sod;
The saints ascend, for glory meet,
And time is lost in heaven and God. 1890

[DEC. 8.] Thou makest the outgoings of the morning and evening to rejoice. Ps. lxv. 8.

When it is evening, ye say, It will be fair weather: for the heaven is red. MATT. xvi. 2.

## AN ITALIAN SUNSET.

WHILE I stand on one of her seven hills,
  Gray old Rome is under my eye,
And a glorious scene my spirit thrills,
  As I gaze on the western sky.

There are gorgeous clouds of vermilion hue,
  And splendors untold beside,
That rise and spread on the arching blue,
  O'er the whole horizon wide.

'Tis the setting sun in his brilliant dyes,
  And what matchless tints are given!
They seem like the light of celestial skies
  O'er the jasper walls of heaven.

How softly on groves of cypress and pine,
  Domes, turrets, and temples old,
The blending glories linger and shine,
  And bathe St. Peter's in gold.

Upon Alban slope and Sabine crown
  The purpling sunbeams play,
And they drop on the winding Tiber down
  Like glimmerings of upper day.

Beyond this brief and enchanting sight,
  I look toward the sky divine—
O City of Light, in a splendor more bright,
  For ever thy glories shine!          1861

[DEC. 9.] Who knoweth whether thou art not come to the kingdom
for such a time as this? ESTH. iv. 14.

Blessed are your eyes. . . Many prophets and righteous men desired
to see the things which ye see, and saw them not. MAT. xiii. 16, 17.

## THE COMING CENTURY.

GOD is writing out the pages
  Of the century's work and worth,
Grandest volume of the ages
  Since th' Apostles left the earth:
    It records the matchless story
    Of the Gospel's later glory.

Lo! a brighter day is breaking
  In the century at hand,
Jesus mightier conquests making,
  Ev'n to earth's remotest land:
    All th' abodes of men possessing,
    Brings he love and peace and blessing.

Vet'rans, weary burdens bearing,
  Heralds of the winning cross,
Reapers, gracious harvests sharing,
  Oft in suffering, shame, and loss,
    Now, their fields to others leaving,
    Palms of vict'ry are receiving.

Ho! ye youthful servants, rally
  To the century's bugle call;
Ne'er with self-born motives dally,
  To the Christ surrender all;
    Come in throngs at his requiring,
    For HIS SAKE your spirits firing!

Glorious now is acting,—being,
At the twentieth century's dawn;
Blesséd eyes such wonders seeing, •
God's great armies moving on!
Take with them your loyal station,
Earnest for the world's salvation!        1890

[Dec. 10.] Lord, I love the habitation of thy house, and the place where thy glory dwelleth. Ps. xxvi. 8.

Whose house are we, if we hold fast our boldness and the glorying of our hope firm to the end. Heb. iii. 6.

## A SANCTUARY MEMORIAL.

What tender memories, Lord, to-day,
Cluster within these hallowed walls,
Where oft thy servants met to pray,
And hear the Gospel's trumpet-calls.

Here rose their grateful praise to Heaven,
Here came the Spirit with the word;
Manna divine to saints was given,
And sinners found by faith the Lord.

In glory now are precious throngs,
Who saw the cross and bore it here,
In scenes of trial sang their songs,
In rapt communion dropt a tear.

Children of this dear mother's name,
If clinging round the sacred place,
Or distant fields their service claim,
O Father, bless with richest grace.

Farewell, sweet spot beloved, farewell!
Thy name shall hallow still our home:
Go with us, Saviour, with us dwell,
And brighter yet make years to come. 1865

[DEC. 11.] Until the spirit be poured out upon us from on high. ISA.
xxxii. 15.
He abideth with you, and shall be in you. JOHN xiv. 17.

## PRAYER FOR THE SPIRIT.

HOLY Spirit from above,
Gift and pledge of Jesus' love,
To this weary soul of mine
Come with rest and life divine.

Blesséd Comforter, abide
In my heart, its perfect guide;
Let me thy sweet counsel hear,
Make the path of duty clear.

Strength impart for every day,
Keep me faithful in the way,
Bid each doubt and murmur cease,
Fill me with thy light and peace.

Now in Zion's anxious hour,
Come with Pentecostal power;
Showers of blessing widely give,
Cause the dead in sin to live.

More and more of Christ reveal,
Fully my redemption seal;
Glorify my Lord in me,
Till his glory I shall see. 1875

[DEC. 12.] He bringeth them out of their distresses. He maketh the storm a calm. Ps. cvii. 28, 29.

In perplexity for the roaring of the sea and the billows. LUKE xxi. 25.

## OCEAN PERILS.

STORM and tempest on the deep!
Wild and high the billows leap;
When shall they in calmness sleep?

Floats a new and noble wreck,
Mid the waves a trembling speck—
Who the fearful gale shall check?

Hundreds crowded, clinging there,
Lift to Heaven their earnest prayer,
Or wait death in dread despair.

Slowly roll the hours away,
Ocean rages through the day,
Nor doth night its terror stay.

Suddenly a mountain surge
Many sweeps from mortal verge—
Passing, wails their solemn dirge.

Who shall calm surviving grief?
Whence shall come implored relief?
Life is loved but seems how brief!

Yonder, see!—a passing sail!
Signal, trumpet, gun, all hail!
Surely now shall hope prevail!

Rescued from a yawning tomb,
Saved from shipwreck's awful doom,
Oh, what joy succeedeth gloom!

1854

[DEC. 13.] Thou wilt keep him in perfect peace, whose mind is stayed on thee : because he trusteth in thee. ISA. xxvi. 3.

The peace of God, which passeth all understanding, shall guard your hearts and your thoughts in Christ Jesus. PHIL. iv. 7.

## THE PEACE OF GOD.

ABOVE the clouds the sky is clear,
    The soothing sunlight fills the air;
No storms invade that upper sphere,
    All is serene and tranquil there.

Such is the peace of God that keeps
    Believing hearts in holy calm;
A blesséd radiance o'er them sweeps,
    And Jesus' love brings heavenly balm.

How shall this peace our spirits guard—
    This treasure passing all our thought?
To trusting souls it is not hard;
    From God's dear heart the boon is brought.

Sincere requests to him be sent,
    In supplication's earnest tone;
Sure will a gracious ear be lent,—
    Confiding souls he loves to own.

Hearts overflowed with thankfulness,
    Mid cares and sorrows all must meet,
Fail not to find, though in distress,
    That peace so restful, large, and sweet.

Who anxious care shall lay aside,
    All burdens to the Lord resign,
Shall in this blesséd peace abide,
    And it will be their guard divine.   1890

[DEC. 14.] They shall be mine, saith the Lord of hosts .. even a pe-
culiar treasure.  MAL. iii. 17.

Beloved in God the Father, and kept for Jesus Christ.  JUDE 1.

## KEPT FOR JESUS.

KEPT for Jesus! for the glory,
　　At the last to be revealed;
Safely led through every danger,
　　For the heavenly kingdom sealed;
Brought to light from sin and darkness,
　　By the Spirit's power divine;
Loved in God and kept for Jesus—
　　Rich and blesséd portion mine!

Kept for Jesus!  Let me never
　　Such a wondrous truth forget;
Let it bind me to him closely,
　　Till my earthly sun shall set;
Let it mould me to his image,
　　Charm me with his precious love,
Make me joyful in his service
　　Till I see his face above.

Kept for Jesus!  Oh, the rapture
　　That inspires my grateful soul,
When I fain would grasp its meaning
　　While eternal ages roll!—
I so sinful and unworthy,
　　Saved by him and sanctified,
Loved and called and kindly chosen
　　For some blessing at his side!

Kept for Jesus! Oh, my Saviour,
    Crucified that I might live!
When I think how thou hast loved me,
    In return what can I give?
Were it all I have or hope for,
    More a thousand times thy due:
Loved in God and kept for Jesus,—
    How it thrills my spirit through!    1890

---

[DEC. 15.] Remember all the way which the Lord thy God hath led thee these forty years. DEUT. viii. 2.

Our brother and God's minister in the gospel of Christ. 1 Thes. iii. 2.

## MINISTERIAL REVIEW.

WHAT hallowed memories, Lord, are here,
    Since souls were first thy servant's charge;
Thou hast sustained him year by year,
    Made field and toil and fruit enlarge.

Sorrow and joy have mingled oft—
    The lot of workmen brave and true—
Through grace they bear the heart aloft,
    And heavenly hope and peace renew.

Blest is the work divinely given,—
    The word to preach, the flock to feed,
To soothe the hearts by anguish riven,
    And sinners to the Saviour lead.

Still, as the years shall come and go,
    May each one beam with light and love,
Harvests of souls thy servant know
    For Christ and crowns that wait above.   1887

[DEC. 16.] This is the day which the Lord hath made; we will rejoice and be glad in it. Ps. cxviii. 24.

The first day of the week, when we were gathered together. ACTS xx. 7.

## THE LORD'S DAY.

BLEST, Lord, thy sacred day,
From morning's welcome ray
  Till evening ends.
Soft on the world around,
Richly where saints are found,
Gathered on holy ground,
  Thy peace descends.

Within thy courts how sweet
To join in worship meet,
  Thy praise to sing.
In prayer we come to thee,
Upward our spirits flee,
We seem thy face to see,
  O Saviour King!

In gospel truth is given
The blessèd bread of heaven,
  On which we feed:
With this our souls grow strong,
To master sin and wrong,
And follow close along
  Where thou shalt lead.

So let each day of rest
Deepen our earnest quest
  Of things divine,
That with us they shall stay,

To us their wealth display,
And daily make our way
With beauty shine.

1890

---

[Dec. 17.] This is none other but the house of God, and this is the
gate of heaven. Gen. xxviii. 17.
Enter ye in by the narrow gate. Matt. vii. 13.

## HOUSE AND GATE.

Glorious is the heavenly mansion,
Where the hosts blood-washed and white
Praise, through all its vast expansion,
Christ the Lamb enthroned in light.

Ours on earth the humbler dwelling,
Yet the house of God and dear:
Echoes of their anthems swelling
Linger in our worship here.

While we keep the paths of duty,
Foretaste of our rest is given;
Jesus makes these walls of beauty
As the shining gate of heaven.

Here, O Father, Saviour, Spirit,
Meet the saints, thy grace bestow;
Sinners, through atoning merit,
Bring thy love and peace to know.

When the earthly house vacating,
For the nobler mansion given,—
To the crowns of glory waiting,
Lead us through the gate of heaven. 1865

[DEC. 18.] I am like a green fir tree; from me is thy fruit found.—
HOS. xiv. 8.

But Christ is all, and in all. COL. iii. 11.

## THE LORD LIKE A FIR TREE.

FAIR symbol divine, from time's earliest bound,
The fir in all epochs and ages is found;
Like Jehovah himself always near to his own,—
The Lamb for them slain before Eden was known.

Unchanging its foliage, unfading its green,
Through summer and winter the fir tree is seen:
Enduring, immortal, God's mercy will prove,
And naught can his care and his kindness remove.

A choice tree is the fir—trace its beautiful form,
From valley to summit, ev'n piercing the storm:
Our Lord hath ascended to glory above,
The Head of his chosen, a kingdom of love.

It thrives in all countries and climates and zones;
So the great Sacrifice for the wide world atones:
Give the tree of the cross in all nations a place,
Till God thro' his Son shall bring home a lost race.

Tall, stately, balm-bearing, its lower boughs swing
Where children for shelter may gather and cling;
So Jesus comes down from his heavenly height,
To welcome the young to his arms with delight.

The temple's high rafters of fir wood were wrought.
And its cherubim portal where entrance was sought;
Our Lord is the door where salvation is given,
And his love is the glorious roof-tree of heaven. 1890

[DEC. 19] I have caused thee to see it with thine eyes. DEUT.—
xxxiv. 4.

Lift up your eyes and look on the fields, that they are white. JOHN
iv. 35.

## THE OUTLOOK.

THROUGH the deep primeval forest
    Lies a pathway straight and long;
On it falls the struggling sunlight,
    Round it hums a summer song:
Sounds of birdlings in the tree-tops,
    Faintest rustling of the leaves,
And that nameless lonely murmur
    Every listening ear perceives.

On the farthest woodland border,
    Through the opening like a door,
Lo! a scene of wondrous beauty
    Stretching far the landscape o'er:
Waving grain along the hillsides,
    Ripening in the friendly sun;
Velvet meadows in the valleys,
    Where the crystal streamlets run.

Graze the herds in greenest pastures,
    Flocks along the hedgerows feed;
Cowbells tinkle in the distance,
    Where the visual lines recede;
Joyous farmers till the cornfields,
    Thrifty orchards greet the breeze;
Cosey homes adorn the roadways,
    Graced by flowers and sheltering trees. 1878

[DEC. 20.]   The streets of the city shall be full of boys and girls play-
ing in the streets thereof.  ZECH. viii. 5.

As thou, Father, art in me, and I in thee, that they also may be in
us.  JOHN xvii. 21.

## THE VISION.

CHILDREN playing in the sunshine,
  Ring their merry laugh and shout;
Happy hearts within each dwelling,
  Peace and plenty smile without;
Joys that spring from highest culture,
  Hope in purest worship found, —
Blessings sought through all the ages,
  Here at last for all abound.

Hearts and hands by love united,
  Each the other's burden bears;
Brothers by the law of kindness,
  Each another's sorrow shares;
Every tender tie regarded,
  Every right and trust secure;
All the varying human currents
  Flow serene and sweet and pure.

Woman holds her queenly station,
  Peer of man in sphere her own,
As in Eden's earliest glory
  By his side her radiance shone.
Walking thus in blended wisdom,
  Light and truth divinely given,
Beauty crowns her glorious scepter,
  Wide as earth and sweet as heaven.     1878

[DEC. 21.] All nations whom thou hast made shall come and worship before thee, O Lord. Ps. lxxxvi. 9.

We look for new heavens and a new earth, wherein dwelleth righteousness. 2 PET. iii. 13.

## THE CONSUMMATION.

WE are in the forest journey,
　　Passing toward the open door,
Catching bright alluring glimpses
　　Of the fields that lie before.
Hear the march of rising peoples,
　　Sounding like the restless sea!
Hail the song of conquering toilers!
　　Hail the dawning jubilee!

Darkness hides beyond the mountains,
　　Sunshine brightens in the vales;
Discord changes into music,
　　Every tone the ear regales:
Ills that trooped through all the ages
　　Vanish from the paths of men;
Sorrow flies from coming gladness,
　　Eden visits us again!

Oh, the beauty and the blooming!
　　Skies have dropt their glory down;
Robed anew in righteous splendor,
　　Earth receives from heaven her crown!
Oh, the countless soul-procession
　　Marching to the Gates of Day,
While Messiah's glorious kingdom
　　Holds its thousand years of sway!　1878

[DEC. 22.] This is the Lord; we have waited for him, we will be glad and rejoice in his salvation. ISA. xxv. 9.

Be ye also patient; stablish your hearts: for the coming of the Lord is at hand. JAS. v. 8.

## THE EXPECTATION.

Æon of the world's redemption,
    Boon to mortals promised long,
Still we wait thy coronation,
    Wait to sing thy victor song!
Wait in toil—our Lord is waiting—
    Wait in patience for the prize;
Wait in faith and supplication,
    Wait in love and sacrifice.

Patriarchs waited on the border,
    Where the landscape stretched away;
Prophets waited at the portal
    Of the joyous Advent Day;
Rapt Apostles saw the glory
    Of the risen, reigning Lord;
Toiling, waiting for its fullness,
    Went in faith to their reward.

Martyrs of the spreading kingdom
    Waited for its regal power;
Gave their lives and labors, hoping
    For the promised noontide hour.
Through the centuries waiting, praying,
    Christ's true church the faith has kept:
Saints all looking for its triumph,
    As in peace and hope they slept.

So they waited, toiled, and trusted;
   So wait we in faith to-day,
Thrilled by sweet and true illusions,
   Gaining treasures that delay.
Faithful souls are more than conquerors,
   All things theirs the ages down;
Having wrought to bring the glory,
   Each shall wear his starry crown.   1878

---

[Dec. 23.] Praise him with stringed instruments and the pipe. Ps. cl. 4.

Give praise to our God, all ye his servants, ye that fear him, the small and the great. Rev. xix. 5.

## THE NEW ORGAN.

Greet worshipers gathered within the church portal,
   Give joy to their hearts, inspiration and strength;
Remind them of music and worship immortal,
   Aid them to be faithful and share them at length.

Bring gladness to spirits depressed and in sorrow,
   Bring calm to the restless in trouble and night;
Strike sweetly the strains of a blesséd to-morrow,
   As faith giveth courage and hope reveals light.

Call in the neglectful by music's attractions,
   Where truth and devotion find way to the heart,
Relief be secured from sin's direful exactions,
   Salvation spring up with the well-chosen part.

Oh, voice of the organ! let Calvary's story,
   As years roll away, to vast thousands be given;
The worshipers cheer as to God they sing glory,
   Akin to the songs of the ransomed in heaven.   1867

[DEC 24.]  His name shall be called Wonderful, Counselor, Mighty
God, Everlasting Father, Prince of Peace.  ISA. ix. 6.

There is born to you this day in the city of David a Saviour, which
is Christ the Lord.  LUKE ii. 11.

## THE BETHLEHEM SONG.

No song was ever heard,
No gladsome voice or word,
Since broke o'er earth the blest primeval morn,
Like the celestial sound
That swept the air around
O'er Bethlehem the night that Christ was born.

Half-dreaming by the rocks,
The shepherds watched their flocks,
But woke, in wonder rapt, the song to hear,
As through the sky-roof riven,
The angel flashed from heaven,
A messenger of mingled awe and fear.

Fear not, the angel said,
But joyful be instead;
Tidings of gladness and delight I bring:
And not alone for you
This revelation new,—
O'er the whole earth the rapturous joy shall ring!

This night in swathing folds
The humble manger holds
The Lord, Messiah, Saviour, born for you.
As thither ye repair
To David's city fair,
That wondrous sign shall meet your eager view.

Then round the angel bright
A host in heavenly light
Confirmed the truth in notes of highest praise.
Glory to God! they sang,
Peace and good will they rang,
In chorus grander than all earth-born lays!

The Lord had come to men;
The Lord will come again;
Is coming now in blest salvation's car.
Dark lands! the joy receive,
Sad souls! your burdens leave,
Transfigured by the glorious Bethlehem Star! 1877

---

[DEC. 25.] Unto us a child is born, unto us a son is given: and the government shall be upon his shoulder. ISA. ix. 6.

Glory to God in the highest, and on earth peace among men in whom he is well pleased. LUKE ii. 14.

## HYMN OF THE NATIVITY.

NEVER, in all the ages long,
Came such a time as Bethlehem knew
When shepherds heard the angel song
O'er Jesus born, the Saviour true!
No boon like that, while earth shall live,
Can God again to mortals give.
Ring out, sweet bells!
In joyful chime,
Your music tells
Of love sublime!
Glory to God! in highest strain;
Peace on the earth, good will to men.

Oh, precious Gift! Oh, gracious Giver!
Bright Bethlehem Star, shine on forever!

Join every heart and every voice,
　　To praise the blesséd Saviour's name;
With heavenly hosts adore, rejoice,
　　As when at first the tidings came.
　　　　His only Son the Father gave:
　　　　He left the throne our souls to save.
　　　　　　Ring out, glad bells!
　　　　　　　　These new-born sounds;
　　　　　　　Your music tells
　　　　　　　　How grace abounds.
　　　　Glory to God! good will to men!
　　　　O Prince of Peace, we hail thy reign!
　　　　We swell the song that ceases never
　　　　Of praise to Christ the Lord forever!

Oh, human souls in all the earth,
　　Awake, and hear the angels' song!
Receive the Christ; your heavenly birth
　　Shall still celestial tones prolong.
　　　　How sweet the strains with joy imbued
　　　　O'er hearts repentant and renewed!
　　　　　　Ring out, joy bells!
　　　　　　　　Afar and near,
　　　　　　　Your music tells
　　　　　　　　The Lord is here!
　　　　Glory to God! who gave his Son!
　　　　Hail his redeeming work begun!
　　　　O Saviour King, all lands deliver!
　　　　Glad angel song, flow on forever!　　1887

[DEC. 26.] O Lord, our Lord, how excellent is thy name in all the earth! Ps. viii. 1.
The name which is above every name. PHIL. ii. 9.

## THE LORD'S NAME.

O LORD! how every work of thine,
  From lofty mount to lowly flower,
Proclaims the bless&eacute;d Name divine,
  Replete with matchless love and power.

The sons of men, where thou art known,
  Rise from their sad and sinful state:
In souls transformed thy grace is shown;
  Thy gentleness doth make them great.

From thy dear name our blessings flow—
  The heart and life and home made pure;
The land we love, the good we know,
  All treasures joyous, true, and sure.

Dark are the souls and dark the lands,
  Where minds debased know not thy name;
Slaves of their sins, in Satan's bands,—
  No worship pure, no heavenly aim.

The rising sun bids night take wing,
  So darkness flies where thou art named;
As beauty clothes the world in spring,
  Thy name gives life where'er proclaimed.

O Lord, our Lord! the name we love
  Be excellent in all the earth,
Till every tribe and soul shall prove
  Its gracious power and glorious worth! 1890

[DEC. 27.]  The day of the Lord is great and very terrible; and who can abide it?  JOEL ii. 11.
Thy wrath came, and the time of the dead to be judged. REV. xi. 18.

### DIES IRÆ—TRANSLATED.

DAY of wrath and woe abounding!
Earth dissolves in flames surrounding,
Seer and Psalmist's words expounding.

Midst dismay and fear attendant,
Comes the Judge in power transcendent,
Searching all with glance resplendent.

Peals the trumpet's blast appalling,
Rending tombs the dead enthralling,
To the throne their myriads calling.

Death and Nature wracked in sunder
See them wake and rise with wonder,
At the Judge's voice of thunder.

Opened are the solemn pages,
Where are writ the deeds of ages,
Whence the world await their wages.

Throned in light the Judge is seated,
Brings to view all things secreted,
Naught exempts from vengeance meted.

Wretched, what have I commending?
Who the daysman me defending,
When the just fears wrath impending?

Sovereign of majestic splendor,
Of free grace the loving Sender,
Save me, Source of mercy tender!

Jesus! think how my position
Caused the anguish of thy mission;
Nor, then, leave me to perdition.

Weary, worn, my soul thou soughtest,
By thy death its ransom boughtest;
Perish not the boon thou broughtest!

Just, O Judge, my condemnation;
Yet, forgiving, grant salvation,
Ere the day that ends probation.

Naught of all my guilt denying;
Shame my face with crimson dyeing;
Spare me, Lord, for pardon crying!

Thou didst Mary give thy blessing;
Didst receive the thief confessing:
Hope from thee am I possessing.

Since my prayers will not avail me,
Let thy goodness never fail me,
Nor the quenchless flames assail me.

Keep me with thy sheep abiding,
From the goats my lot dividing,
At thy right my place deciding.

When the scorners wail in sorrow,
Nor from woe relief can borrow,
Pledge me heaven's eternal morrow.

Still before thee low I bend me;
Balm for broken spirits send me:
Let thy care, at last, attend me.

When, that tearful day appearing,
Man shall rise, the judgment fearing,
And a culprit stand before thee,
Saviour, spare him, I implore thee!        1890

--------◄◆►--------

[DEC. 28.] And God said, Let us make man in our image, after our
likeness. GEN. i. 26.

The name of the Father and of the Son and of the Holy Spirit.—
MATT. xxviii. 19.

### THE TRINITY.

FATHER! thy majesty
Fills heaven and earth and sea;
   God evermore;
From ages past the same,
Thy love a ceaseless flame;
Thy great and holy name
   Our souls adore.

Jesus, enthroned above,
Son of the Father's love,
   Our Lord divine,
Who didst, the world to save,
Dire crucifixion brave,
And conquer death and grave,
   Our hearts are thine.

Eternal Spirit blest,
The new heart's purest guest,
   And perfect guide;
Ever our life and light,
Grant us to know thy might,

Dispel all lingering night,
  With us abide.

To God the Father, Son,
And Holy Spirit—One,
  Be glory given:
Honor to him belongs,
Crown him in loftiest songs,
Praise him, ye ransomed throngs
  Of earth and heaven! 1891

———————————

[DEC. 29.] A name and a praise among all. ZEPH. iii. 20.
The friends salute thee. Salute the friends by name. 3 JOHN 14.

### THE NAMES OF FRIENDS.

WE love our friends, our early friends,
  And those of later days:
How frequent fancy for them sends,
Or joyously their steps attends,
  And notes their varying ways;
How often thought with memory blends
  And brings them to our gaze!

What's in a name? A dear friend's name
  Has much we love and prize:
While changes mark e'en earth's great frame,
The silent autograph's the same,
  A pleasure to our eyes;
The bond of friendship is its claim,—
  It holds what sacred ties! 1865

[DEC. 30.] The Lord's portion is his people. DEUT. xxxii. 9.
Beloved, now are we children of God. 1 JOHN iii. 2.

## FAITH AND TRUST.

Now AM I a child of God,
  Spirit-born from life above,
Bought by Jesus' precious blood,
  Closed in arms of endless love.

Oh, this wondrous truth divine!
  Blesséd peace and joy it brings;
Grace and glory through it shine,—
  Mounts my soul on heavenly wings.

Saved by grace thou didst impart,
  Lord, my all belongs to thee;
Ah, the bliss that fills my heart
  Since I knew thy love for me!

Earth and sky, all nature fair,
  Birds and flowers, dear friends of mine
Brighter, lovelier beauties wear,
  Now my will is lost in thine.

Oh, to trust thy love how sweet,
  Walk with thee through all the days,
Learn faith's lessons at thy feet,
  Joy alike in work or praise.

Jesus! ne'er thy love shall change,
  Nor thy glory full be known;
But my soul shall share their range,
  For thy life infolds my own.          1891

[DEC. 31.] Better is the end of a thing than the beginning. ECL. viii. 8.
What is your life? .. that appeareth for a little time. JAS. iv. 14.

## CLOSE OF THE YEAR.

LIKE a swiftly rushing river,
Rolling grandly, pausing never,
Time is sweeping onward ever.
 Life, on its unresting surges,
 Toward the mystic portal verges.

For a laggard ne'er it tarries;
Past and future as it marries,
All our deeds and hopes it carries.
 One more year of history ending,
 What its record forward sending?

Good achieved and ill rejected,
Wealth of soul and life collected,
Higher hope and worth expected,
 Earth from heaven receiving treasures,
 Heaven from earth augmented pleasures?

When our souls shall be demanded,
May we not go empty handed,
But with precious sheaves be landed
 Where, all seasons bright and vernal,
 Years and lives shall be eternal.   1876

### DOXOLOGY.

PRAISE Father, Son, and Spirit, whom,
 Almighty, we adore;
Who is, and was, and is to come,
 Our God for evermore.   1891

# APPENDIX.

## TO MY WIFE.

DEAREST of all on earth, my love, that golden day wert thou—
That bridal day so beautiful—but thou art dearer now ;
Departing years have shown thy worth and tested well thy love,
And I in thee a treasure have my highest thought above.
      Sweet kindred soul, my own fond wife!—
      A world of bliss mid earthly strife—
I bless thee, kindest Heaven, for this, the choicest boon of life.

The glow of thy affection pure, the beauty of thy mind,
Have round me cast their golden links my willing heart to bind,
Have shed upon my path their rays so sweet, so calm, so bright,
And changed a lonely somber world to one of cheerful light.
      Of earth thou art my Eden fair,
      Awaking joy and soothing care,
The smiling angel of my heart in thought and wish and prayer.

My dearest! when I saw thee first, and met thee as a friend,
And only in acquaintanceship our hearts began to blend,
Strange rapture swept my youthful soul and woke the tender
    flame ;
Unconsciously, at every shrine, I breathed thy tuneful name;
      And day by day, before my eye,
      Came, like a seraph from the sky,
Thy lovely image, darling one, and in my dreams 'twas nigh.

How oft, with light and joyful step, in flowery paths we trod;
Oft, listening to the Sabbath-bell, we sought the house of God;
And many a blissful hour flew by when sitting at thy side,
But happiest was the moment when I took thee as my bride;
      Oh, then, my Beautiful, were given
      Our pledge to each, our vows to Heaven;
And naught hath yet, these lustrous years, our deep affection
    riven.

In mutual hope and faithful trust and sweet confiding love,
Receiving from our Father's hand rich blessings from above,
Amid life's duties, toils and cares, along our pilgrim way,
Together we have come with joy increasing till to-day;
     Thou, in my every ill or fear,
     In every shadow darkening near,
Hast been the Heaven-sent messenger to comfort and to cheer.

Upon our path and in our home hath beamed a precious light,
With charms so new and wonderful, in hope and promise bright;
An angel baby's face and form, and laughing life of glee,
A golden link of love to bind my heart more close to thee;
     Amusing, mirthful, elfin girl,
     A treasure sweet—immortal pearl!
Oh, ever round our darling may celestial pinions furl!

Our little world, so full of joys, with cloudless sky serene,
By sordid souls and vulgar eyes is never known nor seen:
The sweetest bliss we can not find in glittering wealth alone,
Nor does it dwell in royal courts, nor on ambition's throne;
     In hearts of faith and love it springs,
     And blesses those to whom it clings,
Sheltered and sweetly brooded by its soft angelic wings.

Thou loveliest one of all on earth, of my own self a part,
The choicest of celestial gifts, and nearest to my heart—
Oh, never shall this arm forbear my chosen to defend,
And never shall this heart grow cold till life's last pulse shall
     Sweet star of life, whose vigil light     [end!
     Guides as it glows with beauty bright—
Can such affection know decay, or die in death's dim night?

Ah! love that binds the pure in heart is not alone of earth,
It is an effluence from God, and hath a heavenly birth;
Its spirit thrills our wedded souls like music tones divine;
Its holy fire of sympathy through all our path shall shine;
     Then, in those radiant skies afar,
     Where naught can e'er its beauty mar,
'Twill ever beam in glory with the Bright and Morning Star!

## MEMORIAL OF AN ONLY DAUGHTER.

DEEP calleth unto deep! The sky seems falling,
　　Whelmed in wild sea and cloud;
And o'er the waste a sunset gloom appalling
　　Shuts like an iron shroud.

Saviour! till on the waves thy form beholding,
　　Our hearts find no release:
Come through the darkness all the world enfolding,
　　And speak to us thy peace.

Life's brightest hope, the gift most fondly cherished,
　　Home's fairest, loveliest light,
All, in this great bereavement, faded, perished—
　　Day darkened into night.

Didst thou, in hidden love, O pitying Father!
　　Make in our hearts this dearth?
Or, for the happier home in glory rather,
　　Long for thy child on earth?

Her life was beautiful in rich completeness,
　　Beyond her years so far;
For Heaven's pure dawning such a radiant meetness.
　　Like a full morning star.

Her mind was peerless in its ample treasure
　　Of varied gifts and grace:
Wide fields of culture, with a lofty pleasure,
　　'Twas hers with ease to trace.

Wrapt in the tender folds of our affection,
　　Her smile as sunlight fair,
Her words, her presence, like heaven's sweet reflection,
　　Can we the jewel spare?

By weeks of weariness and pain consuming,
　　Pressed to the verge of life,

Her trusting spirit, with an angel's pluming,
　　Soared from the tranquil strife.

The next grand moment, as at once awaking,
　　From wondrous dreaming strange,
Within the gates, her raptured view is taking
　　The City's glorious range.

Oh, the sweet thrill of that survey celestial,
　　The blessed Christ to see !
With dear ones, known and loved in years terrestrial,
　　Again with joy to be !

How deep the pleasure of that high communion
　　To the departed given—
The endless bliss profound in the reunion
　　Of spirits loved in Heaven !

Oh, what were life save this glad expectation,
　　As here our dearest die ?
Thanks, ceaseless, for the glorious revelation
　　Of the blest home on high.

We cannot bring from hence whom God hath taken,
　　But must, submissive, wait—
Wait, in more earnest toil and faith unshaken,
　　Till we shall pass the gate.

Ah, long we for the radiant, matchless daughter !
　　So much of us a part :
Rent are our souls, and tears burst forth as water—
　　O Christ ! bind up our heart.

Ours is the weight of deep, heart-wrung afflictions,
　　And sorrow's toil and night ;
Hers, welcome, beatific benedictions
　　Of spirits robed in light.

Ours, the sore discipline of earth's probation,
　　Where conflicts never cease ;

Hers, victory sure, and endless jubilation,
  In full and perfect peace.

Ours, pain, grief, anguish, in the years impending,
  And death sometime to meet;
Hers, a well-finished work, and life unending—
  This trial scene complete.

It is the Lord:  His wisdom never erreth;
  He would not do us ill;
We must accept as love what he preferreth,
  And trust his goodness still.

She 's near us now, the same sweet, gentle being;
  'T is but a little while—
A step, a lifted veil—and oh, we 're seeing
  Her loving face and smile!

## MINNEHAHA.

[Written in 1855, on visiting the beautiful falls by this Indian name,
meaning "Laughing Water." In 1887 the writer revisited the place,
to reach it passing through the splendid city of Minneapolis with a
population of 160,000, which at the first date had no existence.]

WHEN o'er the prairie first
    The Indian trod,
And on his vision burst
    This work of God,
No wonder he should claim it
    A lovely sight,
    A laughing sprite,
And shouting forth, should name it
    With rapt delight,
      Minnehaha!

Long ages passed, I ween,
    And none came near,

To view this charming scene,
   Its music hear:
Before the forest-ranger
   Heard its sweet clang,
   It rushed and rang;
To human eyes a stranger,
   It smiled and sang,
     Minnehaha!

To summer-blooming flowers
   That fringe the brook,
To clustering leafy bowers
   That on it look,
To the deep vale extending
   Far on below,
   Where echoes go,
'Twas ever sweetly sending
   Its tuneful flow,
     Minnehaha!

When winter's mantling snow
   Lay by its side,
When bright flowers ceased to grow
   Along its tide;
Amid the frost-harps, builded
   By the ice-king,
   Each silver string
With golden sunlight gilded,
   It still did sing,
     Minnehaha!

Stars, in the silent night,
   Might be enchained;
Birds, in their passing flight,
   Be long detained;
And, by this scene entrancing,
   Angels might roam,

Or make their home,
Hearing, in waters dancing,
Mid spray and foam,
Minnehaha!

Methinks there is a strain,
A saddened sound,
A half-concealed refrain,
A requiem found,
And tear-drops, softly falling
Along the steep,
In the wild leap
Of sparkling waters, calling
For them that sleep,
Minnehaha!

The tribes that earliest viewed
This glad cascade,
Wild sons of solitude,
Who hither strayed,
Have passed away for ever!
Come they no more,
Nor hear the roar
Of this bright, laughing river,
Singing of yore,
Minnehaha!

But hardy pioneers,
A pale-faced throng,
Surmounting toils and fears—
Stalwart and strong,
Their Eastern homes forsaking,
In eager quest
For this great West,
Blooms in the desert making—
By thee find rest,
Minnehaha!

Shout, to the sons of peace,
　　A gladsome cheer,
Whose pilgrim-bands increase
　　With every year;
Whose art and taste are giving
　　To lake and land,
　　To prairie grand,
A glory bright and living,
　　With thee to stand,
　　　Minnehaha!

Sing to the rising State,
　　With cities fair,
Whose power and honor great,
　　Her sons shall share:
Bidding all foes defiance,
　　Their happy choice
　　Shall them rejoice,
While Freedom, Truth, and Science
　　Blend with thy voice,
　　　Minnehaha!

Sing on—a hundred years,
　　And then how bright
This glorious realm appears
　　To human sight!
All good things here shall enter;
　　True faith shall beam,
　　And blessings teem;
Our Country's crown and center
　　This spot shall seem,
　　　Minnehaha!

## THE NEW SONG OF FREEDOM.

WRITTEN IN 1863, ABOUT THE MIDDLE AND DARKEST PERIOD
OF THE CIVIL WAR.

FROM the present conflict turning,
 From the sorrows of the past,
See approach the happy morning
 Breaking o'er the land at last,
When the South, in true uprising,
 Loosened from her heavy wrong,
No more slaves her sons comprising,
No more sons her wrong advising,
 Joyous swells her RANSOM SONG!

It ascends from all her rivers,
 From her hills and valleys fair;
From the dew-bent flower that quivers
 In her soft and balmy air;
From her harvest labor ringing
 With the implements of toil;
From the hope her new life's bringing;
From her future freemen singing
 On her sunny, affluent soil.

Sounds of joy o'er broad savannas,
 Waking to a newer life,
Glad recall the old hosannas
 Of the early battle strife,
When, our liberty achieving,
 North and South together stood,
To their glorious purpose cleaving,
And the boon at length receiving,
 Purchased with their mingled blood.

Down the border currents flowing,
 Sweetly rolls the tide along,

Through the tropic bowers going,
  Till the sea repeats the song;
Burdened hearts, the music feeling,
  Catch the glow of Freedom's fire,
And before her altar kneeling,
For their cause to Heaven appealing,
  Grasp the boon their hearts desire.

O'er the snow-clad Rocky Mountains,
  Onward sweeps the anthem clear;
Mississippi's farthest fountains
  Its rejoicing echoes hear,
While they reach far hills surrounding
  Where the wild Comanche dwells;  .
Where Missouri's flood is sounding,
To Nevada's distant bounding,
  Waking all her golden dells.

To the mighty inland oceans,
  And the little lakes between;
To the broad rich prairie-Goshens,
  Herds and harvests on them seen:
Over dale and hillside ringing,
  Where the Susquehanna rolls;
To the Catskills' summit springing,
To romantic Hudson bringing
  Strains that stir all patriot souls.

O'er our sacred fields of battle,
  By New England rock and rill,
The rejoicing pæans rattle,
  And revive at Bunker Hill;
And through all the land extending,
  As a new day's gladdening light,
All our sundered interests blending,
All our stormy conflicts ending
  In the triumph of the right.

Earnest faith the song's inspiring,
   Praise to God, good will to men;
Purer knowledge, all desiring,
   Flows in living streams again;
Schools and churches multiplying,
   All the precious arts increase;
Fruits of labor, self-relying,
Wealth, with generous purpose vying—
   Marks of freedom, skill, and peace.

Onward, Flag of glory, flying,
   Grandest earthly banner, thou;
Higher rise to fame undying,
   Borne aloft by Freedom now!
Thine, O Stars and Stripes, the story
   Of a Nation's wondrous birth,
Symbol of its brightening glory
Won from field and conflict gory,
   Symbol of its power and worth.

---

## "IS LIFE WORTH LIVING?"

READ AT AN OBSERVANCE, MAY 15, 1886, OF THE WRITER'S
SEVENTIETH BIRTHDAY.

LIFE worth living? Who denies it
   But the pessimistic one?
Always dwelling in the shadows,
   Never basking in the sun;
Ever whining and repining
   At what is or is not done;
Looking at the orbs fast setting,
   As they sink beneath the earth,
Not at brighter stars of morning,
   Rising from a heavenly birth,
Glad to render through their splendor
   Homage to creation's worth.

Life in childhood is delightsome,
　　Sweet and charming are its days,
Love and innocence combining
　　In a thousand happy ways—
Heaven descending, with us blending,
　　Angels present to our gaze.
Wonderful the growth and beauty,
　　Lovely forms, unearthly fair;
Mind's fresh budding, eyes so thoughtful,
　　Dimpling smiles and golden hair;
Would we lose it, fail to choose it,
　　Never know the blessing rare?

Sure the youth-time is enchanting,
　　Bubbling, sparkling in its joy;
Soul and body fast advancing,
　　School and books invite employ;
Folly waning, wisdom gaining,
　　Man's fair blossom in the boy.
Nature breathes her benediction,
　　Spreads o'er earth and sky her glow;
Knowledge brings her boundless treasures,
　　Rapture 'tis to be and know—
Bright adorning of life's morning
　　In its sweet and hopeful flow.

Early manhood has its pleasures,
　　Aspirations high and true;
Choices pleading for acceptance,
　　Noble pathways to pursue;
Friends that love us, Heaven above us,
　　Watch the ends we hold in view!
Hearts to hearts responsive beating,
　　Friendships rise to heights divine,
Manly strength and tender beauty,
　　Kindred souls to each resign;
Life's rich sweetness finds completeness
　　In the home's pure sacred shrine.

There's a grandeur in well-doing;
  Acting nobly for the right—
Standing firm for truth and virtue,
  Fighting always the good fight;
Never flinching, error clinching,
  Routing evil through God's might.
Ah! 'tis glorious thus to battle,
  Driving out the hosts of sin,
Helping souls to break their fetters,
  Bringing Christ and freedom in,
Burdens lightening, futures brightening
  Through the victories we win.

Men of true and lofty purpose,
  Women of a kindred mind,
Moved by heavenly inspiration,
  Highest joy in service find;
Ever giving, through their living,
  Greatest treasures to mankind.
All the way such souls are marching,
  Landscapes rise with verdure crowned,
Mortal streams flow purer, sweeter,
  Gardens bloom and fruits abound;
Earth rejoices—all her voices
  Say a Paradise is found.

Wonderful and doubly blessed,
  When we live in others' lives;
In grand deeds and high example
  All our noblest self survives,
Adding measures to the treasures
  Which enrich each soul that strives.
Memories, like the wings of angels,
  Cluster round us to the end;
Showers of grateful benedictions,
  Manna-like, on us descend:
Outward perished?  Still we're cherished
  In earth's brighter, heavenward trend.

Life worth living?  O, my spirit!
   Break thou forth in thankful song
For these years that now are nearing
   That for which I hope and long.
Made victorious, life is glorious;
   Death—and then the heavenly throng!
Oh, the rapturous culmination
   Of true Christly living here—
Blest beatitude of being,
   Lifted to th' immortal sphere,
Where life's story is the glory
   Of the soul's full-crowned career

## DIES IRÆ.

THIS noted Latin hymn, ascribed to Thomas of Celano, about 1250, has had many translators, but none probably was ever satisfied with his version. Of my three, the first, on pages 380–82, I regard as much better than those here inserted with the original. That of 1891 consists chiefly of stanzas written while translating the first; the other, made thirty-six years ago, has been slightly revised. A very interesting account of the Dies Iræ, with various translations, is given in Dr. Philip Schaff's valuable book, "Literature and Poetry," Scribners, 1890.

1 DIES Iræ, dies illa!
   Solvet sæclum in favilla,
   Teste David cum Sibylla.

2 Quantus tremor est futurus,
   Quando Judex est venturus,
   Cuncta stricte discussurus.

3 Tuba, mirum spargens sonum,
   Per sepulchra regionum,
   Coget omnes ante thronum.

4 Mors stupebit et natura,
   Quum resurget creatura,
   Judicanti responsura.

5 Liber scriptus profereter,
   In quo totum continetur,
   Unde mundus judicetur.

6 Judex ergo quum sedebit,
  Quidquid latet apparebit,
  Nil inultum remanebit.

7 Quid sum miser tunc dicturus?
  Quem patronum rogaturus,
  Quum vix justus sit securus?

8 Rex tremendæ majestatis,
  Qui salvandos salvas gratis,
  Salva me, fons pietatis.

9 Recordare, Jesu pie,
  Quod sum causa tuæ viæ;
  Ne me perdas illa die.

10 Quærens me sedisti lassus,
   Redimisti crucem passus;
   Tantus labor non sit cassus.

11 Juste Judex ultionis,
   Donum fac remissionis,
   Ante diem rationis.

12 Ingemisco, tanquam reus,
   Culpa rubet vultus meus;
   Supplicanti parce, Deus.

13 Qui Mariam absolvisti,
   Et latronem exaudisti,
   Mihi quoque spem dedisti.

14 Preces meæ non sunt dignæ,
   Sed tu, bone, fac benigne,
   Ne perenni cremer igne.

15 Inter oves locum præsta,
   Et ab hædis me sequestra,
   Statuens in parte dextra.

16 Confutatis maledictis,
   Flammis acribus addictis,
   Voca me cum benedictis.

17 Oro supplex et acclinis,
   Cor contritum quasi cinis;
   Gere curam mei finis.

18 Lachrymosa dies illa,
   Qua resurget ex favilla,
   Judicandus homo reus,
   Huic ergo parce, Deus.

---

## DIES IRÆ.

### TRANSLATED, 1891.

1 DAY of wrath and awful glory!
   Ends in ashes earth's long story,
   As foretold by prophets hoary.

2 Oh, what fear and tribulation,
   When the Judge comes through creation,
   Making strict examination!

3 Loud the trumpet blast astounding,
   Through the charnel chambers sounding,
   Calleth all the throne surrounding.

4 Death and Nature, shocked and shaken,
   Wonder as the creatures waken,
   To their Judge responsive taken.

5 From the volume, now unsealing,
   Sinful deeds, each thought and feeling,
   Must be tried with no appealing.

6 As the Judge assumes his station,
   Things concealed have revelation;
   Guilty souls their condemnation.

7 Wretch, what plea can I be making?
   Who my case be undertaking,
   When the righteous soul is quaking?

8 O thou King, all kings transcending,
   Yet salvation's gift extending;
   Save me, Fount of love unending!

9 Jesus blest! thy heart was riven
  When my sins brought thee from heaven;
  Lose me not when dooms are given.

10 Sought by thee through much affliction,
   Purchased by thy crucifixion,
   Fail me not thy benediction.

11 Judge of righteous indignation,
   Grant me gracious vindication,
   Lest that day bring reprobation.

12 Conscious of my guilt, and groaning;
   Shame my crimsoned visage owning,
   God of pity, hear my moaning!

13 Thou didst pardon Mary grieving,
   Didst accept the thief believing;
   Hope, thy gift, am I receiving.

14 From my prayers no merit earning,
   To thy grace my soul is turning;
   Shelter me from endless burning.

15 To thy flock in love allure me;
   Sev'rance from the goats assure me;
   Standing on thy right secure me.

16 When thy foes find their punition
   Sharpest fires of dread perdition,
   Call me to the blest's fruition.

17 Suppliant at thy feet low bending,
   Bowed in dust my heart is rending;
   Stay my soul when life is ending.

18 When that woeful day is breaking,
   Man shall rise, from ashes waking,
   Justice might condemned declare him,
   But in mercy, Saviour, spare him!

## DIES IRÆ.

### TRANSLATED, 1855.

1 DAY of wrath! that day appalling,
When the world in fire is falling—
Prophet voice and scroll recalling.

2 What the dread dismay impending,
When the Judge shall be descending,
Searching eye o'er all things bending!

3 Wondrous sound the trump revealing,
All earth's sepulchers unsealing,
Summons to the throne is pealing.

4 Death amazed, and Nature quaking,
See the throngs their graves forsaking,
And their way to judgment taking.

5 From the written book inspected,
Where men's deeds are all collected,
World-awards shall be effected.

6 Hence, the Judge his seat attaining,
Hidden things in light arraigning,
Naught is unavenged remaining.

7 Ah, then, what shall I say, quailing?
Who for me shall plead, prevailing,
When the just man's heart is failing?

8 King of glorious exaltation,
Life and peace are thy donation;
Fount of grace, be my salvation!

9 Jesus! since my sin's sad story
Made thy way so rough and gory,
Let my rescue serve thy glory.

10 Waiting, wearied, thou hast sought me;
On the cross from death hast bought me;
Be not vain what thou hast wrought me.

11 Righteous Judge! thy wrath forbearing,
Make remission free my sharing,
Ere the final dooms declaring.

12 Self-accused, my guilt lamenting,
Of my faults in shame repenting,
Spare the suppliant, Lord, relenting.

13 Thy forgiveness Mary knowing,
Mercy to the robber showing,
Hope on me thou art bestowing.

14 With my prayers though sin is blending,
Kindly, Lord, my soul befriending,
Shield me from the fire unending.

15 With the sheep by thee selected,
Distant from the goats rejected,
Set me on thy right protected.

16 When the curst with fears are riven,
And to fiercest flames are driven,
With the blest my place be given.

17 Low before thee I am lying,
In contrition rent and sighing;
Comfort me when I am dying.

18 Oh, that day of tears and dooming!
When awaked from his entombing,
Man for judgment is assembling,
Spare, O God, thy creature trembling!

---

## NOTE ON "SOMETHING FOR THEE."

INCIDENTS relating to this hymn (pages 135-36) have been often solicited. The following, abridged somewhat, is from Rev. Dr. H. S. Burrage's admirable volume, "Baptist Hymn Writers and their Hymns."

"This hymn, written in 1862, was first published in the Watchman and Reflector, and was copied into various other

religious papers.  Later  Rev.  Robert Lowry requested Dr.
Phelps to furnish some hymns for a collection which he was
preparing.  Among other hymns placed in his hands was this
one, and it appeared in 'Pure Gold' with the excellent music
which Dr. Lowry composed for it, and with which it will al-
ways be associated.  It also appeared in 'Gospel Hymns,' No.
1, and later in numerous collections in this land and in lands
across the sea.  It has been a most helpful  hymn to many
hearts.  A minister in Glasgow says: 'A large family joined
my church lately.  The mother told me she had first of all
happened to drop into our chapel, while a stranger in Glas-
gow, when she was quite overcome, as if her heart were lifted
up, with the people singing

Something for Thee.'

"Professor W. F. Sherwin, a few years ago, was holding a
Sunday-school Institute in Maine, and during the singing of
the third verse of this hymn a young lawyer was so much af-
fected that it was the means of changing all his plans for life;
and, consecrating himself to Christ's service, he devoted him-
self with his whole heart to evangelistic work.  Says Dr.
Phelps: 'I have had requests for autographic copies of this
hymn, and many testimonies concerning its helpfulness.  I
have heard it sung in various and distant parts of our land,
on ocean steamers, and in other countries.  A friend recently
showed me a hymnal in the Swedish language containing it.'

"At the celebration of the author's seventieth birthday,
with other letters, the following words of sincere congratula-
tion from Rev. Robert Lowry, D. D., dated Plainfield, N. J.,
May 13, 1886, were read: 'It is worth living seventy years
even if nothing comes of it but one such hymn as

Saviour! thy dying love<br>Thou gavest me.

Happy is the man who can produce one song which the world
will keep on singing after its author shall have passed away.
May the tuneful harp preserve its strings for many a long
year yet, and the last song reach us only when it is time for
the singer to take his place in the heavenly choir.'"

At the close of the reading of Dr. Lowry's letter, the con-
gregation, filling the First Baptist church, New Haven, Conn.,
at once arose and sang this hymn, a touching scene.